GOLF IN THE TWENTIETH CENTURY
AND THE BOSTON GOLF CLUB

Frank Curtis, the founder and first captain of The Boston Golf Club

GOLF
IN THE TWENTIETH CENTURY
AND
THE BOSTON GOLF CLUB

by

PETER FLYNN

IN ASSOCIATION WITH
THE HISTORY OF BOSTON PROJECT

19 | 97

RICHARD KAY
80 SLEAFORD ROAD • BOSTON • LINCOLNSHIRE • PE21 8EU

© Peter L. Flynn 1997
First published by Richard Kay Publications June 1997
Reprinted with a corrected illustration July 1997
ISBN 0 902662 18 X
Issued as a paperback August 1997
ISBN 0 902662 08 2

Typeset by the publisher initially in Microsoft Word™ and PageMaker™ on an AppleMacintosh™ and output in camera-ready copy which was then manipulated via Rank Xerox Media Server. Printed electronically, in Bookman 10 point typeface for the body of the text, at 600 dpi resolution at 135 pages per minute on a Rank Xerox DocuTech™ 135 Laser Production Publishing System by:

Foxe Laser
Enterprise Road • Mablethorpe • Lincolnshire. LN12 1NB

*To my wife
for her patience and assistance.*

CONTENTS

ILLUSTRATIONS

ACKNOWLEDGEMENTS

In the course of writing this book I have received a great deal of help and information from innumerable people. I wish to thank all of them for their help, without which this history would not have been possible. Those whom I wish particularly to mention are as follows:

Bryan and Philip Cooper.
The Staff of Boston and Lincoln Libraries.
Peter Lewis, Director, The British Golf Museum, St Andrews.
Mrs E A Mackie and Mrs Julie Hall, Administrators, The Ladies' Golf Union, St Andrews.
D E Smith Manager/Secretary, The Boston Golf Club.
Harry Caudwell.
Michael Hobbs Golf Photo Library.

Many people have co-operated in offering photographs for which both the publisher and the author are most grateful. Acknowledgements for individual illustrations are given either in the caption or by the illustration itself. It has not been possible to identify with certainty the origin of all photographs but the most likely source is given. If no source is quoted the author or publisher has taken the photograph. Since ownership of a photograph does not necessarily confer copyright if we have inadvertently infringed anyone's copyright they should contact the publisher.

PRELIMINARY NOTES

For those interested in the history of golf in Lincolnshire, there are excellent books and booklets provided by most of the clubs, and I would like particularly to commend those written on the history of the Sleaford, Lincoln, Canwick Park, Burghley Park, Belton Park, and Seacroft Clubs.

Some golfing terms have been explained in detail for the benefit of non-golfing readers. A brief glossary appears on pages xvi-xvii.

The author will donate any royalties from the sale of the first edition of this book to the 'Junior Section' of The Boston Golf Club.

SPONSORS AND SUBSCRIBERS

The author, the publisher, and the History of Boston Project are most grateful to all those individuals and corporate bodies who, by their sponsorship and subscription, have greatly facilitated the production and publication of this book.

SPONSORS

Dr and Mrs Richard Allday—Boston
Richard Atterby—Sibsey
R. A. Barclay—Boston
Belton Park Golf Club—Grantham
Blankney Golf Club—Blankney
Mrs K. J. Bradley—Fishtoft
Harry Caudwell—Friskney
Bryan and Philip Cooper—Boston
Mr and Mrs R. Hardy—Fishtoft

Sheila and Jim Hopkins—Boston
Garth Isaac—Boston
Barry Johnson, Architect—Boston
Johnson's Seeds—Boston
Kirton-Holme Golf Club—Kirton-Holme
Lincolnshire Libraries
C. and R. Needham—Boston
Sleaford Golf Club—Sleaford

SUBSCRIBERS

Anon
Frederick Ash—Market Deeping
S. F. Ayliffe—Fishtoft
Mr D. A. Baker—Pinchbeck
J. D. Barnes-Moss—Boston
Mrs Marion E. Bavin—Stickford
M. W. Bothamley—Boston
M. Bowman—Boston
F. Bramwell—Boston
Jane Bratley—Quadring Eaudyke
Mr F. Buitelaar—Tetford
John Burns—Boston
Mr and Mrs H. Corns—Boston
J. E. Daker—Boston
Richard Davison—Boston
Mr and Mrs C. Dawson—Freiston
R. Drury—Lincoln
Ted Eaglen—Boston
Martin Fairman—Boston
Mr and Mrs D. Grant—Leverton
John Grant—Woodhall Spa
D. W. Hodgson—Frampton
N. Holgate—Boston
Mr and Mrs F. Holmes—Kirton Skeldyke
Pamela and David Hopkins
　　　　　　—Redwood City, California
Gerry Hopper—Boston
V. J. Hunter—Boston
Malcolm Hyde—Boston

Clive Johns—Boston
Mrs C. E. Means—Kirkby Green
Martin Middlebrook—Boston
K. F. Monck-Mason—Frampton
G. A. and L. M. Mulholland
　　　　　　—Leake Commonside
M. J. Norton—Boston
Jill Nyman—Boston
H. Oldham—Boston
Maggie Peberdy—Frampton
Les Pepper—Stamford
Ernest Porter—Boston
Mrs M. Reed—Boston
Adrian Reynolds—Boston
Peter Reynolds—Boston
Raymond L. Ringrose—Boston
C. J. Russell—Boston
R. Sales—Swineshead
Bryan Skinner—Boston
Mr T. D. Slade—Kirton Holme
D. E. and M. V. Smith—Boston
R. C. Smith—Boston
Ruth Street—Boston
Tim Sylvester—Boston
R. W. Tinn—Boston
A. E. Walker—Boston
Mr and Mrs R. Ward—Sutton Coldfield
Trot Weightman—Wyberton
Colin Woodcock—Boston
Mr and Mrs N. Woodcock—Wyberton

INTRODUCTION

This is the story of how Boston golf club started its uncertain life in 1900 as a small nine-hole winter course, overcame a number of near fatal catastrophes and survives today as one of the best golf courses in a county which can boast of having a large number of first class golf clubs.

Like many other golf clubs of the time any records and minutes have vanished in one or other of the upheavals undergone by the club. They are only available from 1961 onwards and therefore for the greater part of its life I have had to rely on the intermittent newspaper reports inserted when the secretary of the times felt like writing them, and the newspapers felt like printing them.

The early members are long since dead and the memories of the older members who have survived are dimmed with the passing of the years. There will doubtless be corrections needed in this account when memories are stirred and old events relived.

Boston golf club is a fenland golf course. In my, possibly biased, view the fenland course par excellence would be an appropriate phrase. Your fenman is not obsessed with history of the past. He is generally more concerned with the task in hand today whether it is growing excellent cauliflowers or laying a tricky chip as near to the hole as possible. Small wonder therefore that tracking down the information to write this history has not been an easy task. It was astonishing to discover that even the older Boston golf club members were quite unaware that Boston had a golf club prior to 1922.

In playing over the present Cowbridge golf course, the fens and their history are all around, and add to the natural charm of the club.

Situated on the southern edge of the old wastes of the East and West Fens, the last area of the fens to be reclaimed, the skills and inventions of the great drainage engineers are to be seen all around.

The elegant small iron bridge designed by John Rennie, the famous drainage and mechanical engineer, and cast in Derbyshire in 1811, faces the golfer putting on the 7th green.

Just up the road towards Boston, Tom Waterfield's magnificent five sailed Maud Foster Windmill, newly restored to provide high quality flour and excellent refreshments, soars over the landscape. There used to be twenty windmills within a few miles of Boston two centuries ago: now there are but two, and the Sibsey Trader Mill, now under the auspices of English Heritage, only operates on a few selected days each year.

The Maud Foster, West Fen, Cowbridge, Stonebridge and earlier drains, masterpieces of a succession of drainage engineers going back to the 16th century, surround the course. They provide an ever present reminder of the charm of the fens and a good reason to concentrate on the shot in hand if one's ball is to escape a watery grave.

Up towards the club house is a gem of the drainage engineer's skill— the double aqueduct where the flood water from the high lying Lincolnshire Wolds carried in the Stonebridge Drain, is led over the old Cowbridge Drain. Aqueduct Farm, the site of Boston's golf club, was named after it. Playing the course one can invariably see a pair of great crested grebes, a heron, the swooping agile terns, the gracefully elegant swans and the ubiquitous Canada Geese all enjoying themselves within a few yards of the fairways.

One is playing in the centre of one of the most fertile and best farmed areas in Britain and probably the world. Within a few miles radius the skilled husbandry of the fenmen produce the bulk of the cauliflowers and potatoes consumed by the British public. This fact at one point in its history almost resulted in the death of the club.

When the Pudding Pie course flooded in 1949 the committee had great difficulty finding another course because of the price and scarcity of land around Boston. But they never gave up trying and in 1961 the old Boston Golf Club Company Ltd., of Pudding Pie, still alive and kicking, took over another course at Cowbridge, just north of Boston. Boston golf club, like Belton Park which had no golf course from 1914 to 1923, had successfully managed to weather the storm.

The game of golf is affected more than most other sports by the fortunes of the surrounding area and its inhabitants. The nature of their work, their standard of living, their interest in other sports, all affect the progress and development of the local golf course.

The changes which have taken place in Britain since 1900 are of a magnitude which will most likely never again be equalled or approached. They have had a profound effect on the progress of the game of golf. Therefore I have looked at those changes which have had the greatest impact on the history of the Boston golf club. The progress and the survival of the club has been no less affected by the state of golf in the country and by the activities of the adjacent golf clubs.

Some of the most relevent aspects of these have therefore also been looked at. The story of golf however, like most other human activities, is above all the story of the people involved. I have therefore endeavoured to write this book around the activities of those individuals who have had the largest share in the fortunes of the Boston golf club. To a few of them the club owes its present existence.

Frank Curtis the licenced trade business man who started it up and got it going.

Major Oliver Cooper who came back from the Boer and Great Wars to provide the energy and drive to move the club to its first twelve-month course at Pudding Pie Farm by the side of the treacherous River Witham. Charlie Smith the workaholic greensman who bailed the Major and his committee out of their unexpected mudbath at Pudding Pie.

Bryan and Philip Cooper who first saw the potential of Aqueduct Farm as a first class golf course and even more importantly put their own capital at risk when they purchased it on behalf of the Boston golfers.

Bob Barclay and Dick Hardy who charmed the lease of the two Islands from the redoubtable Bert Platt thus allowing the course to be extended to eighteen holes.

Finally I would like to pay tribute to all the committee members over the years who have laboured long and hard to provide my wife and myself and all the other Boston members with one of the best and most interesting golf courses in the county.

Peter Flynn
BOSTON 1997

1890   Belton Park and Burghley Golf Clubs opened.
1891   Lincoln Golf Club opened.
1893   English Ladies' Golf Union formed.
1893   Canwick Park Golf Club opened.
1894   Thonock Golf Club, Gainsborough, opened.
1895   Seacroft Golf Club opened.
1900   Boston Golf Club— nine-hole winter course— opened at Sleaford Road.
1900   Sandilands Golf Club opened.
1900   Lincolnshire Gentlemen's and Ladies' Golf Unions formed.
1900   Lincolnshire Ladies' Golf Union affiliated to the English Ladies' Golf Union.
1900   The Haskell golf ball introduced.
1903   Boston Golf Club moved to Tower Road— nine-hole winter course.
1903   Blankney and Canwick Park Golf Clubs opened.
1905   Woodhall Spa Golf Club (new course) and Rauceby (now Sleaford) opened.
1906   Carholme Golf Club opened.
1907   Surfleet (now Spalding) Golf Club, opened.
1910   North Shore Golf Club, Skegness, opened.
1914   Sutton Bridge Golf Club opened.
1922   Market Rasen Golf Club opened.
1923   Boston Golf Club moved to Pudding Pie— nine-hole twelve-month course.
1924   Men's English Golf Union formed and Lincolnshire Men's Union affiliated to them.
1924   The East Lincolnshire Golf Club opened at Sibsey.
1924   Stoke Rochford Golf Club, Grantham, opened.
1925   Market Rasen Golf Club opened.
1927   The Ryder Cup Competition started— Massachusettes, USA. USA won $9^1/_2$ - $2^1/_2$.
1929   Tubular steel shafts legalised by R. and A.
1931   Fred Caudwell, owner of the East Lincs Golf Club, died following an accident.

1932	The East Lincs' Golf Club wound up.
1932	Boston Golf Club enlarged to twelve holes.
1949	The Boston Golf Club at Pudding Pie flooded and was abandoned.
1961	Aqueduct Farm, Cowbridge, purchased by Bryan Cooper and offered to Boston Golf Club.
1962	(June) Boston Golf Club re-opens. Twelve holes.
1962	Boston Ladies and Gents, affiliated to the Lincolnshire and English Golf Unions.
1965	Louth Golf Club opened.
1977	Cowbridge Island lease purchased by Boston Golf Club for £10,000.
1980	(March) Boston Golf Club: Eighteen-hole course opened: SSS 68.
1987	D Smith appointed full time manager/secretary of Boston Golf Club.
1985	Millfield Golf Club, Lincoln, opened.
1986	Woodthorpe Hall Golf Club opened
1990	Boston Golf Club purchased eighteen acres for £63,000 to be incorporated into the course: SSS now 71.
1990	Horncastle and South Kyme Golf Clubs opened.
1991	Belton Woods Golf Club, Grantham, opened.
1992	Boston Golf Club practice ground opened.
1992	Kirton Holme Golf Club opened.
1992	Kenwick Park Golf Club opened.
1993	Boston Golf Club practice ground extended.
1994	The English Golf Union purchased Woodhall Spa Golf Club.
1995	Boston West Golf Club opened.

A Brief Glossary of Golfing Terms for the Non-Golfing Reader

Ace: A hole in one shot.

Away: Player whose ball is furthest from the hole

Better ball: Two players playing another two with the better score of each pair counting at each hole.

Birdie: A score of one under par for the hole.

Bogey: Now generally taken as a score of one over par.

Borrow: The amount that a golfer has to allow for due to the slope of the green.

Bunker: A pit containing sand; also sometimes called a trap.

Chip: A short shot played on to the green.

Closed: A stance where the back foot is back from the line of play.

Club: The implement used to propel the ball. Divided into 'woods', 'irons', and 'putters'.

Cup or can: The metal container into which the golfer aims to putt his ball.

Cut: The cut off score in a competition at a particular point below which players are allowed to continue to the next round.

Dormie: In match play standing as many holes up as there are left to play.

Double-Bogie: A score of two strokes over par.

Draw: Where the flight of the ball moves from right to left (for a right-handed player. If severe it is called a hook. (The reverse applies for a left-handed player.)

Drive: A shot hit from the tee to start the hole.

Driver: The club used to drive. Usually with a steep faced wooden or metal head.

Drop: Dropping a ball away from an unplayable lie. Penalty shots may be added to the player's score.

Eagle: A score of two under par for the hole.

Fade: Where the flight of the ball moves from left to right (for a right-handed player). If severe it is called a 'slice'.

Fairway: The mown area between the 'tee' and the 'green'

Glove: Used on the left hand to obtain a better hold on the club shaft.

Golf widow: A wife whose husband neglects her for golf.

Green: The putting surface surrounding the hole.

Green fee: The charge made for a round, or a day's golf, for visitors.

(1) Grip: Rubber or plastic material on the top of the club shaft to obtain a better grip.

(2) Grip: The position of the golfer's hands on the club. There are several variations.

Gross score: The player's score before deduction of any handicap allowance.

Halve: In match play to take the same score as one's opponent for a hole or the match.

Handicap allowance: The number of shots to be deducted from a players score to allow players of differing abilities to compete on level terms.

Hazard: A bunker or feature containing water.

Hold: The characteristic of a green which is sufficiently soft to prevent the ball bouncing off the surface: usually achieved by watering.

Hook: Where the flight of the ball moves severely from the right to the left for a right-handed player.

Iron: A club with a steel head. Numbered from 'one' to 'nine' as the angle of the head becomes more sloping. Wedges are irons for use near the green or in a sand bunker.

Lay-up: A shot played to a safe distance from the green.

Lie: Where the ball comes to rest. It can be easy or difficult for the next shot.

Line: On the green the best direction to hole the putt.

Loft: The angle on the face of the club.

Marker: Small flat object to mark the position of the ball on the green before lifting it.

Match play: A competition where one or more players compete hole by hole.

Medal play: A competition where many competitors play and add up the score hole by hole to reach a total.

Nassau: A match played for money where the stakes are on the first nine holes, the second nine, and on the whole round.

Net: The score after deduction of the handicap allowance.

Open: A stance where the front foot is back from the line of play.

Par: The score for a hole expected from a first class golfer in favourable conditions.

Penalty: The adding of shots to a golfer's score for an infringement of the rules.

Pin: The flag stick which marks the position of the hole on the green.

Professional: A golfer who plays for money and his livelihood.

Rabbit: An amateur of only moderate ability; usually playing to a handicap of eighteen or higher.

Relief: Permission under the rules to drop the ball, generally without penalty.

Rough: The area between fairways where the vegetation is much heavier.

Round: The rules stipulate eighteen holes.

Royal and Ancient: After the golf club of St. Andrews who are responsible for formulating the rules of the game in Great Britain.

Scratch: A first-class amateur golfer who can play without requiring a handicap allowance.

Slice: Where the flight of the ball moves severely from left to right for a right-handed player

Splash: The shot description to get a ball from a greenside bunker onto the green.

Stableford: A competition where scoring a net par attracts two points, one over one point, and one under three points.

Standard Scratch Score: Is the score that a scratch player is expected to take playing off the medal tees in summer conditions.

(1) Tee: The area from which the initial drive is taken.

(2) Tee: A wooden or plastic peg on which the ball is placed for a drive.

Tour: The scheduled series of tournaments for the professional golfers.

Unplayable lie: Where the ball can be removed and dropped at a suitable distance, generally with one penalty shot added to the player's score.

Winter rules: Local rules (made by individual golf clubs) where a ball may be lifted and replaced close by to avoid damage to the course.

Wood: A club with a wooden head used for driving or long fairway shots. The wooden heads are increasingly being replaced by metal heads. Normally golfers may carry a driver and two, three, four, or five numbered 'woods' as the club face becomes more angled.

Yardage: The length of a hole or a course.

Photograph of Boston Market Place c. 1900:
around the time when the first golf club was being formed.

A view from approximately the same place today.

CHAPTER ONE

THE BEGINNING

O N THE 18TH OF AUGUST 1900, a small paragraph on an inside
page in the *Boston Independent*, the local newspaper,
mentioned the success of a well known Boston personality,
Councillor Frank Curtis, in winning the Silver Medal Golf
Competition at the Woodhall Spa Golf Club. The article went on
to mention that Councillor Curtis had had several recent
successes there and around the county, and was keen to start up
a club in Boston. He invited any other interested golfers to join
him in forming a Boston club.

Boston in 1900 was a small market town and port with a
population of around 20,000 situated on the River Witham just
before it enters the Wash. It is surrounded by some of the most
fertile land in the country and is famous for its potatoes,
vegetables and flower production.

The name derives from St BOTOLPH, an Anglo Saxon monk,
who reputedly started a monastery where Boston now stands,
around 650 AD, which thrived until attacked and destroyed by the
Danes in 870 AD.

From its early history it was a market town for the surrounding
area and a small thriving port. It received a Charter from King
John in 1204. Its market expanded and it became a centre for the
Hanseatic merchants who helped build it up into what at one time
was the second most important port in the country after London.
It also became a Staple port with the King's authority to trade in
wool, leather, tin and other commodities. Its wealthy merchants
financed the building of a new St Botolph's Church, started in
1309 and finally completed a hundred and fifty years later, which
has one of the highest stone steeples in the county. St Botolph's
church, known as 'The Stump', is a well known landmark and one
of the fine buildings which the town today carefully preserves.

In the fifteenth century the Witham suffered the fate of all the
rivers flowing into the Wash and silted up leading to a gradual
decline in the port.

From the early nineteenth century new attempts were made to

dredge the river and improve the drainage system; and in 1882 a dock was constructed resulting in a new and deeper port. This, with the benefits of the railway system which came to Boston in 1848 led to a great renewal of trade. The rapidly expanding population of Britain required large quantities of potatoes and vegetables, and Boston farmers and the town benefited. Fishing was an important industry and The Boston Deep Sea Fishing and Ice Company owned a large fleet of deep sea trawlers fishing as far away as Iceland and Newfoundland.

All of these developments had, by 1900, given Boston a thriving business community and this was of vital importance to the success of its newly formed Golf Club, which would draw its members exclusively from the business and professional members of Boston society.

Frank Curtis in 1900 was a thirty two year old Londoner who had spent all his working life in the brewing industry. When he was seventeen he had started working for Messrs Worthington, the large brewers, and quickly worked his way up the firm by dint of hard work and enthusiasm. When he was thirty he moved to Lincolnshire on being offered a post with E H Soulby and Sons, a small Alford brewing firm. Over the next few years he helped this firm to expand rapidly to a position where they owned and managed over a hundred taverns all over the county. In the process he had become a large shareholder in the firm and when they amalgamated with Messrs Winch and Co. of Louth he became a joint Managing Director of the firm.

In addition to his business activities he was active in other aspects of Boston life. He was elected a conservative councillor for the Boston West Ward where he gained the reputation of being a keen and hardworking member of the council. He took special interest in public health as a member of the Sanitory Committee, and in public finance. He played a prominent part in local church affairs and was a Freemason and he was Vice President of the Boston Show Committee.

He had rightly gained the reputation of being a person of some vision and stood for the county council where his stated objective was 'to represent the town's interest at county level'. He was a person who 'got things done'. Frank Curtis was also, last but not least, a golf fanatic and travelled widely all over the county to

2.

engage in this sport. He played regularly at Woodhall Spa and had won several prizes there.

There are no written minutes of the Boston Golf Club which have survived from this period. Indeed none would be available for another sixty years. We are therefore dependent on newspaper reports for the story of how the club has developed. However the major golf publication of the time, *The Golfing Annual*, for the year 1900 has the following insert about the new club.

The Boston Golf Club

The annual subscription is one guinea. The number of members is 100. The captain is Mr F Curtis. The Hon. Sec. is the Rev H Garvey. The professional is C Mitchell. The course record is 37. The Club was instituted in October 1900.

The Boston Ladies Golf Club was instituted in December 1900. The annual subscription is ten shillings and sixpence. The membership is 42. The Captain is Mrs A Black. The Hon Sec is Miss Francis South, Conway House, Boston. The play is over the same course.

We have no information giving details of the October meeting when the Boston Golf Club was inaugurated, nor of the December meeting when the Ladies' Club was formed. We have however a full newspaper report of the first General Meeting of the new club which was held in the Peacock and Royal Hotel, Boston, on the 17th December 1900. *The Independent* gave full coverage of this meeting and reported that a large and enthusiastic gathering attended. Frank Curtis, who had been selected captain at the inaugural meeting, took the chair and the Hon Sec, the Rev H Garvey, recorded the events of the meeting. Also present were N Green Armytage, Dr Reckett, Dr Snaith, Dr South, B B Dyer, J Short, H Harwood, C Johnson, E P Smith, S Cooper and C Wood.

The captain outlined the plans for the new club. A set of rules based on the recommendations of the Royal and Ancient Golf Club of St Andrews was proposed and adopted. Details were provided of the Invitation Matches to be played over the new course the following day. Those named as attending the meeting were all well known professional and business men of the town.

The Boston Golf Club therefore dates its existence to October

1900 which makes it one of the oldest clubs to be formed in the county.

THE FIRST GOLF CLUBS IN THE COUNTY

It was not however, by some years, the first Lincolnshire golf club to be formed. In 1890 Belton Park started off its illustrious life, and in the same year Burghley Park, the Stamford club, was formed at a meeting in the George Hotel in Stamford, surely one of the most beautiful settings possible in which to start up a golf club. The start of the new century saw a great increase in interest in the game of golf. It suddenly became popular amongst the well to do members of the community. Interest in the game was aided by its popularity amongst the top politicians in the country, including the future prime ministers Arthur Balfour and Henry Asquith, both of whom were keen golfers.

Lincoln Golf Club had started in February 1891, with an entrance fee of one guinea, and an annual subscription of the same amount. The course was started on the West Common, adjacent to the Carholme Race Course. Lincoln, like Boston and many other golf clubs, would change its venue during the course of its lifetime.

Woodhall Spa also started up in 1891, on land between Tattershall Road and Abbey Lane. The present course is the third laid out in Woodhall, with the site given the blessing of the immortal Harry Vardon, when he inspected the area in 1903, and pronounced favourably on its potential. Vardon had excellent judgement in almost everything he did whether it was perfecting the best golf grip and swing, or selecting a site for a new golf club, and his instincts did not fail him on this occasion. Woodhall would eventually become one of the best courses in Britain. The history of Woodhall Spa Golf Club, and The Boston Golf Club are, as we shall see, much intertwined. Providing Boston with Frank Curtis its founder, was only one of the many favours for which Boston would be indebted to its neighbouring club, situated up the road on the edge of the beautiful Lincolnshire Wolds.

Lincoln, as befitted the premier town in the county, initially had two clubs. The second to be set up was the South Park Club, which started up in 1893 on the South Common. Known today after several changes of name and a change of venue as Canwick

4.

Park Golf Club, it is famous for its beautiful parkland setting, and the magnetic attraction exerted by the magnificent Minster on golf balls rolling about on its putting surfaces, particularly when propelled by Boston golfers.

Playing golf on common land has its disadvantages. There is no privacy and golfers must make the best of frequent interruptions whilst pedestrians, generally accompanied by gambolling dogs, make their way about the fairways. The Carholme Club members became increasingly unhappy about this situation and when plans were discussed to build an Isolation Hospital in the vicinity of the course the Committee decided to seek alternative land. After much difficulty in securing a suitable site they were successful, and in 1903 J H Taylor inspected land at Torksey a few miles north west of Lincoln, pronounced it suitable, and in 1904 a new nine hole course started up. With steady and continuous improvement it is now today one of the best clubs in the county.

Carholme however had not seen the last of golf. The interest in the game by now was growing steadily and in 1906 the West Common saw the resuscitation of golf and Lincoln was soon able to boast of having three first class clubs, Lincoln Golf Club at Torksey, South Cliff Club at South Park, and Carholme Golf Club on the West Common.

Another club already in existence in 1900, which would provide much help in a variety of ways to the Boston club, was Seacroft which started up in 1895. On the southern edge of the Lincolnshire seaside resort of Skegness, a town owing its fame and fortune to its excellent beaches and the railway link which provided access for holiday makers from the Midlands, Seacroft is a genuine links course running along the sand dunes close to the sea.

Around 1900 one of the most beautiful golf courses in the county— Blankney— was laid out on the Earl of Londesborough's estate between Sleaford and Lincoln.

1905 is the official date of the start-up of the club but golf was played there at an earlier date on the nine hole course set in the free-draining heath limestone.

It started as an extremely selective club and the first committee included two Peers of the Realm, one Baronet, M.F.H., two

Reverends, two Esquires, a doctor and two misters. A suggestion early in the life of the club that estate retainers be permitted to join was not accepted.

THE SLEAFORD ROAD LINKS

To construct a new golf course from green fields in 1996 the planning committtee would most probably put the task out to Jack Nicklaus Associates, or a similar specialist golf course construction group. After the expenditure of perhaps several million pounds, many months of hard work by a fleet of bulldozers and earthscrapers, and a good slice of luck to avoid the common pitfalls of bankruptcy, hey presto, we would have a spanking new golf course. Frank Curtis and his committee did not use quite that sort of approach. They did however provide a golf course in a very short space of time, following the inauguration of the club in October 1900.

The Sleaford Road Links, as the committee christened their course, was ready for play two months later, on the 18th December 1900. A large gathering attended an Open Exhibition

1. *The Sleaford Road/Woodville Road playing field today. The site of part of the first Boston golf course: probably its northern border.*

Match to celebrate the opening, when R Ferguson, a well known county player and a member of Seacroft, beat the Rev H E Curtis, a vicar from the nearby village of Langrick, one up. R Ferguson and Frank Curtis then beat the Rev H Curtis and Dr Moxon by an undisclosed amount. In the final match Miss F South, the secretary of the ladies section, and Frank Curtis, beat Dr Moxon and Arthur Black three and two.

The committee had managed this miracle of providing an 'instant golf course' by taking several short cuts. The first and most important was to decide that the new club would be a nine hole course. The exhibition matches were played twice around these nine holes. The great majority of courses in those early days were nine hole courses.

THE CIRCUMSTANCES

The second and most significant short cut was to make the new golf club a six-month course, but rather amazingly played over the winter months from 1 October to the end of March.

To understand the reason for this short cut, it is helpful to examine the circumstances facing Frank Curtis and his committee. They were starting up an uncertain venture that might or might not succeed. None of them were very wealthy individuals, although equally they were not poor. They were not in a position to take very large risks. The possibility therefore of purchasing land for a course in an area comprising some of the very best and most expensive farming land in the country, was out of the question. They cut the Gordian Knot of this problem by renting from a local cattle farmer fifty acres of grassland for the six winter months. He would not require it for his farming enterprise over the winter, since his cattle would be comfortably housed in cattle yards during this period.

This system required very little capital. The working capital needed was low, since the rent would be a fraction of what would be needed for either a full year, or for a summer six months term. At 1994 prices the club would be paying around £50 a hectare, instead of the £250 required for a full twelve months tenancy. There would be no need for expensive course management during the summer months, since the cattle were, in effect, cost free mowing machines. The greens would be fenced off to prevent damage from the cattle during the summer months.

As for the cost of construction? This would not present a problem. All that would be required would be one or two of the club members who could mark out greens and tees, and then push a mowing machine over these areas. In the event this was not required, since the club hired a professional to do those chores. It is most probable that the 1900 members would not have been happy mowing golf course greens. The greens produced by this system might not have been acceptable at Augusta, but then this was not Augusta, and in any event the typical golf course putting surfaces available in those days, would most probably have given our present greens expert, Peter Pearson, convulsions.

Notwithstanding those shortcuts, it is obvious that Frank Curtis must have been an extraordinary character, who did not believe in letting the grass grow too quickly underneath his feet, or on his golf course. There was of course a heavy price to pay for this economy. The silt soils of the Wash are wonderful for growing potatoes and cauliflowers, but they can lie wet in the winter months. This, with the risk of rain and snow, must inevitably have made life difficult for the Boston golfers, and the early scores, as we shall see, reflected the problems that they would face.

The new sport would be competing with other well established games. Cricket and football were the two most popular activities, and teams of both were run by most villages.

Boston had a better cricket team at the start of the century than towards the end and took it more seriously. In March 1900 it was announced that Tom Woodhouse, the Leeds' professional cricket player had been engaged by the Boston team as their professional for the coming season.

The two biggest football teams in the town, Boston Town and Boston Victoria, played in the Lincolnshire Football League. There was great rivalry between them and the managements of the teams were not on the best of terms.

In March 1900, at a meeting of the Lincolnshire Football Association in Lincoln, it was announced that because Boston Town had cancelled their fixture with Boston Victoria and had refused to play them they were henceforth expelled from the

Lincolnshire Football League.

The principal difference however between all these sporting activities was that whereas cricket and football were played by people from the whole social spectrum, golf was initially a sport of the wealthy.

GOLF IN 1900

The Sleaford Road golfers' scores were not of course helped by the equipment then available to play the game. There have been immense strides in the hardware available to present day golfers, to enable them to try and reach their idea of heaven—a single figure handicap. There were no steel or graphite shafted, balanced, and matched clubs, to make life easy. Typically a set in 1900 would consist of six unmatched hickory shafted clubs, made up of a driver, a brassie equal to a three or four wood, a driving iron equal to a three or four iron, a mid iron equal to a five iron, a short iron called a mashie or niblick equal to a seven to nine iron, and a putter. The wedge, the club responsible to a large degree for the greatest improvement in scoring, would not reach these shores until the 1930's, and may well have been the invention of

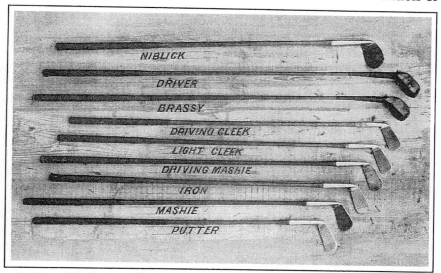

2. *Harry Vardon's golf clubs; taken from his book 'The Complete Golfer'.*

the peerless Gene Sarazan—who delightfully is still using it today, to the consternation of his opponents.

Club heads in those early days came in all shapes and sizes, with the irons scored and grooved in a fashion that would merit instant disqualification today. The hickory shafts common in 1900 were imported from America, having been found to be more whippy and durable than English ash. The wooden heads were commonly of English ash, but more and more were being made of imported persimmon, as the supply of good ash started to dry up. The putter would have an angled face to allow the striker to play a stymie. In 1900, if an opponent's ball on the green lay between the hole and your ball, it had to be played as it lay, which meant bouncing it over, or sliding it around, the offending ball.

This added an important dimension to putting, and many of the old golfers, who had acquired the knack of playing this shot were loathe to see it abolished. Many vital championship matches were won and lost on stymies. It disappeared in 1951 when the rules were changed to allow players to ask for the offending ball to be marked and removed.

The clubs of the early Boston golfers would be carried loose under the arm, or in a simple bag. The hickory shafts, surprisingly, were not a major limiting factor to good golf. Steel shafts, which became available during the 1920s, were certainly more uniform than the variable hickory, but many golfers, including the immortal Bobby Jones, were still using hickory shafts at a much later date. He played with them in 1930, when he performed a feat which it is safe to say will never again be repeated. In that year he won the British and the USA Amateur and Open Championships—the 'impregnable quadrilateral' as the sports writers of the period termed this miracle.

The golf ball used by the Boston golfers in 1900 was, however, much more of a limiting factor to low scores. It was known as the gutta percha and was made of a rubber like gum, from a Malayan tree. This was heated and hardened in a ball shaped mould. It had low elasticity and would feel 'dead' to the present day golfer. It travelled around twenty five per cent less distance than does a modern ball. It did have the advantage of being cheap to produce, and when it lost its shape the club professional could put it back in a mould, apply heat and reform it. It had the even greater advantage for golf committees, that they could have smaller and less expensive golf course layouts than their modern day counterparts.

THE HASKELL BALL

However 1900 saw a striking development in the technology of golf balls. An American, Dr Coburn Haskell, invented a new ball consisting of hundreds of yards of thin rubber band wound around a solid rubber core. This was then covered with an outer layer of hardened gutta

The Evolution of the Golf Ball.

"The Feathery"

"Smooth Gutta"

"Marked Gutta"

"Rubber Core"

"Dunlop Orange Spot"

"Dunlop Junior"

DUNLOP "V"

"The World's longest and most accurate golf ball."

THE COMPLETE DUNLOP RANGE FOR 1914.

THE DUNLOP RUBBER COMPANY, LIMITED, Founders of the Pneumatic Tyre Industry, MANOR MILLS, ASTON, BIRMINGHAM

3. *Dunlop Rubber Company advertisement-1914. Top left: the 'feathery' made of feathers encased in leather, supplanted in 1848 by the gutta percha. Dunlop balls were made on the Haskell principle.*

percha. Its introduction was rapid because Sandy Herd, the Huddersfield professional, acquired one at great expense just prior to the 1902 British Open, and beat Harry Vardon by one shot. His fellow competitors, to his consternation, attributed his victory entirely to the new ball. From then on the Haskell was used by all the professionals, but the gutta percha with its price advantage, continued to be used by most club golfers for many years after the invention of the Haskell. In time mass production would bring the price of the new ball to within the reach of the club golfer.

A spectator at the Sleaford Road club would have seen the men playing golf wearing heavy jackets, and leather boots studded with nails. Most of them would probably be smoking pipes and would continue to do so whilst playing their shots.

THE LADIES

When the Boston club was formed, a ladies section also started. This reflected credit on the Boston committee, since, on many courses of the time, the ladies were not made welcome. The attire of the fair sex was even more inhibiting to good golf than was the men's. Long dresses with two or more petticoats was the order of the day, and for the more ample figures these might enclose a stout whale bone corset, though with experience doubtlessly these were left hanging up in the clubroom. The effect of a whale bone disintegrating at the top of the back swing is too painful to contemplate.

THE MANNER OF PLAY

The golf swings used at the turn of the century by the best professionals would have appeared rather strange and uncouth to our present day eye, used as we are to the smooth straight armed swing of their modern counterpart. Even Taylor and Vardon, early in their careers, favoured a bent left arm and a lunge and sway at the ball. Vardon however, one of the first of the 'scientific' golfers, was by then beginning to analyse the best way of hitting a golf ball long and straight. He would popularize the 'Vardon' overlapping grip, probably first used by J E Laidlaw, a very good amateur player of the period, and a move towards the present day smooth balanced swing.

There are no details, and no one alive today, who knows anything about the plan of the Sleaford Road course. It was laid out on a block of about fifty acres, bounded by Sleaford Road, Woodville Road, the South Forty Foot Drain, and the Cut Drain. The area was permanent pasture for grazing livestock and could soon be turned into a makeshift golf course, with the hazards consisting of hedges containing some mature trees. It is unlikely there would have been any bunkers. Although it would be wettish after periods of rain the fertile soil provided a thick mat of grass

4a. The 'Old' swing of
James Braid

4b. The 'New' swing of
Harry Vardon

13.

that could generally carry the heavy traffic of the golfers. When however there was prolonged rain the course would become unplayable. The greens would be fenced off during the summer to avoid damage from the heavy bullocks and sheep, and these would be mown from time to time. This would be the job of the professional, who traditionally at that period occupied a much more subservient role than his modern counterpart, with his main task being to keep the greens and course in a good state of repair, with any time left over used for mending members balls and clubs, and giving golf lessons. He would be completely barred from the members lounge if the club were sufficiently fortunate to have one. Nothing is known about the background of Mr Mitchell the first club professional.

The tees would be unfenced in the summer, and consequently on the rough side when in play in the winter months. By the side of each tee there would be a wooden box containing sand, for the members to place under their ball. The sandbox would continue to do its duty well into the 30's and 40's, when the present wooden tee started to replace sand. No club minutes have survived to give us an insight into the life of the club. Indeed none would be available until 1962. We depend therefore on newspaper reports, written spasmodically by the club secretaries, for information and these are generally sketchy.

The Lincolnshire Union of Golf Clubs

The first monthly medal played at the Boston Golf Club of which we have details relates to a ladies competition played on February 4th, 1901, and fittingly won by the Hon Sec Miss Francis South, who would become one of the staunchest supporters of the Club.

The Boston Guardian of 23rd February 1901 reported on the second AGM of the recently formed Lincolnshire Union of Golf Clubs. This had taken place the previous Friday, in the Albion Hotel, Lincoln. Mr W T Warrener took the Chair, and the following delegates attended. Mr T Theodore Norton, Belton Park; Mr R H Ferguson, Skegness; Mr E McAmoir, Brigg; Mr W P Newsam, Lincoln South Park; Mr S Shaw, Grantham; Mr F A Gamble, Thonock Park; and Mr H H Dunn, Lincoln.

The Hon Sec commented on the great success of the first County Championships held at Carholme the previous April.

14.

There were 90 competitors. There was a healthy balance sheet. The following officers were elected for 1901. President: the Earl of Brownlow; Vice Presidents: the Earl of Yarborough, the Earl of Scarborough, the Earl of Winchester, and the Hon Harold Finch-Hatton; The Hon Sec and Treasurer Mr W T Warrener and the Hon Local Secretary Mr Theodore Norton. It was decided to hold the County Championship meeting at Belton Park in April. Mr R H Ferguson, Seacroft was elected Captain of the County Team and it was decided to arrange matches with the Golf Union of Yorkshire and Nottinghamshire.

CONTEMPORARY BIOGRAPHIES

5. *The Right Hon. The Earl Brownlow, Lord Lieutenant of Lincolnshire.*

R H Ferguson was the golfer who played in the Exhibition Match to celebrate the official opening of the Boston Golf Club.

In the same year a Lincolnshire Ladies' County Union was formed with Mrs M Wilson as Captain and Miss Luard, 3 Wellington Gardens, Grantham the Hon Sec. This report gives a valuable insight into how golf was developing and being organised in England.

The Lincolnshire Ladies' County Union immediately joined the Ladies' English Golf Union which had been started up in 1893. The men's County Organisation could not follow suit because, as we shall see, their English Union did not then exist.

Lincolnshire ladies started to play against adjacent counties and in 1901 their team, consisting of Miss Gwyn, Mrs E Smith, Miss A Bramley, Mrs Strett Thompson, Mrs M Wilson, Mrs White and Miss Luard, lost to Yorkshire at Belton Park.

THE GOLF UNIONS

The game of golf had expanded rapidly at the turn of the century and had started to change into a major national sport. The problem facing golf officials was how to set up an organisation that could cope with the new demands this involved. The Royal and Ancient Golf Club of St Andrews was by that date the governing body responsible for the rules of the game since being asked to take on that task by the leading clubs in 1897.

In 1900 the R and A Committee also provided advice on the organisation of the British Open. The men's Open Championship had started in 1860 and by 1900 was a well organised event with a first prize of £30.00. It was open to professional and amateur golfers and had already been won by several amateurs by 1900. Not until 1919 however was the full management of the Open taken over by the Royal and Ancient Golf Club of St Andrews. Organising the Open however in those early days was a much less demanding task than running the national golfing scene. What happened was that the individual Counties took on the responsibility for organising the game, and by 1900 when the Lincolnshire County Golf Union was formed most of the County Unions had already been set up. One of their tasks was to organise matches between the best clubs in their county and hold competitions that would identify the best players to represent the county and country in representative matches.

Membership of the County Unions was by invitation. Boston did not receive this much sought after accolade until 1962. You may be assured that Mr Curtis and his successors, including the ambitious Major Oliver Cooper, were only too well aware of the inferior status of their beloved club and this was one of the motivating forces that would inspire them to make progress.

HANDICAPS

The counties did an adequate job of arranging county and inter-county events. There was however one vital role that was quite beyond their ability, and that was organising and running an efficient handicapping system. This had to be done on a national basis since it needed to be based on a fair and equitable assessment of course difficulty and an equally fair and ongoing system of allocating individual handicaps to players. It required a National Union of Golf Clubs to carry out this onerous and demanding duty.

THE MEN'S GOLF UNION

This brings us to one of the most interesting stories in the early history of the game in Britain. Despite the very best efforts of

16.

many keen and leading golfers the English men's clubs resisted the necessary development of a national rather than a county based golf organisation. The Irish male golfers, however, had formed a Union in 1891 followed by the Welshmen in 1895.The principal reason was the reluctance of the counties to lose power to any National Federation. The result was that the handicapping system for male golfers was chaotic in those early days and remained so until, on 13th February 1924, at a meeting in Manchester, the English Golf Union was formed. The very next day on the 14th February a Council was formed at a meeting in York whose role would be to deal with what had become a vexed question, 'The SSS (Standard Scratch Score) for courses and handicapping'.

ISSETTE PEARSON AND THE LADIES' GOLF UNION

If male intransigence had held back the development of their golf organisation the foresight and drive of the fair sex golfers had triumphed. At the Wimbledon Ladies' Club towards the end of the 19th Century one of the great characters of golf was emerging. Miss Issette Pearson, the daughter of a wealthy business man, had taken a great liking to this new sport, and had found she had an aptitude for the game. Like many Victorian ladies of ability she had found that many of the roles that would be open to modern women were closed to her and her peers. Golf was an ideal way of passing the time and she very quickly took charge of the affairs of the Wimbledon Ladies' Golf Club.

She soon made a name for herself and her club as a good organiser of local county and inter-county matches, but she quickly realised that a better organisation was required to get the ladies game on a sound footing. Amongst several outstanding problems, the questions of handicaps caused constant arguments and friction between clubs and players. She sought the help of a local prominent golfer by the name of Dr William Laidlaw-Purves, who had been trying in vain to set up a National Federation for the men's game. Together they made a formidable team with similar views and objectives.

After a great deal of spade work the Ladies' Golf Union was formed at a meeting in London on 19th April 1893 and Issette Pearson was elected its first secretary. She would hold the office for many years and by her drive and energy set the ladies' game

6. *Miss Issette Pearson, founder of the Ladies' Golf Union in 1893.*
[Courtesy of English Ladies' Golf Union, St. Andrews]

7. *Lady Margaret Scott, winner of the Ladies' Open Amateur Championship in 1893, 1894, and 1895*
[Courtesy of the L. G. U]

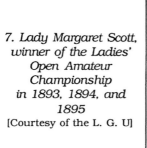

18.

on a solid footing that would remain in advance of that of the men's game until 1924. The Scottish ladies formed their own Association in 1902 and the Welsh ladies followed suit in 1904.

The Ladies' Golf Union Committee led by their formidable secretary immediately set about the problem of working out a fair handicapping system. One of the great advantages of playing golf is that a system has been devised to allow very good golfers to play against players of much lower ability, on an equal footing. Every golfer is allocated a handicap figure. This is the number of shots to be deducted from his score after playing over eighteen holes. A good golfer might have a handicap of 6 and a much less able player one of 27. To operate this system however requires a formidable organisation which can allocate fair handicaps to individual players and can then adjust them at frequent intervals as players improve or deteriorate. But courses vary in their degreee of difficulty and an efficient and uniform system of handicapping requires an assessment for each club of its degree of difficulty.

Issette Pearson solved the problem by getting her inspectors to check each course that was in her Union. The degree of difficulty was worked out as the number of shots that a first class golfer would normally require to play the course. This is the course's Standard Scratch Score. Typically it varies from 67 to 73 and is largely decided by the length of the course. By 1900 the ladies had a good handicapping system in operation. The men's system however was still disorganised and the 'Royal and Ancient' was perpetually embroiled in arbitrating on complaints from clubs and players about losing matches because of the unfair handicaps of their opponents.

Issette Pearson's handicap system has been improved and refined over the years but devising the perfect method has continued to elude the senior organisers of the game.

There remain significant differences in the way the ladies' handicap system operates compared with that of the men. For example the ladies are obliged to hand in four cards each year for their handicap to be adjusted. The men are under no such obligation.

Under the aegis of the English Golf Union in 1901 a Lincolnshire ladies' team played and unfortunately lost to a

Yorkshire team at Belton Park. The Lincs ladies were: Miss Gwyn, Mrs E Smith, Mrs A Bramley, Miss Gilliatt, Mrs S Thompson, Miss B Thomson, Mrs M Wilson (captain), Mrs White and Miss Luard. There were no Boston Ladies' Golf Club members in that team. None would be considered until 1962 when their club would eventually receive the coveted invitation to join the ranks of the 'great and the good' in the Union.

HANDICAP CONFUSION

Prior to 1924 only the ladies' clubs which were members of the Golf Club Union could boast of an adequate handicapping system. The Boston ladies were not members and had a chaotic allocation of handicaps. There is no better illustration of this than the mystery of the handicap of their hard working Hon Sec Miss Francis South. She won the first monthly medal recorded at the Boston Club with an undisclosed score. She then played in a monthly medal in November 1907 with a score of 116-4-112. There is no known record of her ever playing in another competition. How did she acquire her handicap of 4 and then play to 40?

THE FIRST MEN'S MEDAL

Meanwhile the Boston golfers, like all golfers the world over, were much more concerned with their own game and its problems than the politics of the national golfing organisations. The very first report we have of a monthly medal played by the Boston men took place in January 1901. Rain and snow affected the attendance and the scores. The best three were: H Willows 113-24-89. W Bell 117-28-89, H Walford 104-12-92.

It can be seen from these scores that either the course and conditions were dreadful or the handicaps were faulty, or both. The scores for the remainder of the year confirms all these possibilities. In the *Boston Guardian* of February 25th 1901 the following report has been written by an astonished correspondant.

> The Boston Golf Club is not only a successful one as far as membership is concerned but its institution appears to have created an enthusiasm for the game which is quite remarkable. Yesterday (Thursday) we noticed a number of members, heedless of the snow underfoot and driving rain

and sleet which ever and amen swept across the links, playing the game as if their very lives depended on it and apparently without any thought that they would be much more comfortable indoors upon such a disagreeable day.

The infatuation for the game which seizes everyone after handling the clubs or whatever they are termed is difficult to understand by the non-player. The caddies reap no such reward from those who can well afford to distribute a little of their wealth. A lady golfer however confessed that she found it a rather expensive game as she had in a very short time broken 3 pairs of stays.'

E Cooke in the March medal scored a nett 77 and our captain, Frank Curtis, managed a nett 79 playing off 16. There were fourteen members who competed and eight did not complete a card. The lowest handicap player was the Rev H Curtis off 8.

The Lincolnshire Union was already organising a number of county events and a Mixed Foursome was held in May and won by Miss H Thomson and the Rev W L de B Thorold.

MEMBERSHIP

The number of members at the Boston club in those days fluctuated around fifty. This was fairly typical for the clubs of that time and must have pleased the committee. Woodhall Spa when it started up in 1891 mustered forty-five (including visitors). Lincoln South Park in 1893 had a membership of forty-three together with four lady associates.

The Boston members, like those of most of the other clubs, were from the wealthy stratum of society. They comprised solicitors, doctors, vicars, business men, the wealthier farmers, and their wives and daughters. There were many reasons for this limited membership. The population of Britain in 1900 was around 41 million. Today it is nearer 55 million with a much higher percentage in the golf-playing age group. The principal reason however for the small and elite membership of Boston and other golf clubs throughout the land was in the main a social phenomenon. In the early 1900's Britain had just come to the end of the Victorian era. The old Queen died on the 22 January 1901, a few months after the start up of the club, after reigning for 64 years.

21.

Class distinction was at its height during her reign. There were masters, and there were servants, and people knew their station in life. Even the great Vardon would touch his forelock to the meanest member of the clubs he visited, and would not dream of entering a members' lounge. It needed the flamboyant Hagan twenty-five years later to start to put an end to this discrimination.

Despite the introduction of the railway to Boston in 1848 Britain was still a horse-powered society. Being a predominantly farming area Boston depended on the horse to work the farms and provide transport.

Farm workers and most of the farmers worked a sixty hour week, and it was hard, grinding physical work. In 1914 the basic agricultural week was still fifty-eight hours and the wage for this sixteen shillings and ninepence. Other workers in Boston were almost equally hard worked. Ordinary workers had neither the income nor the energy to play golf regularly. The Welfare State was away in the future and there were no state pensions, unemployment benefit, sick pay nor Income Support, to help people in difficulty. Not until Lloyd George and Winston Churchill pushed through the great National Insurance Act of 1911, would a start be made to our present caring society. Any Boston family meeting hard times in 1900 without relatives to help out would quickly find themselves in the public workhouse on Skirbeck Road dressed in rough calico uniforms and treated little better than medieval serfs. Living conditions compared to the present day were appalling.

LIVING CONDITIONS

In 1900 Dr Tuxford, the Boston Medical Officer of Health, wrote in his annual report: 'The insanitary conditions of this town without mincing words is as bad as it can be.' He went on to say that largely because of this situation a quarter of babies born died within a year. The expectation of life in 1900 for a male was 46 years, and for a female 50 years. Today it is 70 and 75 respectively. Boston of course was no worse nor better than all the other towns and villages in the country at the start of the new century.

Many of the older members enjoying themselves playing golf

22.

today, and helping golf secretaries balance the books, would not have survived had they been born in that era. Last but not least, the cost of running golf clubs in those days was very much less than today. Committees could be much more choosy in who they would accept as members than the present generation of treasurers, faced with more and more demands for better and more expensive facilities.

Sometime prior to 1901 another famous Lincolnshire club started up: Sutton-on-Sea Golf Club, now under the name of Sandilands Club. It was already established when in 1908 plans were drawn up for a 'garden village by the sea' called Woldsea in an area called Sandilands and including the Sutton Golf Course. A true links like Seacroft, Sandilands has always been popular with golfers from all over the county, and with the hordes of holiday golfers who descend on the coast each summer. It appeared to be rather informally managed in the early days with the course maintained by a group of local golfers assisted by friendly holiday home owners in the area. Visiting golfers used the services of the local boys as caddies paying them 9d a day—a princely sum at the time.

THE FIRST AGM OF THE BOSTON CLUB

In October the first AGM of the Boston Golf Club was held in the Peacock and Royal Hotel, Boston. This was at the time a coaching inn and one of the best facilities in Boston. It has long since been demolished to make way for the present 'Boots the Chemist' shop but in 1900 not only did it provide comfortable rooms for a meeting but, like many other similar establishments, owned its own brewery and brewed its own beer which was on sale at that time for 1/- a gallon; and it provided stabling for coach horses and private hire.

From the report it can be deduced that problems were already beginning to surface in the new club. There was not a large attendance. Frank Curtis endeavoured to hand over the captaincy but could not find anyone willing to take it on. He therefore continued in the post. It was decided to allow new members to join without payment of an entrance fee. 'Explanations were asked for for the change of the club professional and strong feelings were expressed on the subject.

23.

Several of the committee publicly dissociated themselves from this course of action and the employment of a new man.' The Rev Garvey continued as Hon Sec and Mr Bell as Treasurer. The Ladies' Club also held their AGM with Mrs Black re-elected Captain and Miss South as the Hon Sec. The committee were Mrs Bell, Miss Mawson, Miss Armstrong, Miss Wheeler and Miss Stables. Doubtless the members were finding that golf played in the winter had its disadvantages.

THE FIRST INTER CLUB MATCHES

In March 1902 we have the first report of a match played between Boston and another club. Boston Gents played Spilsby Gents at Boston.

The results were:

Boston		Spilsby	
Rev H Curtis	3	Rev R Barrow	0
F Curtis	11	Rev C Disbowe	0
H Walford	8	H Trinder	0
E Cooke	7	Mr Waller	0
Rev Garvey	8	Mr Robinson	0
Mr Stables	4	Mr Richardson	0

The Rev C Disbowe was the Rector of Skegness, and the Rev R Barrow was the Rector of Skendleby, Spilsby. Both were members of the first Seacroft Golf Club Committee. The scoring system was unusual. However it was calculated that Boston scored a resounding victory.

A problem arises trying to find out any details of the history and background of the Spilsby Club which like many others has long since vanished. The situation is rather similar to Boston, in that the origins of the club is shrouded in mystery. Spilsby like Boston has a keen local history society but the members have no good information on their deceased golf club. It was an area with many keen golfers. No less than six of the Seacroft management committee came from the Spilsby area.

24.

The Motor Car

The horse was the master of the scene in 1900, and would remain so for many years to come, but the country was now beginning to rush into the twentieth century. The newspapers of the day reported a typical court case. 'John Mitcham of 52 Queen Street was charged with driving a horse and cart in a furious manner in Norfolk Street;' He was fined 10/- (ten shillings) and 7/6d. (seven shillings and six pence) costs, or fourteen days in prison. In July 1902 however, there was another rather humorous but historic report: 'The mayor had evidently decided to investigate the contents of Mr Slingby's shop window in the centre of Boston, but unfortunately forgot to get out of his car before he did so, resulting in considerable damage to the car and the window.'

The motor car had arrived into our lives. It would have vast implications for all of society including the new sport of golf. The wealthier members of the community, many of whom were golfers, would quickly take to this new form of transport. Golf committees would from henceforth no longer have a captive membership. Disgruntled players could jump into their cars and travel to a more progressive club. There would be more competition for the limited supply of members between golf clubs throught the county.

The motorists very soon began to organise themselves and in July 1902 the Lincolnshire Automobile Club aranged a run out to Heckington.

The 1902 AGM

The AGM of October 1902 showed several changes. The new captain was the Rev H Garvey. The committee: Rev W Fielding, Dr South, B B Dyer, H Harwood, G Rainey, S Cooper, W Bedford, R Staniland and J Wood. The Hon Sec was Mr Bell. Sam Cooper was a local corn merchant and a member of a family that would have a great part to play in the history of the club.

The ladies AGM provided a valuable insight into the development of the club. 'The professional can give daily instructions. There is a convenient club house where refreshments can be obtained and clubs stored. An American Tournament will be played in November and December with an entrance fee of one shilling. Particulars of the tournament will be found in the Ladies' Club Room, at Mr Bontoft's 93 Sydney Street,' As to who the new club professional was we have no information. The details about the 'club house' are especially intriguing since it denotes an important development in the history of the club.

Number 93 Sydney Street was then an ordinary terraced house and is still so today. It had been built around the time of the start up of the club and was not far from the course. As to what the financial arrangements were between the club and Mr Bontoft we have no details. Did the gentlemen also have facilities there, or was this solely for the ladies?

8. The first Boston Golf Club 'clubhouse' at 93 Sydney Street—as it is today.

FRANK CURTIS DISAPPEARS

There is another unsolved mystery in the affairs of the club during 1902. The man who started the Boston Golf Club, Frank Curtis, disappears completely from the area, with no information as to why, how, nor where he went. The last public mention of him in newspaper reports, is when he played in the Spilsby match in March. Thereafter he vanishes into thin air. There is information that he was given six months salary in lieu of notice from Messrs Soulby and Winch, but why and where he subsequently went is a mystery, given his standing in the area and with his firm. Perhaps it is as well that his disappearance remains a mystery. The salary paid in lieu of notice is rather ominous. As he was a councillor it is possible that the Boston Corporation Minutes for this period could have shed some light on this mystery, but they have unfortunately disappeared.

In November Lincolnshire Ladies played against Surrey Ladies at Belton Park. The Lincolnshire team was: Mrs E Revill, Miss M Revill, Mrs M Wilson, Mrs Marshall, Mrs S Thomson, Mrs E Smith, Miss Gilliatt, and Miss E Wilson. Surrey ladies won 5 $^1/_4$ to 2 $^1/_2$ and within the same month a Ladies team from Woodhall Spa severely beat Belton Ladies 7 points to 1.

COLD WINTERS

1903 started off with weather that would test the resolve of the most intrepid golfer. The January men's monthly medal was played with snow falling. Only two members competed and Mr Bell won with a nett 107. The Boston golfers had learned, in the short time that the club had been operating, that they would have to pay a heavy price for the low rent they had negotiated for a six month winter course.

No one had heard of the 'greenhouse effect' in those days, nor the danger of the earth starting to warm up. The very opposite applied, as there was a run of very cold hard winters at the start of the century. If this was unfortunate for the golfers, it was good news for the traditional followers of the fenman's sport of ice skating. The Amateur and Professional Ice Skating Competitions were regularly held on the frozen fens around Boston and Spalding. Many of the Boston golfers engaged in this sport and several of them, including Fred McGuire and the Arch family, were championship skaters.

W. GARFITT, M.P.

From its inaugeration the Boston Golf Club had elected an eminent committee, and an equally eminent President. Mr W Garfitt, Member of Parliament for Boston, JP, DL, had accepted the honour of becoming the first President of the new club. In many ways, and without casting aspersions on succeeding and present committees, these early managers of the Boston Golf Club were, on paper, of superior social status to their successors. With a Member of Parliament and a wealthy banker as their President, and several church dignitaries to accompany him, the early meetings would in all likelihood have been rather more grave, and most probably less joyful occasions, than their 1990s equivalents.

William Garfitt represented Boston at Westminster as a Unionist MP from 1895 to 1906. He was a highly respected member of the Boston business community. There was at that time no Labour Party, as we know it, in existence. Not until 1906 would 26 Labour MPs under their leader Keir Hardie, take their place at Westminster. The Unionists would be known today as the Conservative Party, and they competed with the Liberal Party for the favours of the electorate.

BOSTON MAGAZINE 1900

9. W. Garfittt, M.P.

As far as is known Mr Garfitt did not play golf. There is no record of him having played at Boston or any other club. He was a conscientious and well liked parliamentary representative for Boston, and involved himself in a wide range of local activities. He was eminently suited to be the first President of The Boston Golf Club.

THE PERSEVERANCE PIG CLUB

Despite the harshness of life in those far off days, it must not be thought that it was all doom and gloom. In fact in many ways people lived a more natural and happy life than their modern counterparts. There appeared to be less 'nervous stress' type illness prevalent. Hard physical work is recognised by the medical authorities to be rather better than some of the modern medicines to combat this problem, and there was no shortage of this commodity for most people of the period. If there was no television, nor radio to pass the time there were other entertainments to compete with golf.

These included magic lantern shows, old time music hall

28.

performances and last but by no means least, and common in all the fen areas, the local pig club evenings.

A newspaper article in February 1902 reported that Mr Garfitt had just renewed his subscription to the Boston Perserverance Pig Club. Boston Golf Club therefore had to share the energy and attention of its President with one of the most popular recreational activities of the fen population. The existence of the pig clubs illustrates clearly the vast difference of life in the early 1900s from that of today.

During the 19th century many of these pig clubs had sprung up over the country and there were a dozen in existence around Boston and South Holland. With meat expensive and scarce in relation to current wage levels, many families had one or two pigs in a pen at the bottom of their garden, or if they lived in the town, any convenient place adjacent to the house. If the pig should die, which any one with much experience of these temperamental animals will know was a frequent occurence, it was a catastrophe for the family. To deal with this situation pig clubs had sprung up whereby the members paid a small weekly subscription, and in the event of the untimely demise of the animal, the club would pay out enough to compensate to some degree for the unfortunate occurence.

In the course of time pig clubs came to play an important part in the social life of Boston and the surrounding fen villages. They would put on a winter programme of entertainment and our President would occasionally attend and preside over the event.

THE GREAT TRIUMVIRATE

The game of golf in Boston and elsewhere was given a great boost by the increasing publicity given to the top players of the period. Today the professional golf players dominate the national and international scene, but at the turn of the century they played a much smaller part in the game than did the top amateur players. The British Amateur Championship, which had started up at Hoylake in 1885, was a much more prestigious tournament than was the British Open. Nevertheless, today those early amateur winners have been largely forgotten, whereas the top professionals of that period have taken their rightful place in the history of the game.

The professional golf scene of the period was dominated by three of the greatest golfers ever to step on a course: Harry Vardon, John Henry Taylor, and James Braid. Between them they would win the British Open on seventeen occasions spanning the years 1894 to 1914. The sports writers of the time christened them 'The Great Triumvirate', and who can dispute their title? They played an important part in attracting new players by playing exhibition matches at clubs all over the country including many of the Lincolnshire courses. The American invasion of the British golf scene was still a few years

[FROM A PAINTING BY CLEMENT FOWLER]

10. The Great Triumvirate

away. Indeed the USA Open, which started up in 1895, was being frequently won by expatriate Scots, and by Harry Vardon himself in 1900. Vardon in his long career almost repeated this feat in 1920 when he was beaten by one shot by another English golfer, Ted Ray.

LADIES' GOLF

Ladies' golf was also making good progress in the country despite the male hostility at many clubs. They had an early stroke of good fortune. At the start up of the Ladies' Golf Union in 1893, they held the first British Ladies' Championship over the nine hole course at St Annes. It was won that year, and the two following years, by Lady Margaret Scott, who not only was a first class golfer who could whang the ball vast distances, but was in

30.

addition a rather beautiful and shapely young girl. This of course did more to dispel the prejudices of all the old army colonels than a thousand lectures on sex discrimination, a phrase quite unknown in those halcyon days.

Scores at Boston continued to be very high by present day standards. The captain, the Rev H Garvey, held his competition, the Captain's Prize, in March and this was won by another cleric, also a staunch supporter of the club, The Rev W Fielding with 95–18–77.

The Rev Fielding, who served for many years on the committee, was a fierce opponent of any form of gambling. He would not permit even innocent raffles to be held for church funds. What would he have said about the occasional lively game of pontoon held in the Boston Club lounge today? Indeed, how many of us who are present day members at Boston would have got past the 1900 committee?

In the early days of the Club as today there were a few families who provided several members for the club. One of the best known of the period was the Arch family, later consisting of father, mother, two sons and three lovely daughters—I have the word of Bryan Cooper on this latter point. They were keen supporters of the club over many years. The father and his sons were also first class, all-round sportsmen, and won titles in skating and cycling, in addition to their golfing mementoes. Mr Arch, Senior won the Boston men's mile scratch cycling competition during the year.

NEW LINKS

The 1903 AGM held in October marked another milestone in the history of the club. The Captain, Rev H Garvey, announced:

> 'New Links have been engaged near to Tower Road, Skirbeck, which are rapidly in the course of formation, and will afford nine good holes of a mile and a quarter in extent. A professional has been engaged from the North of England. There is a Golf House with separate rooms for ladies and gentlemen, and when the course has been got into order, an enjoyable season's play is anticipated.'

11. The one time site of 'The Tower Road' golf course lies in the triangle formed by Spilsby Road to the north, Freiston Road-Tower Road to the west and south, and Tollfield Road to the east extending, as it then did, along a footpath to reach what is now Blackthorn Lane. The approximate site is now occupied by Wing's Meadow and the Girl Guides' building at the narrow western end, and the housing developments around Margaret Drive, Freshney Way, Ashlawn Drive, and extending to Princess Anne Road at the broad western end. Also included now are four schools and a residential home.

The upper panoramic view is approaching the Guides' building: the lower is of Ashlawn Drive from west to east.

CHAPTER TWO

THE TOWER ROAD GOLF CLUB

T O HELP PAY THE EXPENSES involved in moving from Sleaford Road to Tower Road, the club held an evening's entertainment on the 26th October in the Shodfriars Hall, Boston, when members were promised, and no doubt received, 'a most cultured performance'. It included a drama performance of 'Sunset', and Mr F Storr's String Band playing a selection of melodies. Reserved seats were 2/6d, and the balcony 2/-.

The new Tower Road nine hole course, was situated a mile east from the town centre. This area is now largely a modern housing estate, but at that time it was grassland, farmed by a Mr Dion amongst others. It was stocked with cattle and sheep, and consisted of rather rough undulating fields, crossed by drainage ditches. It extended to around 50 acres, made up of half a dozen fields, surrounded by low and broken hedges containing many mature trees, and it was bounded by three roads, Spilsby Road, Tower Road, and Tollfield Lane (now Road).

Mr Dion was an enterprising young farmer who by dint of hard work had built up a considerable farming enterprise. He would have made a first class landlord for the new club. The committee must have remained cautious about borrowing capital to improve the golf club, because the new tenancy was, like the previous one, for a six month winter let, from the 1st October to the end of March. The tenancy must have been somewhat flexible as in some seasons play started earlier. Presumably when the farmer sold his cattle or took them into their winter yards he would allow the golfers access to the course. The land, like the Sleaford Road course, would be grazed by stock during the summer months, and the greens fenced off. The principal attraction for the club was that they could rent a cottage on Tower Road, situated at the edge of the course. This served as a club house and was a vast improvement on the facilities they had had at Sydney Street.

The 1903/4 edition of The Golfing Annual had the following entry:

BOSTON

Instituted October 1900, Annual Subscription £1.1s.
Number of members 60. Captain – Rev H R Garvey, Hon Sec
– B B Dyer, Holgate, West Skirbeck. The course is of nine
holes circuit (1738 yards) at Tower Road.
The hazards are bunkers, hedges and ditches. It is a mile
and a half from the Station (Great Northern Railway).
Boston Ladies Golf Club instituted December 1900.
Subscription 10/6d.
Play is over the men's course.

Unfortunately it does not give any details regarding the
professional who had been appointed. The bunkers were few and
consisted of shallow depressions filled with sand. There were
several deep and wide ditches, separating the fields, that would
constitute quite difficult hazards for the golfers. There is of
course no one alive today who played at the start up of Tower
Road, but even when play finished there many years later, those
who can recall it, remember it as a rough old course compared to
present day standards.

In the 1906 *Golfing Annual* there is an addition to details with
visitors being charged 1/- a day. In the 1911 edition a further
piece of information was given, 'No Sunday play'. Most clubs of
the time, including Boston, had strict rules prohibiting Sunday
play. There were many more clergy in public life in those days
and many of them golfers. As the Boston club can testify, they
were keen and hardworking members. It is understandable that
they would not be keen to have play on the Sabbath. There was
however a move afoot at the time to allow golf on some clubs in
the country on Sunday and hence the insert to avoid
disappointing Sunday visitors.

In the *Golfing Annual* over the next few years there are no
details of names nor information provided regarding greenkeepers,
nor professionals employed at the club.

THE FIRST COMPETITION

The first competition at Tower Road of which we have details
was a men's monthly medal for January 1904. The scores were:

Rev H Garvey 96 14 82; W Bell 108 16 92; Rev H Curtis 104 8 96; C Holland 131 32 99; H Marris 166 32 134. B B Dyer, W Bedford, and S Cooper nil return.

The Rev H Curtis playing off 8 is typical of the incomprehensible handicaps of the period. His previous net scores in competition were 88 and 83. Perhaps the 96 was the last straw since he disappears from the list of competition players after that.

Other players mentioned in competitions held around that time, with their handicaps, were: A Hill 22, G Rainey 30, E Smith 22, Dr Small 22, Dr Wright 22, J Boag 28, A Marris 14, C Taylor 22, Rev J Sykes 28, and H Johnson 30.

At the first AGM for the Tower Road Club, held in October 1904 at The Peacock and Royal, Mr W Garfitt was re-elected President, the Rev Garvey re-elected as Captain, Mr W Bell as Hon Treasurer and Mr B B Dyer as Hon Sec. The committee was: Rev W Fielding, C Wood, R South, E Smith, and W Bedford. Mr W Bell was manager of the Lincoln and Lindsey Bank, one of the many small banks which were common in those days and have long since disappeared. The rest of the committtee was made up of solicitors, bankers, doctors, vicars and business men. The links were opened for play on the 1st September and the chairman commented that they were a great improvement on Sleaford Road.

> Regular labour will be employed on the greens and course.
> Lessons will be available for interested members.

As to who the professional was, how long he remained at the club, and when he left, we have no details. He would, like the professionals at all but a handful of the very best clubs in the country, spend most of his time mowing the greens and keeping the course in order. He would provide lessons to members and anyone interested in taking up the game. Some of them were skilled club makers, and added to their small wage by providing clubs to the players' specifications. The club heads and shafts of this period could be bought in by the professional and made up into the finished article. There was available at the time a wide range of heads and the players of the time spent much energy and got much amusement searching for clubs that would give them another fifty yards on their drive, or get rid of a troublesome slice, just as we do today, and no doubt with as much or as little success. A professional at a club which was only open for the winter season was in a peculiar situation. Was he paid only for six months or did he occupy himself in the summer keeping the greens mown, members' clubs in order, and giving lessons? We do not know.

WOODHALL SPA GOLF CLUB

In 1905 an important event occurred in Lincolnshire golf. The new Woodhall Spa course was officially opened, after a great deal of hard work over the previous three years. This was the third successive course played at the Woodhall Spa club and the great Harry Vardon had a hand in its design. On the 25th February J H Taylor played against the best ball of three club members, A James, W Costobodie, and T Stokes. Taylor won 2 up and went round in 72. The course would not open for general play until May.

12. Col. S. V. Hotchkin, owner of Woodhall Spa Golf Club.

Meanwhile scores at Tower Road were not showing much improvement over those of the old Sleaford Road course. In October, J Boag however did well, and won the monthly medal with 100 28 72. The best gross score noted in the newspaper reports of the year, was W Bell 91 16 75. The lowest handicaps were A Marris 14, the Rev H Garvey 12, and the Rev H Curtis 8. Calculation of an individuals handicap was very much an inspired guess. Like the present day members they were all having great difficulty playing to their handicaps, but it must be remembered that these would generally be much less accurate than those of 1994.

In 1906 the Club President, Mr W Garfitt M P together with his Unionist Party, had a severe shock, as they were swept from power in a landslide victory by the opposition Liberal Party, led by Campbell-Bannerman. Mr Garfitt lost his seat thus ending his

36.

Parliamentary career. He was a keen yachtsman and spent his newly found leisure sailing his yachts, the *Chloris* and the *Shuna*, to far away places. The *Chloris* was a sailing vessel and the *Shuna* a steam yacht. He was evidently a man of means and continued in office as Club President.

Campbell-Bannerman's team, including Asquith, Lloyd-George, and Churchill, were soon hard at work planning the legislation that would lay the foundations for the Welfare State, thus making, as we shall see, future golf club treasurers' work markedly easier. All three were golfers but would have much less time to play the game in the future as they struggled to get Parliament to accept the radical 1911 National Insurance Act and other innovative legislation.

UNIDENTIFIED NEWSPAPER

13. A. J. Balfour (Prime Minister 1902-5) opening the Broadstone course in Dorset in 1908.

One of the reasons for the increase in the popularity of the game at the turn of the century was the publicity gained when the leading politicians of the day became golf enthusiasts. Henry Asquith, Liberal Prime Minister from 1908-1916, was Member of Parliament for East Fife, which included St Andrews and the heartland of the game. Not surprisingly he became a keen golfer. Arthur Balfour, Conservative Prime Minister from 1902-1905, was an avid follower of the game and attended most of the major tournaments. Both were moderate but steady orthodox players. The two 'enfants terrible' of the political scene and bosom

companions, Winston Churchill and David Lloyd George, were
entirely different. Politics was their principal and devouring
interest and any other activity including golf a mere sideline.
Churchill, typically, would play a few holes brilliantly until his
attention became diverted by an unusual bush or bird or
whatever. Lloyd George, the brilliant dynamic young Liberal
radical from Llanystumdwy in Caernarvon— arguably the greatest
Prime Minister of the twentieth century— played a unique type of
game. After striking off, he would march down the course
oblivious to the scenery or the whereabouts of his companion
golfers until he reached the various greens. Golf for him was a
few seconds looking at and striking the ball in between the
Machiavellian scheming as he planned to propel British society
towards a modern, caring way of life.

New names were taking up the game at Boston including W
Pinder, J Shove, and T Horry, all of them off 32. The pound in
those days was worth rather more than its present value.
Numbers 11 and 13 Sleaford Road sold for £240 and £270
respectively in March 1906. When considering the annual
subscription to the Boston Golf Club of just over a pound, and the
value of these houses, it must be remembered that a farm worker
then would be earning around a pound a week for nearly sixty
hours of very hard physical work. The ladies were finding Tower
Road just as difficult as were the men. At their April monthly
medal the best scores were: Mrs Wright 130 36 94, Miss Pooles
156 36 120. Miss Armstrong, Miss G Smith, Miss Wheeler, Mrs
Price, Mrs Boag, and Mrs Dodds nil return.

In May 1906 the Lincolnshire Union of Golf Clubs held their
annual match at Torksey. It opened on Monday with a ladies'
medal competition for the county championships, Miss E Wilson
of Belton Park won the gold medal with a score of 94, and Miss
Bertha Richardson the handicap prize with a nett 91. A mixed
foursome bogey competition was played on Wednesday and won
by Miss Walde-Sibthorp and Mr Lowe 2 up.

The gentlemen's county championship was played on
Wednesday off scratch over thirty holes. The course was 'at full
stretch' and 6350 yards long. Dr J Matthews Duncan, Grimsby,
won the gold medal and county championship with rounds of 89
and 85 — 174.

1905 saw another important event in golf in the county. The Sleaford Golf Club started up. The fascinating story of this club, one of the best in the county and a good friend to Boston during some of the difficult times the club would encounter, is outlined in their excellent guide, written by Brian Harris and Ken Worsencroft. Play started up on the Sleaford course in July 1906, but a team from Boston must have been privileged to obtain an early run over the course, because the 26th May edition of the Boston Guardian gives details of the first match ever held between the two clubs at Rauceby, on Saturday 19th May.

SLEAFORD	BOSTON
Dr G Wilson	Rev H Garvey
C Peacock	A Hill
E Bower	G Bell
Ben Smith	T Horry
H Tointon	J H Taylor
E Teesdale	W Bedford
T Skinner	E P Smith
Rev J Davies	R M Wright
Dr Ewan	J Boag
Capt E Smith	M Bottomley

Boston lost heavily by $8^1/_4$ points to 2

A BRIEF HISTORY OF THE SLEAFORD GOLF CLUB

14. *Major. Gen. Sir Mildmay Willson, K.C.B.—first landlord of Rauceby golf course.*

The Boston players would gain some compensation for the heavy defeat from the pleasure of playing over the delightful course at Rauceby. Laid out over free draining Bunter sandstone it must have seemed like heaven compared to the wettish heavier silt of the Boston course. From its opening it attracted members from all over the country including many from the Boston area, and today remains one of the most delightful courses in the county.

In the same month the lowest gross and net scores recorded to date by a Boston player at Tower Road was 82 11 71 scored by

H Harvey.

There were other sporting activities against which Boston Golf Club had to compete. In March 1906 is a report of a pigeon shoot at Wildmore Fen where the farmer generously provided the targets which were released from cages. These were: 'Some good birds of the old true Lincolnshire Rock breed'. An enjoyable day was had by all participating, presumably excluding the true Lincolnshire Rocks.

Rabbit and hare coursing were equally as popular as pigeon shoots and, similarly, live animals were used. There is no record in the newspapers of the day of any objections being raised against the sports. Most families were too occupied in trying to survive the rigours of the times to worry about the environment or the welfare of the country animals.

SURFLEET GOLF CLUB

Golf continued to increase in popularity. 1907 saw the opening of another South Lincolnshire golf club: the Surfleet Golf Club, now better known as the Spalding Golf Club, opened up towards the end of the year. It had been laid out by the Nottingham professional, Tom Williamson, and it started with the advantage over Boston of being a nine hole course available for play for the full twelve months.

Although Spalding would not officially open until late 1907, there is a record of a match played by a Boston team and a Surfleet team over their course, on Saturday 23rd March 1907.

The Boston team was: Mr T Horry, Mr A Hill, Mr A Marris, Mr M Bottomley, Dr J Taylor, Mr J Shove, Dr R Wright, Mr W Bedford, and Mr J Boag.

The Surfleet team was: A N Other, Rev C J Ward, E T Cooke, Dr G Barrett, Mr C Harvey, Mr F Woods, Mr W Newton, Mr M Savage, and Mr Hamilton.

There has always been much friendly rivalry between the two clubs, and I am delighted to report that we emerged the victor on this first encounter by five and a half, to four and a half points. Like Boston, Surfleet is a true Fenland course with several of the holes running alongside the picturesque and tranquil fen drains and the River Glen. In those early days they had a very much better course than that of the Boston club, and have worked hard ever since to make it a good test of golf. They were good friends to Boston when the club encountered stormy waters in later years, offering the courtesy of their course after the 1949 flooding of the Boston links. The annual subscription of the new course was identical to Boston at one pound and one shilling for the men, and ten shillings and sixpence for the ladies.

The winter of 1907 was very hard with heavy frosts, which did not help the Tower Road golfers but did allow the Lincolnshire fenmen to indulge in one of their favourite pastimes of ice skating. Percy Arch, the well known Boston golfer and cyclist, came fourth at Cowbit Wash in the Amateur Mile Championship, with Walter Pridgeon of Whaplode Drove, one of the best skaters of the time, winning.

An epidemic of scarlet fever closed the workhouse at Skirbeck Road. As a child I well remember the terror of being threatened with being sent off to the workhouse by unthinking relatives. It was a real fear for most working families, any of whom might encounter hard times, and lacking the protection of our current substantial social benefits, finish up in the local workhouse. There was however good news for Boston when Oldrid's Park was handed over as a public recreation ground for the benefit of the townsfolk, initially on a ten years lease, but with the option to purchase for £7,500.

New names were now playing golf for the ladies. The March monthly medal scores were: Miss Armstrong 106 9 97; Miss G Smith 110 13 97; Mrs Price 128 22 106; Miss Pooles 146 36 110; Mrs Dodds 142 30 112; Miss Dolbey 163 30 133. Mrs Black, Mrs Wright, Mrs Boag, Mrs Kitwood, Mrs Wheeler, and Miss G Pooles nil returns.

The Boston ladies, as we see from their scores, deserved full marks for perseverance. The Boston club, in its chequered history, can be thankful for having, from its inception, the backing of a lively and enthusiastic ladies' section. It is no exaggeration to say that in some of the difficult times that the club would encounter, this probably meant the difference between survival and extinction, a fate that many of the early clubs would meet.

The very first away Boston Ladies' match to be recorded was played at Rauceby on 2nd April 1907 when Miss Armstrong, Miss

G Smith, Mrs Black, Mrs Wheeler, Mrs. Price, and Mrs Boag beat a Sleaford team 4 points to $2^3/_4$ points. The Sleaford team members were: Miss M Smith, Miss F Smith, Miss Lowe, Miss Ward, Miss Jenour, and Miss Beaven.

Human nature does not change all that much. Some boys in October caused damage in the new Boston Park to the tune of ten shillings. Boston, like the rest of the country at that time, was in the middle of a depression with farming prices severely lowered by the heavy imports of wheat and refrigerated meat from the prairies of Canada and America. Ominously, there was also rising tension with Germany. With an expanding population, and a growing envy and resentment of the wealth and overseas empires of Britain and France, the German Emperor was under increasing pressure from the Prussian generals to embark on a military escapade.

THE BOSTON MAY HIRING FAIR

There was therefore no great incentive to invest in improvements at Tower Road, nor to move to a better course, although the members were beginning to realise more and more that the present six months winter course was not satisfactory. Life however went on as normal with the Boston May Fair in 1908 being well attended. Plough boys were in demand at £6 to £8 a year; second waggoners at £14 to £16; waggoners at £18 to £22; and grooms at £17. Female servants were sought after, with young girls at £6 to £8; cooks at £18 to £24. Without the help that our generation receive from the 'electrical work horses' of the kitchen, life was hard for working class wives at the start of the century and would remain so for many years. Families of over six were the norm. The chances of most women playing golf were as remote as a visit to the moon.

Most wives of business and professional men of the period, had the help of two or more maids to make life easier and it was mainly due to their assistance that the Boston Ladies' Golf Club flourished. Children up to the age of eleven in many ways had happier lives than their peers of today. Without radio and television to divert them they could play outside to their heart's content, with their regular friends, and with a reasonable diet of simple food, what more did they require for a happy life? It certainly was a more natural existence for them than life today. From that age onwards however it started to become tougher and many of them would then have to start to work in the fields around Boston. In September there were ninety summonses under the new Education Act at Boston Session House for the illegal employment of children.

The Junior Golf section at Boston did not have as many members as it does today. In fact it did not exist.

At the end of 1908, Mrs G Smith won the monthly medal with 108 11 97. A good case for handicap revision? The handicaps as indicated by the scores were still surprising by present standards. Boston Ladies' Golf Club was still not then a member of the Ladies' Golf Union and did not have the advantage of using their handicapping system, which helps to explain the peculiar scores indicated in the competition results. New names continued to join the club, amongst them a Mr H Hudson playing off 15.

Other sports were beginning to compete with golf. In June 1909 the first Boston Lawn Tennis Tournament was held. As is the case today, many members of the golf club were keen tennis players. Since they played tennis mainly in the summer, this did not compete to any great extent with the winter golf played at Tower Road.

The Boston Golf Club AGM was held in October and reported a satisfactory season. There was a surplus in the accounts of £15.14s.2d.

In 1910 the third of the true Lincolnshire links courses started up on the north side of Skegness. A wealthy solicitor, Lawrence Scott, purchased a block of land and had an eighteen hole course designed by James Braid. Scott was a man of great drive and was not content with a typical nine hole course. He also had built a large hotel for £3,000 and could offer holiday makers golf and accommodation known as North Shore Golf Club. It was, and remains to this day, a privately owned golf club with the advantages and disadvantages this involved. The course could not have provided a better opening when a large crowd followed an exhibition match between Braid, Varden, Taylor, and Duncan. It is a very good course, part links, part parkland, with the fine leaved fescue grasses providing excellent lies, and the dunes wonderful bunkers. It would have its good and bad patches but fortunately remains today to help make Lincolnshire one of the best golfing counties in England.

FRED PARKES AND PUDDING PIE FARM

At the end of 1909 a November newspaper report mentioned the sale of a farm that would play a large part in the future history of the Boston Golf Club. Pudding Pie House Farm was sold at auction by Messrs Saul at the Peacock and Royal Hotel, Boston. It lay alongside the river on the edge of the town, and the adjacent banks had recently burst, flooding Pudding Pie Farm. Fred Parkes, a trawler owner in the town, purchased lot 1 – 65 acres for £400. There was no bid for lot 2. Fred Parkes and Pudding Pie would be important names in the future development of Boston Golf Club. Boston at that period had a large deep sea trawling industry, with upwards of 40 boats bringing back large catches of cod and haddock from all the principal fishing areas, including Newfoundland and Iceland. Fred Parkes eventually worked his way up to gain control of this fleet and became one of the most important business men in Boston and Lincolnshire.

Over the next few years the club continued on a steady course. New names became prominent, playing in different competitions. Amongst them were Miss N Staniland, 114 24 90; and Mrs Wrinch, 121 30 91. By this period both the men's and ladies' sections had accumulated a number of cups and trophies. The Harvey Rose Bowl was won in 1910 by Miss M Pooles, in 1911 by Mrs B Swinn, and in 1912 by Miss G E Smith.

Taking part in the 1913 competition were Mrs Mason, Miss M Pooles, Miss A Pooles, Miss B Wrinch, Mrs Wrinch, Miss G Smith, Mrs O Cooper, Mrs Dodds, Miss G Pooles, Mrs Black, Mrs Mawson, Miss Staniland, Mrs Price, and Mrs Kitwood.

Mrs O Cooper was the wife of Major Oliver Cooper who had, like several other members of his family, a profound influence on the fortunes of Boston Golf Club. The Kitwood family were also taking an interest in the new game. In April, at Tower Road, Mrs Price and Mark Bottomley won the Mixed Foursomes. Mark would become one of the best servants the club would ever possess, and its longest serving Honorary Secretary.

With good rail links between Boston, Skegness, and Lincoln there was a considerable amount of golf played over the County.

44.

Walter Kitwood, Boston captain 1912 to 1914, won a competition at North Shore in March 1913.

1914

   1914 is remembered for events other than golf. On 4th August, Britain declared war on Germany, following the attack by German troops on Belgium. There was suprisingly little initial change in the public's way of life, since it was widely felt that it would not take long to achieve victory. Gradually it dawned on everyone that it was going to be a long and bitter struggle. Not until 1916 however would there be compulsory conscription. Long before then Boston Golf Club, like many other clubs up and down the country, lost many of its members, leaving for the front line, some of them never to return from the carnage of the French and Belgian trenches.

   Some of the courses in the county were affected by the onset of the war much more than Boston. Belton Park in 1914 was immediately commandeered by the War Office and turned into an enormous army camp.

   It did not re-open until 1923. Boston, like Belton, was not the only golf club which would be, at some time in its life, temporarily out of action for a long period because of a major catastrophe.

   Meanwhile life in Boston went on as best it could. In November 1914 the men's monthly medal was won with a nett 67 by F Parsons. One of the lowest scores ever recorded at Tower Road. It must be remembered that this course, like the Sleaford Road 'links', was a six monthly course played from October to April 1st. The 1915 Harvey Dixon Rose Bowl was won by Mrs O Cooper whilst her husband was off to the war for the season. The AGM was held in September 1915 at the White Hart Hotel and Mr Pinder presided. Mr Walter Kitwood resigned as captain, and Mark Bottomley was elected in his place. There were now 41 men and 39 lady members. Mr Garfitt was re-elected President. R W Staniland, C H Dunn MP, Dr South and B B Dyer were elected vice presidents. Mr A Norman was elected Hon Secretary and Treasurer. Other members present were C Wood, H Budge, S Cooper, G Robinson, J Towell, W Sharpe, Dr South, B B Dyer, M Bottomley, A Norman, P Staniland and C Dixon, MP. The committee was J Towell, W Pinder, E Richardson, W Kitwood, H

45.

Budge, J Dyson, and George Robinson.

For the first time in the history of the club there was mention of a Greens' Committee. The members were J Pinder, Mark Bottomley and Mr Norman. The task of the members of this committee is onerous on any course but it must have been especially difficult on a six month winter course. The greens were fenced off during the summer months and one of the principal tasks was keeping the fences secure and the cattle off the putting surfaces. At this time there were still no mechanical mowers available, only hand pushed machines. There were early gang mowers pulled by horses available, manufactured by Ransomes (Ransomes, Sim and Jeffries, Ltd) but it is highly improbable that a set of these was owned by the Tower Road Club. There was no need for them on a winter course.

The accounts showed an income of £79 and an expenditure of £71 – a balance of £8 – rather different from its 1994 counterpart.

THE EFFECT OF THE WAR

The effects of the war began to affect the club membership badly and it was decided to discontinue the monthly medals. Five members of the club were already away on active service. They were Major Oliver Cooper, 2nd Lt. Basil Wood, 2nd Lt. George Holland, Captain G H Scott, and Assistant Paymaster Street.

Miss Poole was elected the Ladies Hon. Secretary. Her father, Alderman William Poole, would be a future mayor of Boston and his three daughters staunch members of the Ladies Golf Section. On November 6th 1915 it was announced that: 'The links are now playable although not of course in perfect order.' With the difficulties of coping with problems brought on by the war restrictions, and rationing of newsprint, less information was appearing in the local newspapers.

Despite the hostilities the committee were still seeking to improve the club. It was announced in November 1915 that two new fields had been added to the course. It must have been a late season, or perhaps it was because of work needed to add the two fields to the course, but the course was not ready for play until Saturday December 2nd of that year. The ladies continued to play their competitions and in January 1916 Miss Andrews won with a score of 98 12 86.

46.

With casualty lists appearing in every edition of the local newspapers, and many families losing loved members, reports of entertainment activities including golf, became more and more rare.

No further golf reports were to be found until the end of the war, which ended when the Armistice was signed by the German Government on the 11th November 1918. The Club however had managed to survive and permit play to continue, largely because of the importance of agriculture to the country's survival, and the fact that many members were in reserved occupations connected with food production.

1918

Shortly after the end of the war, the Boston Golf Club held the AGM on November 22nd 1918 at the White Hart Hotel, Boston. Only a small number of members attended. Mr Mark Bottomley continued as Captain and Mr A Norman as the Hon Sec and Hon Treasurer. The club like most of the other clubs in the county was obviously having a hard time to survive.

The captain reported a resolve to ' . . . keep the club going to tide it over the effects of the War, in the hope that it would improve before the end of another year.' On November 30th it was announced that: 'The links are now ready for play.' Newspaper reports were still scarce and little is known of the affairs of the club at this period. On August 9th 1919 it was announced that 130 acres of land at Skegness, including the North Shore Golf Club, had recently been purchased by the Allied Bank of Nottingham.

On October 25th it was announced that the Boston Golf Links would be open for play next Saturday.

The Peace

Following the end of the war the country took many years to get back to normal. Most families had suffered personal tradgedies with the loss of father, brother or other close relatives. It would require many years before the scars of their losses healed. There was however an atmosphere of great relief that the country had managed to weather the storm. Furthermore after four years of hardship and stress, people were ready for some enjoyment and relaxation.

Leisure activities throughout the country began to thrive. Many people had cash to spend, saved up during the war when there were few goods to buy. They now proceeded to spend it. Factories were soon at full production and there were plenty of jobs available. Wages had risen substantially during the previous four years. Farm prices had been high during the war despite the controls and farmers and farm workers had been obliged to work even harder than normal because of the shortage of labour. Farming areas like Boston benefited from these conditions. All those changes meant that the country was experiencing an 'economic boom.'

The larger clubs in the county returned to a more normal programme fairly quickly and in September 1919 there were newspaper reports of the Open Days held at Carholme, Woodhall Spa, and Seacroft.

The Boston Golf Club, like the other clubs over the county, also started to benefit from these changes and get back in to some sort of routine. The Ladies' AGM was held in October 1920. Mrs MacTaggart was elected Captain and Chairlady. The President elected was Lady Weigall and the Hon Secretary Mrs Bottomley. The Committee were Mrs O Cooper, Mrs W Kitwood, Mrs S Cheavin, Mrs H Mawson, Miss N Staniland, and Miss Gilliatt. In February 1921 the Boston Gents played Surfleet at Boston, the first post war match recorded. The team was: G Robins, Dr Mowett, H Hutson, P Ostler, W Bedford, W Horry, and G Robinson. Boston won both the singles and the doubles.

GEORGE ROBINS

Sometime during the period around 1910 to 1912, the club had taken on a greenkeeper called George Robins. Prior to moving into the cottage at Tower Road he had lived in Main Ridge, and worked for some time with a large Boston building firm called Sherwins. He was also a skilled gardener. George Robins had a son, also called George, who started to caddy for some of the Tower Road members when his father took over the duties of greenkeeper. He soon showed an aptitude for the game. After playing at the Boston club for several years he would eventually become a professional golfer. Many others of the early

48.

professionals including Braid, Vardon and Hagan all learned their profession starting off as caddies. George Robins Senior never took much interest in the game having taken the job as greenkeeper rather late on in life. When he took over the post he eventually moved into the club cottage on Tower Road. The cottage was a typical small fenland house and the three upstairs rooms were taken over by George Robins, leaving a room for the ladies and one for the men downstairs. It was lit by gas, Boston having had its own gas lighting supplied by the Boston Gas Light and Coke Co Ltd since 1807. Boston streets would not be lit by electricity until 1924, much later than most comparable towns, but in 1910 gas lit thorium mantles provided most of the lighting of the town houses. In the country areas however Boston golfers

15. The Tower Road 'clubhouse' in 1933 after it had been purchased by Mr S Belton. His two children, Allan and William, are seated on stones prior to the drive and forecourt being prepared for laying tarmac.

would rely on paraffin lamps and candles for many more years. Light refreshments were provided by George Robins' wife, for the members and their guests. The facilities were not sumptous, but were a great improvement on 93 Sydney Street. Most clubs at that time were not very much better off in the way of club facilities.

George Robins' son at an early age started playing in matches for the club. The first mention of his name is in the February 1923 match against Surfleet. When he left school at thirteen he was apprenticed to Harry Maddison a barber who had a shop next to the Red Cow in Bargate. Golf must have seemed much more attractive to him than cutting hair and he had ample opportunity to improve his game. A contemporary of George Robins Junior, Geoffrey Horton, who was born just after the turn of the century, but still retains a good memory, is certain that George Robins Senior took over as groundsman at Tower Road around 1910, since Geoffrey attended the Tower Road School with George Robins Junior around that date. George Robins Senior and Junior would play important parts in the history of the Boston Golf Club over the next few years.

MAJOR OLIVER COOPER

In March 1921 a golf match was held at Tower Road between the captain's team and a team led by the club secretary. Major Oliver Cooper was the captain and his team was: G Robinson, F Parsons, C Fleet, Mr Street and S Cooper. The team of Mark Bottomley the secretary was: W Bedford, P Ostler, J Towell, Mr Scrimshaw, and G Robins. George Robinson

THE BOSTON MAGAZINE

16. Oliver Cooper.
He was ambitious to provide
a twelve hole golf course in Boston.

became a successful newspaper proprietor, as did his son Lionel, who would also become a keen member of the club. Their gift of the back copies of *The Standard* newspapers, to the Boston Library, together with *The Boston Guardian* was instrumental in providing information to allow this history to be written.

Just as important however to the history of The Boston Golf Club, were the team members, Oliver Cooper, Sam Cooper, Mark Bottomley and George Robins. George Robins would later be appointed the golf professional to the Boston club, before he moved off to become the professional at the Sleaford club in 1924.

Sam and Oliver Cooper were brothers, the sons of William Mansfield Cooper, a successful corn merchant in the town. Sam, according to his son Bryan, was the first person in Boston to have plumbing installed in his bathroom. Mark Bottomley, also in the corn trade dealing in malting barley, would become the longest serving secretary of the Boston club, and someone who helped steer it successfully through some of its most difficult moments.

The club captain, Major Oliver Cooper, as we shall see, became an important member of The Boston Golf Club. The photograph of Lance Corporal Oliver Cooper, just returned from the Boer War in 1902, suggests a brisk, confident and ambitious young man. He gained rapid promotion in the army, eventually becoming a Major in the 1914-1918 War. Returning safely home, he became keen on golf and quickly got involved in the management of the club. He served as captain for many years, and provided the impetus for its development towards becoming a successful all-year round, twelve hole course.

Major Cooper's team won that match by four matches to three. He had much in common with Frank Curtis and was not content to be second best at anything he was involved with. Tower Road was very much a third class golf club at that time compared to many others in the county. The boom the county was experiencing put committees in the frame of mind to spend and improve. Membership at Boston jumped from 90 in 1921 to 140 by 1923.

In December 1921 Mr F Scrimshaw broke the course record with 91 28 63— the lowest nett score ever recorded at the Tower Road 'Links'.

At the AGM of October 1921 a good balance was recorded

'despite the extra costs of fencing the greens, new stiles and gates'. The Boston club was no different from many other much larger clubs in those days who fenced greens to keep off grazing stock, often with indifferent success, to the fury of greenkeepers and players coping with deep hoof marks from hungry Lincolnshire Red bullocks.

In 1922 the Surfleet Golf Club decided to extend their course to eighteen holes. They also announced increased subscriptions from £1 to £2.10. 0. for gentlemen and from £1 to £2 for ladies, a staggering increase by any standard and a reflection of the inflation in prices and wages brought on by four years of war. They hoped to leave the eighteen holes for winter play and return to the nine hole layout for summer golf— presumably to halve the wear and tear on the course during the wet winter months. The Lincoln clubs also were improving club facilities, as was the Sleaford club. With motor cars becoming more and more popular, the pressures on the Tower Road committee to improve their club was severe. One improvement the ladies arranged was to obtain the services of Mr Harry Cawsey, the Seacroft professional since 1909, to attend on certain days of the week to provide lessons.

The Seacroft committee continued to improve their club and facilities. It was reported in 1922 that they had pensioned off their horse which had given them sterling service for over 20 years and purchased a new ACTO motorised mower which would allow them to cut their fairways. It would be many years before Boston could afford a luxury such as this.

THE WALKER CUP

In 1922 there was a major development in British and American golf. George H Walker, President of the United States Golf Association, donated a Cup for a competition between teams of American and British amateur players. This soon settled down to a biennial event. The American golfers dominated the event winning twenty-one out of the first twenty-two matches.

THE END OF TOWER ROAD

At the AGM in September 1922 there was an historic announcement. Members were informed that Boston Golf Club would shortly be moving to a new golf couse. It would be

52.

constructed at Pudding Pie Farm, which lay alongside the River Witham on the south side of the town, two miles from the station. A large meeting unanimously supported the move, which gave the Boston Golf Club all-year round golf for the first time in its history. It was a brave decision. The accounts for the year showed a balance of only £30.17s.6d—not a princely sum to launch Boston golfers on their first 'twelve-months' course. It was a proud moment for the club. The proposition to agree to the move was proposed by the captain, Major Cooper, and seconded by Mr Robert Isaac. A member of a family who would provide Boston with one of its most successful town centre stores, he and his family continued to play a prominent part in the affairs of the club for many years. The club was not at that time flush with cash. The captain explained the financial situation, and asked for voluntary offers of assistance from those attending. There was a good response and £180 was promised to assist with the expenses which would be incurred with the change of course. Major Cooper explained that the club had obtained a favourable lease from the owner, Mr Fred Parkes, who by this time owned a large fleet of trawlers, fishing from Boston. It included a future option to buy at a favourable price.

THE LANDLORD

After purchasing Pudding Pie Farm in 1909 for £400, Fred Parkes had become the successful wealthy owner of a fishing fleet. On becoming the owner of the farm, it had not taken him long to remedy the breach in the river bank. He acquired, for a knock down price, two old barges, filled them with ballast, and sunk them in the hole in the bank. He covered these sunken boats with brushwood faggots, and the river Witham laden with silt did the rest, sealing the breach almost immediately. This was a typical example of the drive and initiative which would make him a millionaire. He then successfully farmed the land himself for a few years, before letting it off to a tenant farmer.

Born in 1879, one of six children, by dint of hard work and natural entrepreneural talent he built up a successful business from starting work as a labourer in a fish stall. Thriftily he saved part of his wages each week, and eventually purchased his employers' business. Boston at that time was an important fishing port. Fred Parkes went into the cod drying business, taking over a large field by the side of the river, not far from Pudding Pie, where he dried his cod strung up on moveable trollies. He then expanded into exporting large quantities of cod roe. He had the gift of recognising good business opportunities, and the drive to exploit these situations. By 1914 he owned his own trawler. By 1919 he was on the board of the Boston Deep Sea Fishing and Ice Company, which owned a large deep sea fishing fleet. Not long afterwards he gained control of this company. Over the next three years he made steady progress until an incident occurred that almost ruined his company.

Unfortunately for him and the Boston Corporation, on the 28th February 1922, the *S S Lockwood*, a large ship carrying coal bound for Hamburg, went aground in the River Witham near Boston, blocking the way into the docks. Fred Parkes offered to assist the Council by effecting its removal. After many difficulties he succeeded in this task, but mistakes had been made in the legal agreement between the Boston Corporation solicitors, Fred Parkes, and the company owning the *S S Lockwood*. He was refused payment for all his efforts and expenses. A legal battle

17. Fred Parkes' cod drying field, not far from Pudding Pie Farm.

then started. It was decreed by the courts that the contract was unenforceable against the agents acting for the ship owners. It had not been signed 'Under Seal'. It was null and void. One can imagine the fury of Fred Parkes at this decision. The judge may not have had any alternative but to find against the Boston parties but Fred had carried out his part of the contract and expected to be paid. Both Fred Parkes and the Boston Council incurred heavy financial losses, because of the court's decision, and subsequent legal actions. He felt a deep sense of grievance over the way he had been treated, and it was one of the reasons why, shortly afterwards, he moved his fleet and business to Fleetwood. Given the character and business acumen of Mr Parkes, it would not however have been the principal reason for his exit from Boston. Fleetwood must have offered greater business opportunities.

He still, however, owned Pudding Pie Farm at that date, and it was let to a Mr Clark who farmed it as a tenant. The *Lockwood* incident may well have been the incentive for Fred to lease Pudding Pie Farm to Boston Golf Club when Mr Clark decided to give up farming. It's an ill wind . . .

THE LAST COMPETITION

The last competetition held at Tower Road, was the ladies' Harvey Dixon Challenge Cup, in May 1923. This had been presented to the club by Mrs Harvey Dixon in 1910. It was won for the third time by Mrs P Arch. Because of her unique triple victory the cup became the property of the winner, and was presented to her by the ladies' captain, Mrs S Chevin.

CHAPTER THREE

THE PUDDING PIE GOLF COURSE

THE FOUR GREAT WASH RIVERS, the Witham, the Welland, the Nene and the Ouse, have posed terrible problems for the fen drainage engineers, from the time of the Romans, on to the work carried out by the great Dutch engineer Vermuyden, and down to the present time. These rivers, flowing through the flat fens around the Wash, meandered all over the adjacent valuable arable land, causing destructive floods every few years. The Dutch engineer's solution to the problem was to cut straight channels for the great volumes of water, back at the point where the land levelled out from the uplands and the meandering started. This enabled the rivers to flow faster, and thus sweep the silt, which was clogging up the waterways, out to sea.

In one of these straightening operations, carried out around 1860 near Boston, a block of marshland was enclosed and subsequently drained. The farm built on this area was named Pudding Pie. The name came from the saucer shaped depression formed by the two flood banks surrounding this area, one running alongside the river, the other an inland bank running alongside Fishtoft Road. This then was the area purchased by Fred Parkes in 1909, and let to Boston Golf Club in 1922. The move to the Pudding

TRAWLINGS OF A LIFETIME

18. Sir Fred Parkes, the millionaire business man.

Pie course brought about some of the most traumatic and dangerous years in the history of the club, and it came within a whisker of causing it to founder.

MUD PROBLEMS

There were several reasons for this. The first was that hitherto the club had been running an extremely low cost golf course and in Pudding Pie they had moved on to one that would involve much more expense.

One cannot get a cheaper method of running a course than to rent it for six months during the winter. Leasing Pudding Pie immediately involved the club in the full costs of running a twelve month course, with the high summer maintenance expenses involved in cutting the greens and fairways. There was also the capital required to purchase the machinery and a horse to do this work. Tractors were still away in the far off future.

But there were other major problems with Pudding Pie which the committee had under estimated in their enthusiasm to move to a better course. It is one thing playing golf on thick, centuries old, permanent pasture. It is quite a different kettle of fish, taking over an arable farm with bare fields, and trying to get it quickly grassed down to a state where it will take the heavy traffic of hundreds of hefty golfers' feet.

When Fred Parkes had sealed off the hole in the bank he had left the golf club with another problem. The land had not long since been covered with sea water. The soil was of a heavier texture than Tower Road and contained a higher percentage of clay. When clay is saturated with salt water it 'deflocculates'— loses it's crumb structure and becomes a sticky mess. Today we understand the chemistry responsible for this change and can move quickly to rectify the situation. It was less well known however in 1923, and Boston Golf Club found themselves in great difficulty trying to cure it.

Many years later, on the Cowbridge course, the greens were inadvertantly irrigated with salt water. It gave this later committee many headaches before they rectified the problem, and there were farmer members on the committee at that time who knew a great deal more about the problem and its solution than the 1923 Pudding Pie members. The Pudding Pie committee were blissfully unaware of the headaches they were about to face grappling with their mudbath. Last but not least the club could not afford to pay two rents, one for Tower Road, and one for Pudding Pie, while they changed courses. The committee had therefore opted for a quick move to save a year's rent at Tower Road.

The 1923 AGM

At the 1923 AGM held in October and reported in the Boston Guardian—there are no club minute books surviving from that period—a new president was in the chair, Councillor E Richardson. There was a large attendance. Major Oliver Cooper, the club captain, explained that the new course had been thoroughly drained under the expert supervision of Mr Charles Gilliatt. The previous April there had been a balance of £114, but since then the club had spent £300 on the new course. There was now a deficiency of around £200. The club had been obliged to pay £100 to the outgoing tenant Mr Clark, for tenant right, and the grass reseeding that he had carried out on the course. The deficiency would rise to £300 by the time the course was open for play.

Officers elected were: President: Coun E Richardson; Vice Presidents: R Staniland, W Kitwood, W Porter; Hon Teasurer: Mr T Stamp; Hon Sec: M Bottomley. The committee were J Towell, S Cooper, A Ingamells, W Horry, A Parry, W Cheer, G Robinson, and Dr Mowett. It was hoped that the course would be fit to play by 31st October. The heaviest roller in the county had been kindly loaned to the club by Mr Booth of Woad Farm and they would soon get the course in good order. It was likely that the membership subscription would go from 25/- (£1.5s.0d.) to two guineas (£2.2s.0d.). The membership could be raised to 200. By letting some of the fairways for sheep grazing the annual rent of £150 would be substantially reduced.'

Questions from the Floor

In questions from the floor, Mr Percy Arch asked whether the decision to move quickly from the old course to the new course, could be put to the members. The chairman replied that the decision had already been taken by the committee, to make the move immediately. Mr Arch objected to this decision and said that many members, including himself, felt the course could not possibly be fit for play in time, and the committee were making a serious mistake.

58.

The meeting closed with obvious worries being felt by many of those atttending. Mr Arch's forecast unfortunately proved correct, to the serious embarrassment of Major Cooper and the committee. No golf was played at Pudding Pie that winter because of the unsatisfactory state of the course. On May 3rd 1924 the Boston Guardian had a brief article saying that about fifty members of Pudding Pie had joined the Sleaford Golf Club. Jim Arch, son of Percy Arch, now over 80 and living in Kingston-on-Thames, recalls that his father always felt that the continued use of 'the heaviest roller in the county' had contributed to the problems at Pudding Pie.

THE GOLF ANNUAL 1924

The 1924 edition of the *Golfing Annual* gives the first insert for the Boston Golf Club at the new Pudding Pie course.

> The Membership is 186. The Hon Sec M Bottomley, Greenkeeper W H Cope, nine holes, Boston station $2\frac{1}{2}$ miles. Visitors 1s 6d a day, 5s a week, 10s a month. Sunday play with caddies.

George Robins Senior had not moved with the club to Pudding Pie but his son remained a member, and a keen and improving golfer. Not much is known about Mr Cope but he may have found the problems facing him at Pudding Pie beyond his abilities. He left after a year, and the new greenkeeper was a local man, Charles Smith. Good luck and bad luck tend, as we are all aware, to balance out. The club had encountered its fair share of the latter over the past year, but this was well outweighed by the good fortune in finding Charlie Smith, who would be their salvation in overcoming the problems at Pudding Pie.

Meanwhile the clerical lobby had lost the argument banning Sunday play. The club had obviously felt it must follow the example of other clubs in the county and allow this. With the increasing use of cars, the green fees of visitors were becoming more and more useful to help balance the books and pay for the improvements taking place at most courses.

A DIFFICULT AGM

The 1924 AGM held on the 10th May was an extremely difficult one for the committee and Major Cooper. Under less resolute leadership the Boston Golf Club, could very easily have foundered at this vital meeting. There was a small attendance. Major Oliver Cooper, not one to duck his responsibilities, was in the chair. The accounts showed a bank deficit of £185, but there was a balance in hand of £114. It was decided that some of the fairways would be let off for sheep grazing, a common practice on many courses at that time, including Belton, Lincoln, and Sleaford. This could be set against the annual rent of £180. There was a discussion about raising the annual subscriptioon to two guineas.

The income for the past year included: Men's subscriptions £78, ladies' subscriptions £49, rent income of land for grazing sheep £20, sale of crops £20. Fortunately the offer of financial assistance from members to set up the new course, more than balanced the severe drop in subscriptions resulting from the resignations from the club. The costs incurred were: Tenant right to Mr Clark for work done in reseeding the arable fields £200, wages and insurance £150, other work on the course £39, stock feedstuffs £29. Alderman E Richardson tendered his resignation as President. Alderman Tom Kitwood was prevailed upon to accept this post

THE CAPTAIN CRITICISED

Major Cooper said:

> There had been criticism in certain quarters, and he would take part of the blame that there had been no golf played on the course this winter. All he could say was that he thought the committee's decision to move to the new course when they did was correct. The course had recently improved beyond all measure. If they had not moved, the club would have been £100 worse off because they would be paying rent for both courses.' Some members said that: 'he had an axe to grind', but the only axe he had was to give members better conditions for their golf than they ever had had before. It was no light task being captain but he would do his best.

Mr Mark Bottomley was unanimously re-elected Hon Sec. He said that he and Major Cooper had not always been in agreement. He never thought they were doing the right thing moving to the new course. He and Mr Robins were the only two to vote against

60.

the committee's recommendation to make the move. Mr Harry Cawsey, the Seacroft professional, had agreed with them. However they had now got the new course and would now have to make the best of it. Mr T Stamp was elected Hon Treasurer, Dr Mowett and Mr S Cooper resigned from the committee. Mr Tyson and Mr R Isaacs were elected in their place.

Whilst the Boston golf club committee were suffering, other clubs in the county were steadily improving. In June the Rauceby Club had a major exhibition match between Ted Ray, Oxley; Tom Williamson, Notts; Arthur Havers, Coombe Hill; and Charles Whitehouse, Lansdowne—all well-known professional golfers. It was played in front of a very large attendance and they scored 79, 76, 73 and 76 respectively. Ray who won the British Open in 1912 at Muirfield would be the last British winner of the US Open, in 1920, until Tony Jacklin's victory in 1970. Havers was the victor at the 1923 British Open.

No Fear of Lost Balls on the Fairways

There is a report in the Boston Guardian in July 1924: 'Boston Golf Course is now in a sufficiently good condition to admit of an enjoyable game. If players keep on the 'fairways' there is no fear of lost balls'. The latter is rather an ominous statement but it must be remembered that many of the courses of the day had 'rough' that would be unacceptable by today's standard. Many of them including Sleaford, Lincoln, Belton, and Surfleet made an additional income by letting substantial areas of the course for hay, as well as sheep and cattle grazing, to neighbouring farmers. Balls landing in the areas set aside for hay were frequently lost. The advantage of the system to the club however was a reduced work load of fairway mowing, and the extra income in rent.

Percy Arch, one of the Pudding Pie golfers most dissatisfied with the course, had a victory in January 1924 which would have softened the misery of playing at Boston—he won the Silver Challenge Cup at North Shore with a 78. The event had been postponed by heavy snowfalls. Despite the shortage of transport, keen golfers still managed to take part in competitions at courses all over the county. He and his wife were also amongst the large list of guests attending the Surfleet Golf Club Ball held in February. Problems would still be encountered at Pudding Pie for many years. Indeed it would always have the reputation of being a wet course. Charlie Smith however, from then on, started to work like a Trojan, digging and cleaning out drains and ditches, and steadily but gradually improved the course for its members.

THE SIBSEY GOLF COURSE

Oliver Cooper and his committee must have felt rather happier, at the end of May, now that they had safely passed the hurdle of a very difficult Annual General Meeting, and with the prospect of dry weather to improve the course. Then another bombshell struck.

On Saturday July 26th 1924, the Boston Guardian carried a large article headed,

'GOLF AT SIBSEY'

> A few weeks ago we announced that through the enterprise of Mr F J Caudwell of Sibsey a new 18 hole Golf Course is to be made in the village. We also stated that Mr J Taylor, ex-champion, and Mr Hawtree, a well known golf course designer, had inspected the fields and had pronounced favourably on their suitability. Within a few days of their visit, Mr Caudwell put on his staff of workmen to start the construction. The fairways and greens have now been well cut out, together with much rolling. As we intimated, nine holes will be made this year, and nine the following year. It is expected that the nine holes will be open for play in a few days time.

Then follows the details of Messrs Taylor and Hawtree's report, and the layout of the course. On 23rd August it was announced in another newspaper report that the new golf course at Sibsey, which would be known as The East Lincolnshire Golf Club, had appointed a fulltime professional to manage the course, provide lessons, and sell and repair the member's golf equipment. His name was Mr E Muggleton. He had started playing at the age of 13, and had been professional at the Leicester, and the Mid Berkshire golf clubs. Since joining Sibsey he had played three times with a best score of 35. He was a fully qualified clubmaker.

19a. Fred Caudwell, owner of the (Sibsey) East Lincolnshire Golf Club.

19b. A bill for golf clubs supplied by E. T. Muggleton, golf professional at the East Lincolnshire Golf Club.

EAST LINCS. GOLF CLUB,
SIBSEY,
LINCOLNSHIRE.

15 / 6 / 1924

Mr J Pearson

Dr. to E. T. MUGGLETON,

EXPERT COACH AND
. . CLUB MAKER. . .

	£	o	J
1 Driver		18	0
1 Spoon		18	0
1 Iron		12	c
1 Mashie		12	c
1 Putter		12	c
1 Bag		12	c
	4	0	0

63.

20. *The Sibsey golf course—The East Lincolnshire Golf Club course—was on the opposite side of the Sibsey-Frithville road to the Sibsey Trader windmill and overlooked by it. (The mill is now a listed building in the care of English Heritage and which mills on occasion throughout the summer.)*

64.

CHAPTER FOUR

THE EAST LINCOLNSHIRE GOLF CLUB

THE BOSTON GOLF CLUB COMMITTEE must have been stunned by the news of the new golf course. Sibsey is only five miles north of Boston. It had at that time its own railway station which had been operated by the East Lincolnshire Railway from its start up in 1848, but had just been taken over, on 1st January 1923, by the London and North Eastern Railways. Visiting golfers could easily travel from the station to the new course. It was easily reached by car from Boston, Skegness and surrounding villages although cars were still of course very much of a rarity in 1923

Everyone connected at that time with the local golf situation, was well aware that there was a very limited number of potential golfers in Boston and the surrounding area. It was obvious to all concerned, and especially Major Oliver Cooper and his committee, that the new course would be in direct competition with the Boston club. With the worry of the poor state of his course, the club's financial liabilities, and the disaffection amongst many of the members, this development could not have come at a worse time.

Mr Fred Caudwell, Manor House, Sibsey, at that time was a successful farmer managing 1,000 acres of a range of Lincolnshire soils. Much of it was under grass, and at Sibsey he had a large herd of Lincoln Red cattle, and lowland sheep grazing some of this permanent pasture. It is one thing however, having sufficient grassland to lay out a golf course and quite a different matter altogether to do so. Notwithstanding that it was a much easier task in those days than it is today, it was nevertheless a formidable operation requiring courage, skill and capital. To begin with it would have to do at least as well as his farming enterprise if it was to be a satisfactory business proposition. However he was much better placed to start up a golf club than most other individuals. He had the land and provided he got the permission of his landlord he could set about forming a golf club. He was a tenant of Admiral Drax, who lived at Charleborough Park, near Bournemouth. The Admiral had been a serving naval officer who had seen action at the naval Battle of Jutland and was a reasonable and accommodating landlord. Thus permission was forthcoming.

FRED CAUDWELL

There is however a mystery surrounding the whole venture. There is no record that Fred Caudwell had ever previously played the game of golf. He was not a member of the Boston golf club nor any other club in the area. As far as is known, and Harry Caudwell, his son, who also farms not far from that area today, can vouch for this, he had not played much if any golf before he started up the Sibsey course. Why therefore plunge into a new and uncertain venture, when he could more easily carry on with his successful farming operations?

Fred Caudwell was at that time in his early thirties, well built and a good all round sportsman, who had played several sports including soccer, cricket, and tennis. He was well liked and a good mixer. He had many friends in the area. It is also something of a coincidence, that his decision came at the same instant that the Pudding Pie committee were having serious problems with their golf club. There is therefore the possibility that some of his friends who were dissatisfied with the problems and prospects at Pudding Pie, had persuaded him to carry out this venture. Whatever the reason, once he had decided to push ahead with his golf course he tackled it in a most efficient and professional way.

THE PUDDING PIE RESPONSE

Meanwhile, an article in the *Boston Guardian* on August 30th 1924 reported on a recent meeting of the Pudding Pie committee. Mention was made of the great improvement that had taken place on the new course. The captain acknowledged that mistakes had been made in getting it back to grass and that:

> a bad atmosphere had surrounded the whole undertaking. Players early in the season had found it much too rough. The committee were determined however to improve this situation as quickly as possible, and to assist with this they had decided, several months earlier, to employ George Robins, son of the old Tower Road greenkeeper and a well known member of the club, as club professional and

66.

greenkeeper. This had been highly successful and with two exceptions the greens are now far better than those on the old course ever were.

The fairways are also improving by leaps and bounds. The committee are committed to going full steam ahead with the course improvements. A number of silver trophies are in the possession of the club and special competitions are to be arranged for these. The committee feel that if members will play the course they will be more than surprised at the improvement. They are of the opinion that they can rely on the loyalty of local sportsmen to support the Boston Golf Club, now that most of the difficulties have been overcome.

Major Oliver Cooper and his committee had made the response that one might expect from them in the face of the threat from the new club.

Developments which had been taking place however behind the scenes, tend to confirm that Fred Caudwell had further plans in mind in connection with his new club and the Pudding Pie Golf Club.

THE TAKE-OVER BID

Following the start up of The East Lincolnshire Golf Club, it was very quickly evident to the Pudding Pie committee that Fred Caudwell was tackling the start up of his new golf course in a most efficient and serious manner. In a small farming community like Boston, communications between the business and professional men of the area were good. All those interested in golf in the area were soon aware of most aspects of the situation with regard to the Sibsey and the Boston golf clubs. Many of them soon made up their mind to play and enjoy their golf wherever it was best available. There was a simple way out of the dilemma. In a very short space of time many of the Pudding Pie members had also joined Fred Caudwell's course. Most retained joint membership, although a few who were disenchanted with the problems at Pudding Pie resigned, and either joined the Sibsey club, or went further afield to Rauceby or Woodhall. Over the next few weeks there were further develpments and approaches made formally and informally to the Pudding Pie committee, and matters came to a head when the Boston club announced that an Extra Ordinary General Meeting would be held in September, in the Drill Hall,

Boston. A full report of this was given in the *Boston Guardian* on Saturday 20th September 1924.

An Extra Ordinary General Meeting

The president, Alderman T Kitwood, explained to the large gathering, that this was an important meeting where the future of The Boston Golf Club would be decided. Recently complications had arisen which might be regarded as prejudicial to the general welfare of the club. Various committee meetings had been held and he was going to report on them. A new golf course had been opened by Mr F Caudwell at Sibsey. Some time ago Mr Caudwell approached your committee asking if they had any offer to make to him. Some members here had already joined Sibsey. Your committee are under a heavy financial burden in the shape of a seven year lease at Pudding Pie, and a bank guarantee. If they did not get the necessary support they could not carry on. A special meeting of the committee had therefore been held, and it was decided to ask Mr Caudwell to attend and to find out what terms he would be prepared to offer, in the event of an amalgamation of the two clubs. It was also decided to ask Mr Fred Parkes if he would be prepared to sell Pudding Pie to the club at a less price than stated in the option to purchase, in the event of the club deciding to carry on. This had been done and the meeting tonight has been held to give the members the opportunity to decide whether to amalgamate with Sibsey or continue at Pudding Pie.'

At this point the Chairman called on Mr Watts, a Turf Specialist employed by Messrs Sutton and Co., Seedsmen, Reading, to report on the state of Pudding Pie. Mr Watts said that in his opinion, 'with a little attention to certain matters a considerable improvement will take place in a short time.' The problems had been caused by:

1. Indifferent farming of the land in past years.
2. Poor cultivation on some areas in preparation for seeding.
3. Bad weather after seeding.

The ground was very weedy. The hardest part of the work is now over. When suitable bunkers have been constructed it should be a good course.'

The chairman then dealt with Mr Caudwell's offer to the
club.

'1. He will give a sum equal to half of the first annual
subscription in respect of all members transferring
to Sibsey.

2. The offer is conditional to closing down Pudding Pie
Golf Club.'

THE KNIFE EDGE

The chairman then intimated that Mr Parkes would be
prepared to accept a sum that the committee considered
reasonable, for the purchase of Pudding Pie. Mr Isaacs
asked what the present membership was. The Hon Sec. Mr
Bottomley said it was around 140. There had been eighteen
resignations, with five members joining at Sibsey. The
Annual Subscription was now two guineas. Dr Mowat said
'The course had greatly improved and that we should now
stay at Pudding Pie.' Mr W Kitwood said 'The views of the
committee should be given backing'.

Major Cooper, the captain said: 'That if they could get
sufficient members to subscribe £300 a year they would be
able to meet expenses.' He was asked what would be the
income if all members paid their subscriptions. 'It would be
£240'. Mr Ingamells said: 'Mr Caudwell did not appreciate to
the full extent the benefits he would derive if the club moved
to Sibsey. If two thirds of the members did not want to
amalgamate then that settled the question.'

PUDDING PIE SURVIVES

Mr O Giles then moved a resolution to the effect that the club
should continue. Mr Bottomley seconded this proposal, and it
was put to the vote. The resolution was carried unanimously.

Thus passed a critical moment in the history of the Boston Golf
Club, when it only just managed to avoid being taken over by one
of the most remarkable characters in the story of Boston golf. It is
easy to be critical of past events when one is aware of later
developments. Fred Caudwell's offer at the time was not
unreasonable, and could possibly have been beneficial to the
members, given the poor state of Pudding Pie and the ever present
risk of future flooding. He had an inland club, safe from the flood
waters of the Witham. He had made great strides in fashioning it

69.

into a golf course, which was already, in the first year of its life, in very much better shape than the wet Pudding Pie course. He had a nice cottage available which he was rapidly turning into a pleasant club house. He had already enrolled a nucleus of good golfers. He was employing a skilled and experienced professional golfer to manage the course, provide lessons, and keep members' clubs in order.

There was however a factor which had not been mentioned by the president in his opening description of the situation, but which counted far more with the Boston committee and members than all these undoubted advantages possessed by the East Lincolnshire Golf Club. The Sibsey club belonged to Fred Caudwell, whereas the Pudding Pie club belonged to its members. This difference, as the future would show, would be of critical importance to the survival of both clubs.

THE BOSTON GOLF CLUB LIMITED

Whatever else the start up of the Sibsey golf club did for the Pudding Pie Club committee it certainly galvanised them into activity. Another Extra Ordinary General Meeting was held on October 11th 1924. The committee took the important decision to form the club into a Limited Company. It would be called The Boston Golf Club Company Limited, with share capital of £1,000. The committee had obviously taken legal advice on this move. There were two principal advantages. If the club were to become bankrupt its liabilities would be limited to the paid element on the issued shares, thus protecting the financial liabilities of the directors. There was obviously a doubt in their minds as to the viability of the club. The other advantage was that it would help the committee raise extra capital towards the cost of improving the club.

It would cost £40. 0s. 0d. for the legal documentation to form a company. It would not be compulsory for members to purchase shares, but the committee hoped that as many members as possible would do so to assist them to finance the extra costs involved in getting the new course into good order. The first directors would be T Kitwood: chairman; Major O Cooper, A Ingamells, Mr Isaac, G Robinson, Mr Wheeler, A Parry, J Towell, Mr Tyson, W Stamp, and Mr Bottomley. The club was in debt to

70.

the bank for £300. The committee members would put up £300 of the share capital. If the club members would subscribe the remaining £700 they could start the legal proceedings immediately to form the company. The club membership was at that time 176 exclusive of the twenty to twenty-five members who had enrolled since the last meeting.

THE LADIES AND EXTRA HOLES

Mr Marris wanted to know if the club planned to construct any more holes. Major Cooper said that: 'It is better to have nine good holes than an indifferent fifteen. There are some adjacent grass fields that can be acquired in the future.' He added that: 'when some ladies have been round all the nine holes they do not want to go round any more.' Mr. Barclay said that the problem of taxation would have to be studied carefully. The proposal to form a limited company was carried unanimously. The chairman also informed the meeting that the committee had considered the possibility of purchasing Pudding Pie but had decided not to proceed with this at present.

It was still not a golfing ladies' world. In February 1925 the Surfleet club debated whether the ladies should be invited to the annual dinner. The decision went against the suggestion.

THE FIRST BOSTON PROFESSIONAL GOLFER

The Sleaford club was making good progress in improving its clubhouse and other amenities. It was decided to pay the professional a wage of 30/- a week but his duties would also include supervising the work on the links. A new professional had just been appointed. He was George Robins Junior, the son of the old Tower Road greenkeeper, and recently appointed professional at Pudding Pie. Why George Robins decided to leave Boston and move to take up the professional's post at Rauceby is not known.

The Sleaford club was by this time a much more successful and thriving club than was Pudding Pie and the offer of a secure full time professional post must have seemed much more attractive than a less certain future at Pudding Pie. He was the first Boston man to become a golf professional and went on to make a successful career in his chosen profession, later moving to the Leamington Spa and Coventry golf clubs. The Boston

71.

committee must have felt that they could not afford at that time to employ a full time professional, and the post was left vacant for several years.

The club had thus successfully survived the difficult year of 1924. How would it fare in the future against the up and coming Sibsey club?

THE ECONOMIC DEPRESSION

Meanwhile the inhabitants of Boston like those in the rest of Britain, Europe, and America, were at that period, trying to cope with difficulties of a greater magnitude than those facing the Boston golfers. The economic boom which had followed the end of the Great War was starting to run into difficulties. The inherently unstable free market system of Europe and America was starting to slide into the 'bust' phase of the boom-bust cycle. The massive reparations which France, and reluctantly, Britain and America, had forced on Germany, were adding to this problem, and causing in that country a period of unparalled inflation. At its height, several million marks were required to purchase a cup of coffee. These conditions were eventually to blame for the rise of Hitler and the 1939-1945 Second World War. Unemployment had already started to soar in Britain. When Churchill, not in his element as Chancellor of the Exchequer, put Britain back on the Gold Standard at an unrealistic rate in April 1925, it precipitated a great deal of industrial strife, culminating in The General Strike of May 1926.

These problems had an immediate and increasing effect on all leisure activities, including the fortunes of the Pudding Pie Golf Club. Money became more scarce as did new members. Golf committees throughout the county began to cut back on club and course improvements. Fortunately for Boston, the plan to build a new clubhouse with the cash raised by the changeover to a limited company, was well advanced before the full effects of the depression were felt.

CO-OPERATION WITH THE SIBSEY CLUB

The immediate concern however at Pudding Pie and Sibsey was to work out how best the two adjacent clubs could maintain amicable relations. To the relief of the committees and members,

72.

it worked out much better than any one could have hoped, thanks largely to the personality of Fred Caudwell and the good sense of the Pudding Pie committee. Fred Caudwell made it clear from the start up of his club, that he intended to maintain good relations with the Pudding Pie club. The Boston players helped by many of them becoming members of both clubs. The Sibsey club quickly acquired the reputation of being a friendly and pleasant golf club, and Fred Caudwell and his wife worked hard to make the Sibsey course a success. During its lifetime it was reckoned to be 'rather rough' from the state of its fairways, much of which was old rig and furrow grassland. It had however the advantage of being drier, and easier to play under wet conditions, than the Boston course.

THE NEW CLUB PAVILION

In July 1925 the new club pavilion at Pudding Pie was officially opened. It was a large wooden structure, raised on bricks and wooden stilts three feet above ground level. The risk of flooding

21. *The new golf club pavilion at Pudding Pie; opened in July 1925.*

73.

was a constant worry to the committee and well founded as events would show. It was situated at the edge of the course, inside the Fishtoft Road flood bank. It was a spacious building for the period, with separate large lounges for the men and the ladies. There were facilities available for refreshments to be served for members and visitors. The Pudding Pie farm buildings were on the other side of the Fishtoft Road from the course and the clubhouse, and the greenkeeper and his wife lived there. Nothing is known as to the cost of the pavilion, or who erected it, but we do know that the ladies under their captain Mrs H Mawson and their president Mrs M Bottomley worked hard and successfully to make it attractive in a short space of time for members and visitors. The ladies' committee in 1925 was Mrs Parry, Mrs E Gilliatt, Mrs D Arch, Mrs Bradley, Mrs O Cooper, Mrs Cheavin, Mrs Giles and Mrs F Day.

In May of that year the Lincs Golf Union, following their Annual General Meeting, held the annual dinner and dance at Woodhall Spa dancing in the Golf Hotel's new ballroom. Over 80 guests attended and danced to the Bonzo Band from Boston. Pudding Pie was still not a member of the *élite* group of clubs who were members of the County Golf Union. In June the improved links at Sutton on Sea were officially opened with a well attended exhibition match played by Arthur Havers of Coombe Hill, who won the Open in 1923, and Tom Williamson, the Notts professional. There had been a nine hole course there since 1903, extended to eighteen holes in 1910, but the new course was much improved and became a favourite links seaside club for golfers from all over.

PROFESSIONAL GOLF

The Great War had effectively checked the growth of the British professional competition programme, but from 1921 it started to grow and expand. The monopoly of British golfers winning the British Open championship, was broken by an influx of top class American golfers. In the 1920s the British Open was won on no less than eight occasions by players from the States including the charismatic Walter Hagan who had his first of three wins in 1922 at Sandwich. The young Bobby Jones won his first Open in 1927 at the Mecca of golf and his favourite British course, St Andrews.

74.

The winning days of the Great Triumvirate of Vardon, Taylor, and Braid, were largely over and the new generation of great players, including Hagan, Bobby Jones, Sarazan, Barnes, Duncan, Mitchell, and Hutchinson would dominate the scene in the 1920s. All except Abe Mitchell would win the British Open and he could outdrive them all. Putting was his Achilles' heel.

The best golfers of the time were however having problems making much of a living from their skills. When Walter Hagan won his first British Open in 1922 at Sandwich his first prize was £75. This was an improvement over the winnings when it first started back in 1860, when Willie Park was presented with a trophy and no cash prize. There were of course no appearance payments or commercial sponsorships available at that period or until well after 1945, and in the twenties the best players had to play frequent exhibition and prize matches to remain solvent.

One of the most common arrangements was for two professionals to team up for these exhibition matches and the current tournaments and to share the profits and their winnings. During the twenties Abe Mitchell teamed up with 'Galloping' George Duncan, the Hanger Hill professional, so called after the rapidity of his play. Duncan was one of the great characters of the then golfing scene and rather like the great Max Faulkner of later years. He enjoyed life and golf, and could smile and joke whilst still concentrating on the shot in hand. Together they toured the States to compete in the US Open and give exhibitions. The American golfing public would flock to see Abe Mitchell knock the ball out of sight, just as we do today with John Daly. He was the longest hitter of the ball amongst professionals of his day, and not until 'Slamming' Sam Snead appeared on the scene was his supremacy challenged.

THE RYDER CUP

In 1925 Mitchell became the personal golf coach to the wealthy seedsman Sam Ryder, who on the advice of his doctor had taken up golf. Golf was now very much an international affair, and matches had already been played between the best American and British teams. Sam Ryder, no doubt encouraged by Abe, who was a personal friend of many of the American players, donated a trophy subsequently known as the Ryder Cup to be played for in these matches. Fittingly enough at a preliminary first Ryder Cup match played at Wentworth on the 4th June 1926, Abe Mitchell and his friend George Duncan teed off first, playing against Walter Hagan and Jim Barnes, whom they beat rather easily 9 and 8. The publicity given to these Ryder Cup matches, involving the flamboyant Hagan and his teams, was highly beneficial to Pudding Pie and all the other golf clubs throughout Britain, now anxious to increase membership.

The 1920s and the start up of the Ryder Cup co-incided with a period where some of the greatest golfers of all times visited Britain competing for our Open. The list of the Open winners over that decade was: George Duncan, Jock Hutchinson, Walter Hagan, Arthur Travers, Walter Hagan, Jim Barnes, Bobby Jones, Bobby Jones, Walter Hagan, and Walter Hagan.

Robert Tyre Jones, or Bobby as he was known to friends and fans, and Walter Hagan were arguably the two greatest golf personalities thus far in the history of the game, with Hagan the extrovert par excellance doing everything with style and panache, and Jones the greatest gentleman of them all. His character combined the natural dignity of an ambassador, with an inborn modesty, that captivated his great following in Britain. There were no more delighted fans than those in Britain when in 1930 he won the four great golf championships of the world— The British and the USA Open and Amateur Championships— 'The Impregnable Quadrilateral' as the sports writers of the day christened the event: a feat that it seems safe to say will never be equalled, and one which he managed using his trusty old hickory shafted clubs.

MAJOR COOPER RETIRES

Life at golf courses up and down the county carried on as best they could despite the deepening of the economic depressionn. In May 1925 there was a sad announcement by the Pudding Pie club. Major Oliver Cooper was retiring from work, and the captaincy. He had decided to move to the New Forest, and would therefore have to relinquish the post. He was glad the club's future now looked assured and he would miss his friends. It had been an extremely tough few years for the Major, and he must have left with the feeling that the bullets and shells of the Boer and Great War, were rather easier to deal with than the slings, arrows and golf balls, of outrageous fortune he had encountered around Boston. He was not however the last member of the Cooper family to play a crucial role in the fortunes of the club.

There was still cash available at some golf clubs for improvements, despite the ever deepening depression. Surfleet planned to spend £1,000 on a new pavilion in late 1925. The new Sibsey club was also making progress. The members played for a handsome trophy, the Johnson Cup, recently donated by A de B Johnson. It was won in September 1925 by Mr Jack Killingworth. There were twenty three entries and eight qualifiers, including J B Arch, R Reynolds, A Reynolds, Mr Mawson, A Ingamells, W Chattell, and T Barnes.

At Pudding Pie in October the committee decided that some of the greens should be returfed.

The Sibsey Golf Club held its AGM in the new hall at Cornhill Lane, Boston in October 1925. Captain H C Marris took the chair and there was a fair attendance. The committee elected consisted of: Capt H Marris, Dr Jennings, Dr Braithwaite, Messrs. F Barnes, J Arch, A Reynolds, E Bailey, C Holland, A de B Johnson, H Hutson, O Giles, A Rysdale. The chairman reported that 'conditions at Sibsey over the last year had greatly improved'. He went on to say that he wanted the most cordial relations maintained with the Boston club, and there was ample room for two clubs in the area. They were extremely lucky to have Mr Caudwell run the course for them. Mr Caudwell was the real proprietor and 'stood the racket' for the whole thing. They were indebted to Mr Caudwell for financing the club in a way which the committee would never have dared. When the club obtained more members prospects would be good, and they would construct more holes. He was of the opinion that more people would cease to go to Rauceby and play at Sibsey instead.

Mr Caudwell was extremely anxious to get the ladies' committee to come along and say what they wanted doing, and act in conjunction with the men. A ladies' secretary was required and would be of great help to the club. The committee was taking steps to apply for a licence. The ladies' committee members were: Mrs Arch, Mrs Braithwaite, Mrs Caudwell, Mrs Giles, Mrs Yates, Mrs Johnson, Mrs Day, Mrs Barnes, and Mrs Weston. The committee were asked to consider appointing a lady captain.

The captain's comments about the role of Mr Caudwell in the SIbsey club is interesting and was doubtlessly the critical factor when it came to the decision by the Pudding Pie members whether or not to amalgamate with the Sibsey club. The Pudding Pie club belonged, like the present Boston club, to the members. They could elect, or dispense with, any member of the committee, as they wished. At Sibsey this was not the case. The club and course belonged to Mr Caudwell, and as we shall see this was crucial to the future of Sibsey.

The organisational ability of Mr Caudwell was first class. There were soon a good number of club and inter-club competitions and fixtures arranged. In October 1925 Mr and Mrs P B Arch won the Caudwell Cup. In the newspaper reports of the time, it occasionally becomes difficult to sort out which club is involved, because of the overlapping membership. In November Miss D Mather won the Cheer Cup, and in the same month Mr Hutson beat Mr P Ostler to win the Thomas Cup. On December 19th 1925, Boston Golf Club held its first ever Christmas Ball in The Assembly Rooms, Boston. It was a great success.

MARK BOTTOMLEY HONOURED

Scores at Pudding Pie did not show much improvement. The Cooper Challenge Cup was won in May 1925 by H Hutson, with 96 14 82. The Coney Challenge Bowl was won in the same month by Mrs Clifton. The Sibsey scores were not much better. In 1926 Jim McGuire won the April monthly medal with 102 24 78. Fred Caudwell was still learning the game, scoring 112 24 88.

The Pudding Pie AGM was held at the new golf pavilion in May 1926.

22. *Mark Bottomley honoured by the Pudding Pie committee. He is shown after winning the Kitwood Cup at the Rauceby course at Sleaford in 1928.*

The president, Alderman T Kitwood, congratulated the ladies for their efforts in decorating the lounge, and providing much of the furniture, curtains and carpets. The Captain, Mr A Parry, congratulated the Hon Sec, Mr Mark Bottomley, and said that the committee wished to show their appreciation for all his efforts over many years, by making him an Hon life member . . .

Mark Bottomley continued to serve the club for many more years. and became the club's longest serving Hon Sec.

. . . The club has made good progress over the past year and many new members have joined. We now have 113 men, 108 ladies, and five juniors. We have weathered the worst of the storm, and the committee now feel they can safely introduce an entrance fee of one guinea. The course has greatly improved and much of this has been due to the efforts of the groundsman, Charles Smith, who is an indefatigable worker.

A list of many members of the Pudding Pie Club of that period can be found in the competition for the 1927 Woodthorpe Cup in Appendix C

CHARLIE SMITH

Charlie Smith, who became greenkeeper at Pudding Pie shortly after it started up, remained groundsman at Pudding Pie for many years, playing a vital part in turning it into a useful golf club. No one could make it a first class golfing course. It had too many natural limitations for that. With constant hard work however, and using his skills, acquired as a farm worker on local farms, to dig ditches, lay drains, returf poor greens, and carry out the 101 tasks required to maintain and improve Pudding Pie, he gradually and steadily improved the course, changing it from something of a mudbath, into one that was acceptable. It never approached the standard of Rauceby and remained light years behind Woodhall as a test of golf, or as a pleasant enjoyable course, but it became sufficiently good to retain its membership. Many of its members, and especially the better golfers, however, also joined these better clubs around the county.

Despite the existence of railways, transferring to a new distant club or having a day out playing over a different course was still extremely difficult for many golfers. Cars were still a rarity although golfers were largely the wealthier members of society. Horse drawn coaches and traps still lined up outside the railway stations to carry visitors to their destinations.

ROBIN SMITH

23. Charlie Smith the greenkeeper at Pudding Pie golf course mowing the greens accompanied by his daughter-in-law and dog.

Charlie Smith was a native of Boston and after leaving school at fourteen he worked on farms around the town acquiring the skills that would be so useful to the golf club. Early on in the course of the 1914-18 War he volunteered for service, and joined up in the Lincolnshire Regiment. After managing to survive the war he returned to Boston, and started working for a Mr Percy

Smith, a local dentist who had also built up a business growing and selling rose bushes. Here he gained a reputation as a skilled rose grafter, and a hard working and reliable man. He was about thirty when he moved to Pudding Pie farmhouse, and took on the job of greenkeeper. He turned out to be one of the most valuable servants the club would ever possess. He was an extremely hard and diligent worker keen to do a good job and work any hours required to complete the task.

This was vital to the club because all that he had at his disposal were a few pieces of not very good horse machinery including a farm mower, roller, and scarifiers. He had a hand pushed mower to cut the greens.

His main helper was a horse called Kitty that had some Shire and some Welsh cob blood, amongst other less well determined breeds, running in her veins. Kitty grazed a paddock against the farm buildings, which she shared with a cow called Polly. Thus Mrs Smith produced her own milk, and made her own butter and bread. She also served refreshments in the clubhouse, 'A pot of tea, a cucumber sandwich, and a cake for sixpence', as her son Robert, now over 80, recalls. As a boy, he caddied on the course for the members and recalls hitching lifts from the town on the barges and fishing boats heading out to the Wash past Pudding Pie. He would jump off opposite the Golf Club and then swim ashore.

What Charlie Smith possessed, that was especially important to the club, was his skills as an all round farm worker. He could plough and manage the temperamental silt soils of the Wash, cut a hedge, dig a ditch, clear a drain, repair buildings, mend implements, catch moles and do all the other jobs that meant the difference between success and failure in turning Pudding Pie from a wet old hole into a playable golf course. He was not a clock watcher and finished the task in hand, no matter what time of day. He took a pride in the course and his work. Over the course of the years he spent at Pudding Pie, his efforts bore fruit, and in the absence of the complicated and expensive equipment available today to run a golf course, his dedication over the difficult times facing the club, could well have spelt the difference between success and failure.

MICHAEL GOODLIFFE – W.W.JOHNSON & SON LTD.

24. A typical one horsepower 60" mower in 1923. Charlie Smith had two 36" horse drawn mowers by 1928.

ARTHUR CHAMBERS

He was assisted in his task of course management by Arthur Chambers, who worked in the corn trade for Sam Cooper, Bryan Cooper's father. Mr Chambers was able to invite various turf and, grass experts along to the club, get their advice and suggestions and with Charlie Smith available to do the hard work, the course improved steadily year by year. Arthur Chambers put in a great deal of work at this period and in the future, helping to improve the course, getting expert advice on management, and siting of greens and tees, and later on helping to replan the course extension. It always tended to be a wet course, but gradually the wet areas were drained, the greens better managed, and life made tolerable for the golfers. Charlie Smith was greenkeeper until around 1940, when his wife retired because of ill health and Charlie took a road job with Boston Corporation. Altogether he had been greenkeeper for around 15 years and had helped the club survive some of its most difficult moments.

82.

PUDDING PIE GOLF COURSE

There is not much information available on the planning and laying out of Pudding Pie. A scaled model was built in the Infantry Drill Hall in Boston in 1922 when the move was first put to the members. Major Cooper and Arthur Chambers had major roles in the planning, but the other committee members must also have been involved. It was laid out originally as a nine hole course, with the principal feature being that it ran alongside the river Witham. There was a high flood bank, and thirty yards of marshy rough, between the river and fairway. This was always wet because of seepage from the river. On the other side of the course adjacent to Fishtoft Road, ran another flood bank that was much older, but there was a critical difference between these two banks. The Corporation had the responsibility for the repair and maintenance of the Fishtoft Road bank, but the golf club was responsible for the upkeep of the River Bank. This difference became, at a later date, of critical importance to the future of the club.

Like all fenland fields, Pudding Pie farm was cut up by large ditches. There were four of these, with some partly lined by hedges. At first these were the principal hazards, but in time bunkers were built around the course. It started off as a nine hole course, like the majority of similar golf clubs of the period, and was 2,687 yards long. No Standard Scratch was ever allocated to the course but its bogey rating, roughly equivalent to our par system was thirty-seven. Two of the so called bogey five holes were 414 and 429 yards long, however, which would have put them into the par four category of today's reckoning. The clubhouse was adjacent to the course. On the opposite side of the road lay the Pudding Pie farmhouse and buildings. The clubhouse was a large wooden building erected on wooden pillars three feet high for flood protection. It had a large central lounge, and on either side of the building were locker rooms for the ladies and gentlemen. On its front, facing the course, there was a large veranda. The lounge overlooked the veranda and the course, and at the back of the lounge was the bar and kitchen. The club professional had a small wooden shed at the side of the pavilion, where he carried out club repairs and kept a stock of clubs and balls. Pudding Pie farmhouse was inhabited at various times by the current professional, or the greenkeeper. Sometime in the '30s the clubhouse was burnt down and was re-built along similar lines to the first building.

Co-existing with the Sibsey Golf Club

Following the initial shock of having another golf club start up just down the road, Pudding Pie and Sibsey settled down to a rather uneasy co-existence. Both clubs made steady progress improving their courses and planning club and inter club competition programmes. There was however, inevitably, competition for players, as there was between all the adjacent clubs in the county. The number of people who could afford the time and money to play golf, was still extremely restricted compared to the present day, and not improving in the difficult economic climate of those years.

By 1929 the depression had not improved and on the 24th October 1929, Black Tuesday, the American Stock Market collapsed, losing 30 billion dollars, and further damaging not only the economy of the USA, but soon afterwards, that of Britain, France and the rest of Europe. Despite the recession the membership at Pudding Pie had risen from 180 in 1925 to 250 in 1929 helped by the fact that golf was steadily becoming less exclusive. Unemployment however was starting to bite into these figures. At the AGM in May 1930, T Tyson was elected captain. He commented on the difficult times the country was going through and how the depression was affecting everyone including the Boston golf club. There was a small balance in the account of £8.10s. and had Mr Cheer and others not worked hard to raise money for the club they would have been obliged by the bank to issue new shares to keep the club solvent. The president, Alderman Tom Kitwood, commented that he was pleased the club was managing to survive although not under the most favourable conditions. Boston ladies and gentlemen continued with a good programme of matches with local clubs. In September 1930 a team of Boston ladies including Mrs Cheer, Mrs Poyser, Miss Kidd, Mrs Arch, Miss Sidorn, Miss T Francis, Mrs Banks, Miss Cheshire, Mrs Spurway and Mrs Kirkby played the ladies of

84.

Sandilands' golf club and were comprehensively defeated 7 $^1/_2$ points to $^1/_2$ point. Lincolnshire was now a full member of the English Golf Union and in January 1931 Mr A A Taylor and Mr H Ridley were elected to represent the county on this committee. The Boston golf club was still not deemed to be of sufficient quality to be a member of the E.G.U.

TRAGEDY AT SIBSEY

The golfing scene around Boston however was completely changed on the 30th July 1931. Fred Caudwell was cutting a long pole with a circular saw in a shed at his farm when the saw jammed and the pole shot back and struck him a severe blow in the abdomen. He was rushed to hospital where he underwent a major operation, but despite the best endeavours of the doctors he died six weeks later on the 18th September. His family, the villagers of Sibsey, and his wide range of friends including all the members of both golf clubs, were stunned by this tragedy. He was only forty-one years old. His widow as might be expected never quite got over her loss. She was fortunate that her family, the Bowsers, from nearby Friskney, were able to assist her and her young son, Peter to run the farm.

Understandably she felt unable to continue with the East Lincolnshire Golf Club, and when the lease expired at the end of March 1932, the course was closed and crops were soon growing on some of the fairways. It was a sad ending to an ambitious and successful attempt to create an inland golf course. In many ways Fred Caudwell had made a better attempt at it than golfers with much more experience. Who knows what he might have achieved had he lived?

Today the old Sibsey course is an unrecognisable part of the attractive countryside around Sibsey. The stately Trader windmill looks down on the old fairways once the scene of fierce golf battles with their tales of good luck or bad luck, long putts sunk and short putts missed. Life must go on however and the Sibsey members were soon playing their golf at Pudding Pie, Seacroft, Sleaford or Spalding. The Pudding Pie committee would have been less than human if mixed with the sadness over the loss of Fred Caudwell, was some relief at the extra members and the healthier bank balance that would come to the Boston club as a result of the tragedy. The decision to reject Fred Caudwell's offer had been much closer than the vote at the E.G.M. would indicate. Golf could very easily have disappeared for a long period in the Boston area.

Tubular Steel Shafts Legalised

The 'twenties' did usher in an event that would benefit all golfers and help bring the game into the present era. In 1929 the R and A allowed the use of hollow steel shafts and thus opened the way to the mass production of cheap and reliable matched sets of golf clubs. The hickory shafted clubs in the hands of the best golfers could be just as effective, but good sets were expensive. For the amateurs of Pudding Pie and elsewhere, tubular steel gradually replaced the old wooden clubs, but mixtures of the new and old continued in use for many years. Better golfing equipment, in the form of golf bags and shoes, became more common, assisted by the lead provided by the dress conscious Walter Hagan and his friend, the Prince of Wales, later King Edward VIII, who was himself a keen and first class golfer.

CHAPTER FIVE

THE 1930s

T HE 1930S WAS A DECADE when most people had more important things to think of than golf. Unemployment soared from one and a half million in 1923 to nearly three million in 1932. Most golf clubs in the county lost members, as people economised on leisure activities. In 1930 the Seacroft Golf Club reported that to help make ends meet, wages and salaries would be cut by 10% and subscriptions raised from three guineas to four guineas. No dividends would be paid to shareholders for a further year. Farming was having just as hard a time as industry, with many good farmers going under. Pudding Pie was saved from the worst effects because it gained members from the now defunct Sibsey course. The Boston club entered the thirties in better condition than ever before thanks to Charlie Smith's hard work. He had recently laid three new greens and there were now thirty-seven bunkers spread over the course. He had had part time assistance from Mr Wilkinson with this work, and Mr Fixter, the Woodhall professional, had provided valuable advice in placing these in the best possible positions. It was announced in late June that: 'the Boston Course is in splendid condition. The hay has been removed and playing conditions are of the best.' The membership, which had stabilised at 250 at the beginning of the decade, actually rose to 280 in 1934, but by 1936 this had dropped to 260.

By 1930 golf was competing successfully with the other sports around Boston. In November 1930 J Mather, the captain of the Boston Rowing Club, complained that: 'too many of the members were taking up golf to the detriment of their rowing.' New names were being seen in the Boston competitions, including Miss L Enderby, handicap 32; H Senior 24; E Turner 24; T Carter 11; Mrs Playle 27; P Rysdale 24; and H Trevitt 24.

There was however a sharp reminder that there were other events taking place outside golf. In July the German airship the Graf Zeppelin passed over Skegness. Germany at that time was undergoing horrific inflation for which Europe would pay a high price in the not too distant future. In August seven inches of rain fell on Boston causing widespread flooding, and Pudding Pie disappeared under water for several days. Mrs Hamer had been having a wonderful season in 1931, winning The Cheer Cup, The Coney Bowl, and The Emma Bottomley Rose Bowl. The depression was still affecting everyone and the dreaded workhouse was still a frightening institution. In November the Spilsby workhouse master was sent to prison for various misdemeanours. There is no evidence that a resident in any of the county workhouses ever succeeded in joining a golf club. In fact very few working class members would gain access to this sport over the next couple of decades. But events were looming on the horizon which would change all this.

THE LINCOLNSHIRE GOLF ALLIANCE

A newspaper report in November 1931 reported a meeting that had taken place at the Seacroft golf club some weeks earlier. It reported the formation of the Lincolnshire Golf Alliance which would arrange competitions where amateur golfers. and golf professionals would combine to compete against each other. This was a historic meeting and the 'Alliance' concept something of a watershed in the organisation of the game. The early years of golf had been dominated by amateurs, and the professional game and the professionals themselves, were rather looked down on by the wealthy amateurs who dominated the sport. This is illustrated by the first committee of the Lincolnshire Union of Golf Clubs which included the Earls of Scarborough, Brownlow, Yarborough, and Winchilsea amongst its members. That the game greatly benefited from the efforts of the Earls and Lords who dominated the management structure cannot be doubted. They provided many of the courses and much capital in those early days. It did however create much resentment in the professional ranks and slowed down the uptake of the game amongst the population at large. Harry Cawsey, who had provided coaching for the Boston ladies at Pudding Pie, was elected the first Alliance captain. At one of their early meetings W Pearson and E Muggleton from Sibsey scored 87 6 81. Henceforth the professionals would slowly but steadily dominate the game culminating with the superstars of the '70s and '80s.

88.

In January 1932 it was announced that the Pudding Pie course would be extended to twelve holes. 'The three extra holes will add 1,000 yards to the course. Six holes will be around the outside so that by using them again the full eighteen holes can be played.' The new layout had been designed by Arthur Chambers. The course now extended to 5,865 yards including seven bogey five holes and an eighteen hole bogey of 76. However, only two of the bogey fives would be regarded as par fives today and the likely SSS would be around 68. The newly enlarged course was opened on 21st May, with Miss Betty Francis, the lady captain and Arthur Chambers driving off to celebrate the occasion. At the AGM held earlier that month Mr R Isaac, who presided, congratulated Mr Chambers as the sole architect and planner of the extension, and Mr Charles Smith, for all his hard work in carrying out the alterations. There had been many members join from the Sibsey club, and a warm welcome was extended to them.

The Pudding Pie Club now had a full programme of competitions for trophies for both the ladies and gentlemen, most of which are still competed for today. There were also matches played against most of the adjacent clubs in the county. Boston ladies beat Surfleet ladies in August 1933 with a team including Mrs W Hamer, Mrs D Arch, Miss T Francis, Mrs W Cheer, Miss B Francis, Miss N Carter and Mrs Scrimshaw. Boston acquired a new professional when Ernest Muggleton joined the club from Sibsey in 1932. He stayed only one year leaving the club without a professional for a period. The course was still in a very rough condition by present day standards and scores were correspondingly higher. In June 1932, R Reynolds won the monthly medal with 98 14 84—a score that is unbelievable today. It was reported that 'all the rough grass on the course had been cut and carted away'. There were many new names to be seen in the lists for the competitions. In April 1933, the Boston Mayor, C Fleet, playing with Mr R Hardy, Willoughby House, won the Winter League. Richard Hardy who farmed just outside Boston had a son also called Richard, who would play an important role in the later history of the club.

In 1933 however, the fairways and greens were reported to be

BOSTON GOLF CLUB

The
SIGNAL SCORER

Player .... H'cap ....

Date .... Won + Lost — Halved O

No	Yards	Bogey	Stroke Index	Strokes	Putts	Result	No	Yards	Bogey	Stroke Index	Strokes	Putts	Result
1	201	4	7				10	430	5	4			
2	414	5	3				11	190	3	11			
3	110	3	18				12	307	4	14			
4	270	4	12				13	251	4	15			
5	115	3	17				14	414	5	6			
6	429	5	5				15	429	5	8			
7	500	5	1				16	500	5	2			
8	306	4	9				17	306	4	10			
9	286	4	13				18	307	4	16			
Out	2731	37					Home Out	3134 2731	39 37				Home Out
+	........)			Bogey Result				5865	76				Gross
													H'cap
													Nett

Marker's Sig. ....

23

'in first class condition'. In July 1933, J Bowman won the Woodthorpe Cup, beating Cyril Dawson. Cyril Dawson became one of the best golfers produced by the Boston club and at his best he played nearly to scratch. He represented the county on many occasions. In May of the same year playing in the Thomas Cup he set a course record with a score of 73 8 65, the bogey of the course being 76.

BOSTON LADIES' FIRST OPEN MEETING

In October 1933, Boston Ladies' Golf Club held their first ever open meeting. Mrs J Bowman, with a gross 92, won the scratch event. Two Spalding ladies won medals. Miss Groan with 95 30 65 and Mrs Harvey with 94 19 75. A 65 was a miraculous score in those days and no doubt the winner's name attracted some noise and comment at the prize giving ceremony. After lunch Miss Betty Francis and Miss Wright of Boston won the bogey competition on minus four. The event was voted a resounding success and a tribute to the Pudding Pie Ladies' organising ability and it would be made an annual event. In June 1934 the inter county Midland League matches were held at Seacroft, Nottingham, and North Shore. Later in the month the Bottomley Bowl was won by Miss M Carter and the Roberts Cup by Mrs Laughton. Cyril Dawson and Miss Carter won the mixed foursomes. Mrs Cheer got a hole in one on the fifth. Boston Gents dealt a severe blow to a team from Blankney beating them eight matches to one. The Pudding Pie team were: Messrs Dawson, Carter, Thompson, Rastall, Ostler, Horry, Richardson, Nicholson and Margerison. Boston Ladies however were not so fortunate and lost to Belton five matches to three. The ladies were Mrs Bowman, Mrs Hamer, Miss Tommy Francis, Miss B Francis, Mrs W Cheer, Mrs Arch, Mrs Carter and Mrs Wright.

THE CURTIS CUP

Ladies' golf in Britain received a boost in 1932 when the Curtis Cup matches started. Two American sisters, Harriet and Margaret Curtis, both very keen and able golfers, donated a cup to

25. *The SIGNAL SCORER opposite was marketed to many golf clubs around the country. There were 28 pages + cover with space for club and course details, thirteen 'score cards', and local retail advertising.*

be played for biennially between teams of British and American leading amateur golfers. The Americans demonstrated the strength of Ladies golf across the Atlantic by winning the first match and holding onto the Cup for the next twenty years.

Boston now had a thriving Junior Section organising their own competitions. The Sinclair Cup, the first presented to the section, won on its first outing by C Coppin, son of Councillor T Coppin.

At the ladies AGM the president was Mrs W Kitwood, captain Mrs Hamer, the Hon Sec Mrs W Cheer and the committee: Mrs J Bowman, Mrs A Parry, Mrs W Wright, Mrs J Laughton, Mrs M Bradley, and Mrs T Tyson. Mrs Giles won the Emma Bottomley Bowl. This was not suprising as she was a rapidly improving golfer. She won the October monthly medal with a score of 101 32 nett 69— one of the best ever net scores to be recorded by a lady over the Pudding Pie course.

In June 1934 a Midland Golf Match was held at Seacroft and amongst the clubs competing were Seacroft, Torksey, Hawkstone Park, North Shore, Blackwell and Hollinwell. Hawkstone Park in North Shropshire at Weston-under-Redcastle is one of the most beautiful courses in Britain set out amongst striking red sandstone outcrops and surrounded by the lovely Shropshire countryside. Later it would become famous for producing Sandy Lyle. His father, Alex Lyle, was professional there from 1955 to 1986 and when the owner Lord Hill died he was a member of a syndicate of local businessmen who purchased it for the extremely modest sum of £60,000. Alex. Lyle was one of the old school Scottish professionals who did so much to spread the gospel of golf throughout Britain and the rest of the world. The memory of the golf lessons I received from him are still fresh in my mind: 'Don't swing that club too far back, laddie,' was his advice, which worked wonderfully for his famous son but alas not so well for the author.

By a unique and fortuitous coincidence for British golf, a few miles up the road at the Oswestry Golf Club a young professional, a contemporary and friend of Sandy, was learning his trade and on his way to becoming a golfing super star— his name was Ian Woosnam. The golfing world was extremely fortunate when

Harold, his father, took up golf at the nearby Llanymenoch course quite late in life. On my visits to his small dairy farm near Ellesmere we used to swap golfing stories. I played then at the Oswestry Golf Club where Ian would later be the resident professional for several years.

Seacroft was by this period regularly holding major golfing events. In 1934 it hosted the English Ladies' County Finals and later the English Ladies' Close Golf Championship.

The ladies were by this time steadily wearing down the golfing establishment's idea of what proper young ladies should wear on a golf course. Hemlines had been steadily rising up from the ankles and by the '30s were hovering around the knees.

One of the competitors in the Close Golf Championship at Seacroft was a Miss Gloria Minoprio, a former conjurer's assistant and a member at Littlestone Golf Club in Kent. A tall strikingly beautiful girl she arrived in a chauffeur driven yellow Rolls Royce attired in beret, sweater and rather tight fitting black trousers. Her performance on the course posed a serious problem for the male sex amongst the large gallery who followed her. Their dilemma was that the lady had another highly unusual habit— she only carried one club—a long iron, and the chauvanistic males found difficulty in deciding which was the more interesting— her extremely attractive figure, or her equally interesting golf swing. Unfortunately her progress in the competitions tended to be of short duration. Sadly she later married a Polish gentleman who took her off to Canada. The golf club manufacturers however breathed a considerable sigh of relief.

GEORGE HEMPSTEAD

In December 1934 George Hempstead, the golf assistant from Sleaford, was appointed to the post of Pudding Pie professional. He had trained under George Robins at Sleaford and was twenty years old. He had been with Mr Robins for five years and then spent some time with Mr Robins successor, Mr Leslie Fixter. Leslie was brother to Alf, later the Woodhall professional. George Robins moved to Leamington Spa Golf Club and stayed there for many years. There were three Fixter brothers, Alf and Leslie became professional golfers and the third, Frank, was reckoned by his brothers to be the golfing duffer of the family and could only

93.

play to five. Their mother had been stewardess at Woodhall Golf Club in the period 1910 to 1930 working for the indomitable Colonel Hotchkin, and her sons learned the game at Woodhall with his encouragement. Alf, winner of the Lincolnshire Open Championship and Lincolnshire Professional Championship on no less than ten occasions, is still very much alive today and can recount innumerable tales of past golfing incidents, many of them involving the old Colonel. On one occasion he was caddying in the morning round for the Colonel playing in a foursome and partnered by the distinguished golf architect Sir Guy Campbell. The Colonel's partner put the ball into a very thick gorse bush at the edge of the seventh hole at the Woodhall course. The Colonel with great difficulty and much damage to his tailored plus fours and backside, eventually got the ball out and onto the green.

When the match, playing in the afternoon, reached the seventh, Alf and Sir Guy was astonished to find that the offending bush had disappeared and furthermore there was no trace of any bush having been in that location. One of the little advantages of playing on one's own golf course! Woodhall Spa, then as now probably the best course in the county, was host to many important events of the time and in March the county golf trials were held there. Mr L Bacon and T H (King) Bowman were selected. 'T H' was nicknamed 'King' because of his supposed resemblance to King George V. He was one of the best golfers to come out of Lincolnshire, played for the county and England on several occasions, and was a good friend to the Boston golf club. The ladies' and

MURRAY BOWMAN

26. T. H. 'King' Bowman. Six times Lincolnshire champion, English international, and Seacroft course manager.

men's County Unions, were active as normal, with a full programme of events. In August, Notts Ladies played Lincs Ladies at Wollaton Park. Notts won four matches to three. The team did not include any player from Boston. In 1935 the Sandilands club

94.

was elected a member of the Lincolnshire Union of Golf Clubs, an honour which still escaped the efforts of the Pudding Pie club.

NATIONAL AVIATION DAY

Britain was steadily moving into the twentieth century. More cars were appearing on the roads and occasionally they ran over some unsuspecting pedestrian. There was consternation in Boston in 1930 when one proud motorist came to collect his car and found that it had been stolen. Aeroplanes were beginning to be seen in the skies over the fens and when June 15th 1931 was designated National Aviation Day, 7,000 Bostonians turned out to see Sir Alan Cobham bring his fleet of aeroplanes to the Boston aerodrome where they performed aerobatics to an astonished gathering.

Since Louis Bleriot had successfully flown across the English Channel in July 1909, steady progress had been made in air transport, accelerated by the demands of the 1914-18 War. International golf today depends on the jet airliner. Walter Hagan would continue to spend several days on a liner crossing the Atlantic for all of his Ryder Cup matches, but the spectacle witnessed in Boston on that day marked a significant step forward in the history of golf. The jet liner today is as important to the golf super stars as are their golf clubs.

HARD TIMES

The entertainment provided by the Flying Circus helped take the minds of the townsfolk away from the more pressing problem of simple survival. Farming like every other industry was suffering from low prices. Many good, well run farms went under. William Pearson of Freiston Hall was adjudged bankrupt in 1933 with deficiencies of over £40,000, a colossal sum in those days, caused by poor prices and an unfortunate severe and widespread flood. Farm wages and the income of every business in Boston felt the knock-on effect. These conditions were also affecting every golf club, and even popular well attended courses like the Sleaford Club started to feel the pinch. At their AGM in 1932 their Hon Treasurer reported a large drop in income and their committee decided temporarily to suspend their entrance subcription and reduce their ground staff. As already noted Boston was helped by the windfall increase in their membership caused by the closure of the Sibsey club.

Another step forward, with Britain steadily moving into the twentieth century, came in 1935 when Pudding Pie got a telephone line. Mark Bottomley the Hon Sec became Boston 717. When the Boston Golf Club started up in 1900 there were only 3,000 telephones in the country, but by 1930 this had risen to 2,000,000. Car registrations which numbered 15,000 in 1905 had leapt to well over 1,500,000 by 1930. The Old Age Pension was nil in 1900, 5/- (five shillings) when first introduced in 1909, and doubled to 10/- in 1926. The average weekly wage was then 47/- (£2.7s.0d.). The standard of living of everyone was gradually rising for those fortunate to have a job, with beneficial effects on the potential number of people who might be tempted to play golf.

WATER SHORTAGE

One essential, the shortage of which continued to plague the Boston area, including the golf club at Pudding Pie, was good drinking water. The flat fens lay many miles from a source of clean water. Outside the town of Boston many inhabitants still relied on water from the roof, collected in cisterns, or shallow wells, for their supplies. Many of the present members of the Senior Section of Boston golf club, including the inimitable Ernest Wilson, remember as children collecting water from the cistern, a brick lined tank sunk into the ground and fed from downspouts from the cottage roof. They would empty this into a patent clay filtering jar and trust that the cloudy fluid was reasonably healthy to drink, which it frequently was not. In October 1935 the medical officer reported that out of seventeen wells and cisterns tested in the villages around Boston sixteen were contaminated. In times of drought water was carted around the villages sometimes in Boston itself, and sold by the bucket. In September 1935 following a drought, water was sold at Old Leake at 1d a barrel. Not until the new Fordington pumping station came into operation in 1936 did the situation begin to improve. No doubt many games of golf had to be cancelled from attacks of 'Boston Tummy'. Meanwhile the economic depression showed no signs of abating. In 1923 there were 1,500,000 out of work and by 1932

96.

this had risen to nearly 3,000,000.

The Lincolnshire ladies' team were also having a hard time losing, in August 1935, to a Nottinghamshire ladies team by four matches to three. The match was held at Wollaton Park.

VISIT OF WALTER HAGAN

Pudding Pie had an eminent guest in August 1937. Walter Hagan came to play an exhibition match. It was arranged that he and the famous Australian golfer Joe Kirkwood would play George Hempstead and Cyril Dawson. Unfortunately, Joe became ill on the evening before the match, which was a great shame for Pudding Pie golfers, since he was one of the best 'trick' golfers of the period and had given demonstrations all over the world. He would hit full drives with every club including the putter, place three balls on top of one another and hit out the middle, swing three clubs simultaneously at three golf balls and knock them all over 200 yards, together with a host of other unbelievable trick shots.

27. Walter Hagan, the great, American golfer, plays at Pudding Pie 1937. He is seated second from the right. On his left is George Hempstead, the club professional, and on his right the club secretary, Mark Bottomley.

28. Bobby Jones and Walter Hagan before their famous challenge match in 1926 over 36 holes. Hagan won 12 and 11. He was seldom beaten in match play.

29 Joyce Wethered, later Lady Heathcote Amory: English Ladies' champion on four occasions 1922, 1924, 1925, and 1929

In the event of Joe's illness, Hagan played the better ball of the two Boston players and won three and one. Boston members recall how, after the match and refreshments in the club house, nothing loth, he took a few balls out on the course and demonstrated his skill with his famous wedge. He had one of the best short games, including putting, amongst his peers and this earned him his glittering list of prizes. From 1914-1937 he was the superstar of the professional circuit winning, amongst many other majors, our Open on four occasions. He was captain of the American Ryder Cup team on six occasions. He was one of the all time 'greats' of the game and had a charismatic personality. Because of the awe he generated in his opponents he was practically never beaten in a match play.

He was equally at ease gambling with millionaires at the London gaming tables, or playing poker with his fellow American professionals. On friendly terms with the Prince of Wales, the future King Edward VIII, who was a keen golfer, Hagan did more than anyone else to lift the status of his fellow British and American professionals. When refused access, as were all professional golfers of the day, to the member's lounge during a competition, he would refuse to enter it later for the prize giving ceremony. Instead he would collect his trophy and cheque at the ceremony which he would insist be held in the car park and, to the acute embarrasment of the club president and committee, depart with all his friends in his Rolls Royce down to the nearest inn to celebrate.

The author owes a special debt of gratitude to the peerless Hagan since he was responsible for earning him his first million. Playing at Boston a few days after reading of this astonishing visit he ventured this information to his opponent Geoffrey Wood. Geoff, a very good golfer and knowledgeable about golf matters, dismissed this information rather scornfully whereupon I ventured to wager him a fiver for his pound. 'A fiver—I'll give a million to your fiver'. Sorrowfully I have to report that he has not yet met his debt. However I am prepared to commute it for a double whisky and unless this is forthcoming within one month of the publication of this book, he may be hearing from my solicitors.

THE PEERLESS BOBBY JONES

The thirties saw the rise of another group of great professional golfers to join the existing super stars which then included the peerless Bobby Jones, Walter Hagan, and Gene Sarazan. This new group included Henry Cotton who won the Open in 1934 and 1937, 'Slammin' Sam Snead, one of the most graceful and longest hitters of all times, and Byron Nelson. In 1945 Nelson won 18 out of 31 tournaments on the American Circuit, including a run of 11 consecutive victories. One could put a considerable bet that this feat will never again be repeated.

Bobby Jones retired from the professional circuit in 1930 after winning the four major Majors—the USA and British, Open and Amateur Championships. He then spent the rest of his golfing career on golf administration and in planning and starting up the last of the 'Major' competitions, the US Masters at Atlanta, Georgia, in 1934, constructing in the process one of the most beautiful courses in the world.

Ladies' golf also had made steady progress during the thirties, with a dramatiic increase in the number of women taking up the game. Joyce Wethered who became Lady Heathcote Amory, the best of a number of great British lady golfers, was coming to the end of her illustrious career by the mid thirties. Rated by Bobby Jones to be the best swinger of a golf club, man or woman, with whom he had played, she was the supreme lady golfer of her age. She won the English Ladies' Championship five years in succession and was practically unbeatable in match play.

Woodhall continued to host important competitions. In September 1935 the Central England Open meeting, a three day event, was held there and T H Bowman and his wife lost in the final of the knockout mixed foursomes.

The Stableford System

In October 1935 an important event took place at the Surfleet Open Day. The Stableford Scoring System was used for part of the competition. This is a method of scoring on a hole by hole basis, with two points for a par, three for one under, and one for one over par, all net of handicap allowance. It was invented by Dr Stableford of the Wallasey G. C. in 1930 and is beloved by high handicap players. For many 'Rabbits', including myself, this invention has added more enjoyment than almost any other golf innovation. The winner J Duval, scored 45 points and the two runners up R Carter and S Roberts from Boston scored 43. This was the first report in a local newspaper of a competition when this system was used.

The Surfleet club had improved their course over the previous few years and were fairly new to hosting important competitions. In November 1935 The Lincolnshire Golfing Alliance held their competition there and sixty-four players attended. Pudding Pie unfortunately was not yet in this favoured category.

On the 25th January King George V died and was succeeded by his son, King Edward VIII. For the first time we had a monarch who played golf, if we exclude Mary Queen of Scots who was keen

100.

on the game and infuriated the Scottish nobles by playing when she should have been mourning the death of her husband. These gentlemen however were quite easily infuriated, but perhaps it was carrying the love of the game rather too far.

The Pudding Pie golfers continued to play a full set of home and away competitions. In a mixed foursome on October 2 1937 Jessie Wright and E Nettleton won with a nett 67, Mrs Skene and Mr B Cooper coming second with 69. In the Woodthorpe Cup, P Arch beat C Dawson 3 and 2. C Dawson had previously beaten R Reynolds and E Nettleton. In the same month the Boston men beat Rauceby $4^1/_2$ to $^1/_2$, the team being: R Thomson, C Dawson, E Nettleton, R Thursby, J Arch, A Wrigley, T Carter, H Rothery, R Callaghan and F Collart.

It was announced in October that there would be an innovation in the form of a Club Championship which would become an annual event involving prizes for handicap and scratch players. In November at the Inter County Meeting at North Shore, Lincolnshire gained a notable victory.

GAS MASKS

The situation in Germany became more and more worrying. There were disturbing reports in the newspapers of the harsh treatment meted out to the German Jews and the demands and attitude of Hitler became more strident by the day. There was an ominous entry in the Standard of November 1937. 'Fourteen cases of gas masks had arrived for distribution in Mablethorpe'. Those for Boston arrived at the beginning of 1938. Not an auspicious start to the New Year. On a cheerier note there was a good photograph of Robert Reynolds newly married to Miss Molly Thacker.

In April The Boston Ladies beat a team from Sleaford four matches to two. The ladies' team was: Mrs Moore, Mrs Arch, Mrs Wright, Mrs Isaacs, Mrs McNight and Mrs Skene. Later in the year the ladies halved a match again with Sleaford, the team on this occasion being: Mrs Colliar, Miss Francis, Mrs Carter, Miss Clifton, Mrs Moore, Mrs Kitwood, Mrs Arch and Mrs Wright.

Another revolution was taking place. The horse which had provided power for work and transport for thousands of years, was on its way out, replaced by the internal combustion engine.

In May the Sleaford club announced that a new tractor was to be bought, and electric lights installed. When the first tractor was purchased at Pudding Pie is not known, but it would most likely have been rather later. Bryan Cooper can recall that it gave a considerable amount of trouble because it was hitched to the old horse machinery, rollers and mowers, and the bearings of these kept on seizing up under the strain of the extra speed.

FINANCIAL WORRIES

The AGM was held in May 1938 at the club house. Robert Isaacs was elected to the chair. There was a loss of £166. It was suggested that non shareholders should be encouraged to purchase shares. The recession was causing problems to Pudding Pie, as it was to many clubs over the county. The chairman said that the financial position was worrying. The president re-elected was Alderman T Kitwood: the vice-chairmen, Mayor J Mountain, W Kitwood, J Towell, A Chambers, and G Clark. The captain elected was S Margerison, the vice-captain R Saville, the Hon Sec M Bottomley, and the Hon treasurer Mr Williams. The committee were: F Harden, J Nettleton, R Reynolds, H Rothery, B Cooper, and P Arch. The chairman suggested that there was not enough co-operation between the ladies and gentlemen. Mr Williams, the treasurer, said that in the past, twenty-seven members had guaranteed the bank overdraft up to £700. This needed to be reviewed. Most guarantees were for £10 with some others for £5. Mr Nettleton said this was an opportunity for members to show how keen they were to help the club survive and carry on. The treasurer said that 600 out of the 1,000 shares on offer had been taken up. It was obvious that the committee were becoming worried about the financial position. The effects of the prolonged recession was affecting most clubs in the county, and many had succumbed. Pudding Pie was vulnerable because the course was not and probably never could be a 'good' course, since it was inherently wet and sticky, lying alongside the river. It was looking more 'dated' compared to the better courses like Woodhall, Sleaford, and Seacroft. It was much easier for disgruntled members to get into car, train, or bus and play golf elsewhere.

But there was another greater worry facing the committee. The River Witham was only a few yards away from the course. Like all

102.

the Wash rivers it could rise anytime and wreak havoc with the surrounding countryside. This had always been a risk facing the low lying fens and on many occasions in the past there had been much loss of life, in addition to flooding of the countryside. What was particularly exercising the minds of the committee was that the flood bank was becoming more and more eroded. They had persuaded the Boston Corporation to dump rubbish and hardcore to strengthen it, but what it really required was a major civil engineering project to safeguard the course and this was entirely beyond the resources of the club. In April 1938 in a high flood tide the river bank burst a few hundred yards below Pudding Pie. A large area was flooded. This incident highlighted the risk to the Boston committee.

The Cinema

Golf is primarily a recreational game and in competition with any other forms of recreation that might develop. In February 1936 the Boston Odeon Cinema opened at a cost of £50,000 and seating 1,500. It is difficult for the young golfers of today, to imagine how powerful a grip the cinema had on people at the time of the opening of the Odeon. In the absence of most of the entertainment now available, it attracted almost everyone, to see the new stars of Hollywood who could transport their audience away from the harsh realities of the Thirties. People would go as often as their pockets would permit. The Saturday afternoon matinee was the high point in out youthful lives, where my friends and I could see Tom Mix and the Lone Ranger shoot their way out of all sorts of predicaments. Believe it or not, but it is absolutely true, at the small cinema I used to attend in Perth the price of admission for this feast of visual entertainment, was one penny and two jam jars. What the management did with all those jam jars was not of the least concern to their young audience. With a packet of Woodbines costing 2d and a large helping of fish and chips for 4d; and these were the old pence at 240 to the pound, life was satisfactory for those with the requisite number of pennies. Alas these were scarce for the average family.

In September 1937 Miss Betty Francis, down to a handicap of $6^1/_2$, won the Eclectic with a gross 81, nett $74^1/_2$. In May 1938 the Lincolnshire Alliance held their championship competition and it was won by W Robertson. Alf Fixter professional at Woodhall and his brother Leslie professional at Rauceby, scored 152 and 153 respectively. On September 11 1938, George Hempstead the young Boston professional married Miss Mildred Pike. He had been in post at Pudding Pie for the last four years. In September the Woodthorpe Cup was won by Dr Sheehan, who beat C Dawson. The Cooper Cup was won by F Pearson 93 24 69, a very good score for the time. R Gresswell, 80 8 72 and Dr N Bloom, 90 17 73, were runners up. Boston golfers like other golfers in the county liked to play at other courses. In September H Rothery and Dr Sheehan won first prize in the North Shore Bogey competition.

The eigth annual competition of the Central England Open Mixed Foursomes was held at Woodhall. It was a three day event and, like all the events held at Woodhall, well organised and enjoyed by all the competitors. There was ominous news pending. On the 1st October 1938. volunteers started digging trenches in Central Park and 20,000 gas masks were issued in Boston. In the same month Pudding Pie held its club championship. Cyril Dawson had the best gross score of 77 and H Rotheray the best nett of 70.

The Boston ladies played Rauceby ladies. Boston won two matches to nil. The Pudding Pie team was Mrs J Coney, Miss T Francis, Mrs Moore, Miss Wright, Mrs Killingworth, Mrs Giles and Mrs Shove. Mrs Coney would become thereafter one of the longest serving lady secretaries the club possessed. In December the men played Woodhall at Boston. Woodhall won by 12 points to 4. The team was: C Dawson, B Pitts, R Thomson, R Reynolds, D Gresswell, J Walker, J Coney, A Reynolds, R Killick, K Wellberry, J Margerison, F Harden, T Bycroft, B Cooper and H Rothery.

1939 AND THE SECOND WORLD WAR

1939 was a year to remember for events other than golf, but for most members at Pudding Pie and the other courses throughout the county they preferred to carry on and hope the politicians would avert a war. In February The Lincolnshire Golf Union recommended only four courses be used for the amateur championships, Holme Hall, Seacroft, Torksey, and Woodhall.

The Pudding Pie AGM was held in February. S Saville the chairman gave an interview in advance to the Boston Standard to

104.

explain the problems of the club. He said that:

> Pudding Pie was at present in an unhappy position. There was a deficit of £100 and although the 220 members had helped by agreeing to an increased subscription the income was still too low. The annual expenditure of the club at present is £600 and the income is £500, despite large economies. The MP for Holland with Boston, Mr H Butcher, had given valuable support by sending a cheque to become an Hon Member. The professional Mr George Hempstead is always available to give lessons. New members can be assured of a warm welcome. The course is in excellent condition and its smooth greens and wide fairways present a picture calculated to gladden the heart of any golfer. There had been tremendous improvements since it started in 1923. During the past year six new tees had been remodelled and returfed. In March the Annual Subscriptions had been raised by 10 shillings a year. In the past few years thousands of pounds had been spent improving the course and it had never been better.

The Boston golf club like many other clubs was obviously experiencing difficulties. The Sleaford club at Rauceby on the other hand was now coping with the depression much more successfully. They had the advantage of a sandy, well drained, and naturally beautiful course, and golfers on a day out obviously preferred playing there to Boston. At that time many of the Boston members were also members at Rauceby. There they had 200 members, with visitors' green fees of £199, and a total income of £887. In April at Boston the Easter competition was won by Bryan Cooper, with a score of 90 16 74. R. Thomson was second with 78 6 72. J. Margerison won the Horry Cup with 92 18 74.

The threat of war was starting to provide an upturn in business as invariably happens, with the expenditure on war materials and a rise in demand for food, providing a boost for business and farming. In May, Spalding reported that they were also doing rather well, turning their deficit of £89. into a surplus of £14. Their income was £957. Cyril Dawson 2, and Lionel Robinson 13, tied for the Anderson Cup. Dawson by this time was obviously one of the best golfers produced by Boston and won the replay. He was having a good year going on to win the Thomas Bogey Cup two up.

INSOLVENCY AND WAR.

At the AGM in May 1939 there was a slight improvement in the finances. Robert Reynolds was elected captain, and Jack Arch vice-captain. There was a loss on the year of £72. Mr Senior, the Hon treasurer, said that despite this, all the shareholder's capital had been used up and the club was in deficit by £240. There were no liquid assets and the club was virtually insolvent at this point in time. Only the backing of the club's guarantors was keeping it going. The Captain's Prize in August was won by R. Reynolds 73 7 66, one of the best scores ever produced at Pudding Pie. R. Isaac was runner up at 94 24 70. The winter league was won by C. Dawson and H. Rotheray. Boston ladies beat Rauceby ladies by four matches to three. Meanwhile the international situation with Germany became more and more worrying.

WAR

On 3rd September 1939, following the invasion of Poland by Germany and their refusal to withdraw, Britain declared war. Golf once more became a very secondary consideration in the lives of Boston people.

Life must go on however and the golf clubs in the county, initially unaffected, were gradually and inexorably caught up in the tragedy. Blankney just managed to change from a nine hole course to eighteen holes in April 1940 before the wind down came.

CHAPTER SIX

THE 1939-45 WAR AND AFTER

AS HAD HAPPENED during the Great War, the effects of the hostilities were felt gradually over a period. In October 1939, one of the documents that would bring back vivid memories of the time, was distributed to the townsfolk of Boston and the surrounding area— 45,000 ration books were issued for use. These small rather insignificant booklets with their pages divided into small numbered squares very soon came to dominate the lives of the housewives of Britain as they grappled with the problems of exchanging the coupons for quite limited amounts of meat, tea, sugar, butter and other rationed foods. Very soon the rabbit population of Britain was being chased and harried from burrow to burrow to supplement scarce meat. Ration books remained in use during, and for many years after, the end of the war as Britain was short of the dollars required to pay for the import of any commodities other than essentials. Exotic fruits were very soon displaced from the Atlantic convoys to make way for munitions and essential foodstuffs. A most vivid memory is of a holiday in Southern Ireland in 1948 when my friends and I first encountered delicacies in the form of bananas and pineapples. We were not quite certain which part to eat and which to discard.

In September 1939 the 'blackout' laws came into force, to avoid giving landmarks to German bombers. From then on, anyone allowing lights to be seen after dusk through any windows, including Pudding Pie lounge, would soon be told to put the light out by an air-raid warden or the irate local bobby— if indeed neighbours or passers-by had not already shouted: 'Put that * * * light out.'

Newsprint was one of the first commodities to be rationed, and from thenceforth few details would emerge of the progress and problems of Pudding Pie. Golf professionals were not regarded as being in a vital occupation and George Hempstead was soon 'called up' to join the Royal Air Force. Many other Pudding Pie golfers joined the armed services— some of them never to return.

Competitions ceased at many clubs and Seacroft was typical in cancelling all events except those held for war charities' fund raising. By 1940 German air raids were taking place over much of Britain including Lincolnshire. Some clubs were affected more than others by many different aspects of the war. The War Office took over Rauceby hospital, and the Sleaford course became virtually a rehabilitation centre for wounded and sick R.A.F. personnel. Belton Park was not as seriously affected as it had been in the First World War. It survived because the members were prepared to carry out most of the greenkeeper's duties themselves. Later in the war the U.S. Airforce had a large base at Barkston Heath and were offered free use of the course.

The Dam Busters and Others

Woodhall Spa became the centre of one of the largest concentrations of bomber air bases in the country, with thousands of bomber attacks launched on Germany from its vicinity. The famous 617 Dam Buster Squadron under Guy Gibson had their base in the area, and the members played frequently on the course. The clubhouse and the local hotels contain many mementoes left by grateful R.A.F. personnel, recalling those wartime days. Sandilands was in desperate straits after losing much of its holiday business. Had it not been helped by generous benefactors it might not have survived. The Lincoln club at Torksey suffered as much as any other in the county. Cross bunkers were dug on the fairways to prevent enemy aircraft attempting to land, and the War Agricultural Committee 'persuaded' them to plough up part of the course for much needed arable crops. The Seacroft Golf Club suffered severely from the war and paid membership dropped to under 200 in 1940. The club fortunately survived by drastic economies involving salary cuts and halving the number of greenkeepers.

Pudding Pie Farm.

The Pudding Pie club benefited from being in an area of intensive farming. Many of the players were classified as being in reserved occupations and too valuable to be released from food production. The War Agricultural Committee soon commandeered eighteen acres of the course to be used for cropping thus reducing it to a nine hole course. Bryan Cooper came to the assistance of the club, and he and Sidney Belton, an agricultural contracter, ploughed, planted, sowed, and harvested the crops, including wheat and potatoes. It is probable that without the substantial income raised from their sale and free labour and materials provided by the Cooper Farms, the club in its straightened financial circumstances would, like many others, not have survived the war.

Marker's Score	Hole	Length	Bogey	Stroke Index	Score	Won + Lost – Halved 0	Marker's Score	Hole	Length	Bogey	Stroke Index	Score	Won + Lost – Halved 0
5	1	301	4	6	4		4	10	301	4	7	4	
4	2	414	5	3	5		5	11	414	5	4	5	
3	3	165	3	14	4		3	12	165	3	16	3	
3	4	99	3	15	3		3	13	99	3	18	3	
5	5	430	5	1	6		6	14	430	5	2	5	
2	6	190	3	11	3		3	15	190	3	17	3	
4	7	286	4	9	4		4	16	286	4	10	4	
6	8	270	4	13	5		4	17	270	4	12	3	
4	9	307	4	5	3		4	18	307	4	8	3	
36		2462	35		37		36		2462	35		33	

Player _____ Sheehan

Handicap _____ 7

Event _____

Date _____

6 inches

BOGEY PLAY. *The score of every hole.*
Holes Won _____ Holes won or halved
Holes Lost _____ must be recorded
Result _____

2462
2462
4924

Bogey 70

MEDAL PLAY.
Gross Score _____ 68
Handicap _____ 7
Net Score _____ 61

Marker's Signature _____

30. *The score card of the Pudding Pie course now reduced to nine holes.*

All the other sporting activities around Boston were affected just as much as golf. The Boston Bowling Club closed for 'the duration'. Situated in the centre of some of the best farming land in England potatoes and vegetables were not in short supply: meat however was scarce and tightly rationed. Many of the local sportsmen reverted to old fenland pastimes—rabbit snaring and duck shooting. The marshes bordering the Wash were the habitat, then as now, of thousands of geese overwintering from Siberia and other cold climes. Using old supplies of cartridges, many sporting fenman supplemented their scarce sausages with a few Brent and Pinkfoot geese. There was rather less talk of

109.

conservation during these desperate years, when our survival hung in the balance. Indeed the word was never used. The inimitable Kenzie Thorpe, the old fen poacher and tutor of Sir Peter Scott and James Robertson Justice, reckoned he had shot 250 swans in addition to countless hundreds of ducks and pheasants during these war years.

At the 1941 Boston Golf Club AGM the auditor reported that income had dropped from £688 to £506. The president elected was R Isaac, the captain S Saville, the Hon Sec Mark Bottomley, the Hon treasurer L Robinson, and the committee: Dr J Pankhurst, Dr Darlow, B Cooper, R Peck, J Walker and O R Reynolds. There was a plea for members to pay their annual subscriptions as soon as possible to assist the club's low finances.

There is little information on the ladies' section during the war, but Mrs Jane Coney became the Hon Sec and remained in this office for many years. It is likely the lady captains would have been chosen from Mrs Buchner, Miss T Francis, Mrs Cheer, and Mrs Isaac. After George Hempstead left for the war, a greenkeeper, Mr Fidderman, took over. Nothing is known about him, nor when he left. There are no minutes avaiable and no newspaper reports for the period of the war. Around this time Charlie Smith's wife suffered from ill health and he left the club. Charlie took a job with the Boston Corporation working on the roads, a common occurrence for farm workers no longer able to do the hard physical work on the farm. Mr Walter Ruskin took over from him and stayed in the Pudding Pie farmhouse.

On the 8th May 1945 Germany surrended unconditionally. Not until August however, did all hostilities cease, when Japan surrendered following the dropping of atomic bombs on Hiroshima and Nagasaki. Pudding Pie was still alive, but only just, and faced the difficult task of surviving during the immediate post war conditions.

GEORGE HEMPSTEAD

Several Pudding Pie golfers were killed in the war. One of the most unfortunate was the club's professional, George Hempstead, who had joined the Royal Air Force in 1940 and had served as a skilled maintenance fitter on Spitfires in Scotland. Towards the end of the war, in 1944, George flew south in an RAF aeroplane to join his wife for some well earned leave. His pilot got into difficulties over Yorkshire and crashed on one of the moors. George was killed and Pudding Pie had lost a good servant.

THE POST WAR ERA

In 1945, like every other golf course, the Pudding Pie committee had to take up the threads from when the club had virtually gone into hibernation in 1939. They were faced with an entirely different world. The troops coming back from the war and the civilian population, including many women who had been doing skilled and responsible work, had an entirely different outlook on life from their pre-war equivalents. The social situation that had been the norm when The Boston Golf Club started up in 1900 had gone with the wind of two horrific wars. The membership had then been restricted to the wealthy business and professional families who had the money and time to take up golf. The changes that had taken place in the fabric of society over the intervening half century had been immense. The demarcations between the different social groups had virtually disappeared. Henceforth most golf clubs in the country would accept anyone who could afford the entrance subscription and could get a member to introduce them. Applicants still had to be accepted by the committees and some exclusive clubs managed to remain so, largely by virtue of the high cost of joining, but they were very much the exception.

This was good news for club treasurers who had the task of resuscitating their clubs. Many were on the verge of bankruptcy following ten years of depression and six years of war. The factories however made the transition from producing tanks and shells, to cars and sewing machines, very much more easily than the economists predicted. For the present they had no competition from Germany or Japan. After the scarcity and rationing, people wanted entertainment and a better quality of life. With the help of the American dollar loans to purchase scarce raw materials, the factories boomed, employment was high, and wages were double what they had been at the onset of the war. Certainly the cost of living had increased by 50%, but most families had more money to spend than they had had in 1939 and this assisted all leisure activities including golf. The returning soldiers soon showed that they wanted a bigger share of the national income by throwing out the 'Caretaker Government' led by Churchill. Whilst they liked him as a wartime leader, they did not trust the Conservatives under his leadership to manage the country. A Labour government under Clement Attlee was elected to lead the country in July 1945.

THE WELFARE STATE

They were not disappointed initially, as there followed a stream of commendable social legislation— The National Insurance Act 1946, The National Health Service Act 1946, and The National Assistance Act 1948: this latter once and for all banished the spectre of pauperism which had haunted every working class family for five centuries. We had entered the era of the 'Wefare State'. All of these measures gradually but steadily affected golf club membership. If we look at the present membership of most golf clubs today, many of those playing do so by virtue of the benefits of those post war Acts. Unfortunately the gnomes of Zurich and elsewhere felt that the British were up to their old tricks of spending before earning. They started selling sterling and landed the Labour Government in a severe balance of payments deficit. General Marshall came to Attlee's aid in June 1947, to provide the country once more with vital dollars.

THE LADIES' GOLFING SITUATION

If democracy was working to the benefit of the men, the same thing could not be said for the lady golfers. Their men folk still rather grudgingly recognised their presence on the course at many clubs. At a large number up and down the country the ladies were not permitted entry to the principal lounge but were restricted to the ladies' lounge. It was not simply a matter of prejudice against the fair sex, since neither the club professional, nor his fellow professionals, were permitted the freedom of the clubhouse at many of the best clubs in the country. Most clubs also, including Boston, did not cater for the ladies being elected on to the major management committees, nor allow their presence on the board of directors of the Golf Club Company Limited. The lady captain and secretary eventually were allowed to 'sit in' as observers at many of the golf club committee meetings, but had

112.

no vote. Whereas many ladies did not object greatly to the men running the affairs of the club—they had their own section to manage—many did feel strongly about the restrictions on the use of the club facilities. The Boston ladies' and gentlemen's sections have throughout the years under review 'got on' with each other extremely well, as has been the case in most clubs, but doubtlessly future generations will be surprised at the 'post Mrs Pankhurst' ladies being quite so tolerant of the male chauvinism of the period.

Considering the number of women who had held down senior and responsible jobs in industry and the Armed Services during the War, it was surprising that more ladies in the mould of the indomitable Issette Pearson did not come along to rectify this state of affairs. Perhaps it was because many of them chose to continue holding down responsible jobs, rather than spend too much time in golf committee meetings. With the assistance of the ever increasing number of electrical kitchen aids however, many of them managed to hold down a job, manage a family, and still find time for golf.

A development which would change the life of everyone was steadily gaining ground. Television broadcasting was coming to more and more homes. In 1947, 15,000 licences were issued and by 1950 this had risen to 3 million. It was bad enough for the poor old golf secretaries having the outstanding state of the next door course brought to their attention by aggrieved members. It was rather more serious when the wonderful greens and club facilities at the USA Masters and Open could be seen and studied by every member of a British golf club. The advertising of the game and the encouragement given to potential members however far outweighed these disadvantages. Golf was clearly seen to be a worldwide sport, with fabulous rewards for the best players.

A New Professional

After George Hempstead's tragic death in 1944, the club appointed, in 1947, a new professional called Walter Hill. He qualified for the Daily Mail tournament in April 1948. Unfortunately as happens to the best players from time to time, he had an off day in the tournament and finished near the bottom of the field. His grandson Christopher, inherited his golfing genes and around 1990, as a sixteen year old, won several competitions at Boston, off a single figure handicap. He left shortly after with the intention of becoming a professional golfer.

The AGM in September 1947 had the largest attendance for ten years. The president re-elected was George Robinson, the captain was Gilbert Buchner, The Hon Sec Dr J Pankhurst and the competition secretary C Dawson. The committee included H Frost, R Thursby, R Peck, F Harden, W Robertson and B Cooper. At an earlier meeting of shareholders L Robinson and R Isaac were re-elected directors of the Golf Company. C Williams and C Dawson were elected new directors. The profit and loss account over the last year had improved and showed a surplus of £89, thanks to the income from the part of the course ploughed up for arable crops. The expenditure was £657 and the subscription income £355. The accounts were audited by Mr F Odling. There was a spirited discussion on the need to increase the subscriptions.

In 1948 further plans were announced to tackle the perpetual problems of providing good quality drinking water for the area. Since the Corporation had acquired the Water Undertaking in 1931 much progress had been made in reducing the widespread incidence of disease and infant mortality caused by infected water supplies. A mains supply was provided at a cost of £44,000 to bring fresh water for the first time to nine parishes including Fishtoft, Carrington, Sibsey, Westville, Revesby, Thornton-le-Dale, Frithville and Langriville. The members of the club from these areas must have been delighted with this announcement, freeing them from their dependence on infected shallow wells, and roof top water collected in undergound cisterns. It is probable that the Pudding Pie clubhouse and farmhouse were connected to this new water supply. The quality of life for everyone was steadily but surely improving.

In July of the same year the Labour government under Clement Attlee saw The National Insurance Act and The National Health Service Act come into operation on 5th July. Many golfers in the present lively Boston Senior Golfers section who have benefited from hip joint replacements, heart bypass operations and a whole host of other medical developments, can especially thank the skills of the NHS surgeons and the 1948 Act. In the same month

114.

Boston men visited Rauceby— and were beaten.

The condition of the river bank continued to worry the committee as the Witham continued to whittle it away at an increasing rate. Another £180 of scarce capital was expended by the club to dump protecting hardcore along its edge. This had followed an expenditure of £250 the year before, constructing a huge inland 'blister' against an especially weak section. The problem of the upkeep and repair of the flood bank was bleeding the club of scarce capital needed for essential course improvements. Other clubs in the county were lengthening their courses, improving their clubhouses and generally making life more pleasant for members and visitors alike. To fall too far behind them in providing good course facilities would mean future financial trouble for the club. At a committee meeting the president George Robinson announced that the club now had a £60 deficit. The captain, Gilbert Buchner, said that the club was investigating a way of getting rid of this perennial problem of the dangerous flood banks.

THE END OF PUDDING PIE

In October 1948, the Captain's Day competition was won by Geoff Bradley with 91 24 67. Other scores were Robert Reynolds 77 6 71, T Byecroft 86 9 77, and G Clark 92 14 78. A new name was appearing on the score lists— Master Peter Reynolds Junior scored 93 24 69. He and his brother David would become prominent club members. The scores required to win these competitions were steadily improving. In November a ladies' team lost at Woodhall Spa.

1949, another fateful year for the club, started with a report of the Christmas competition. Tom Byecroft won with Bryan Cooper runner up.

At the end of February bad weather was forecast for the area. This was worrying, since it coincided with the Spring high tides. Steps meanwhile were being taken by the Pudding Pie committee to avert, once and for all, the spectre of flooding of the course. The committee had been in prolonged negotiations with Boston Corporation, to persuade it to take over the upkeep and repair of the Witham flood bank. Their idea was to offer the Corporation the deeds of the course in exchange for them taking over the repair and maintenance of this bank. The club would then lease the course for an annual rent of £200. A meeting of the Dock Committee was arranged for Tuesday 1st March, when it was hoped the agreement would be signed and sealed.

At eight o'clock that Tuesday morning the flood bank burst, a tidal wave swept over the greens and fairways, and when the committee met later that day the course was six feet under water. The Corporation's legal advisors warned them against proceeding with the takeover. That decision spelt the end of the Pudding Pie Golf Club. Its life had been short, and full of problems and headaches, from its start up in 1923 through to the 1949 flood. Would its loss be a curse or a blessing? The committee on that fateful and stormy day, so near and yet so far from safety, must all have felt like jumping into the swirling muddy waters covering their beloved if troublesome course.

31A. The flooded Pudding Pie golf course. The photograph was taken by Harry Fountain from the bridge of the S. S. Corfell in March 1949.

31B.

31B. and 31C. These two views of the area that was once 'Pudding Pie' golf course were taken in 1996, 47 years after the photograph 31A. on the opposite page. 31B. was taken from the river bank at approximately the equivalent position to 31A. 31C. was taken from the inner, Fishtoft Road, flood bank of roughly the area where the clubhouse once stood.

31C.

CHAPTER SEVEN

THE GREAT FLOOD

ON THAT FATEFUL MORNING, Tuesday the 1st March 1949, the Witham outflow met the piled up sea water, driven by gale force easterly winds gusting in from the Wash This colossal volume of sea water met river water, swollen by run off storm water, pouring down from the Lincolnshire Wolds. When the 8.00 a.m. spring high tide added its effect, the flood defences along the Witham were overwhelmed. A thirty-five yard wide gap was torn in the Pudding Pie flood bank. Hundreds of thousands of gallons of water poured through the gaping hole and, within minutes, the fairways and greens of the golf course were six feet under a sea of muddy water.

A large area of the town of Boston, like the golf course, was soon also under water. The famous Boston Parish Church of St Botolph, with its massive stone built tower, among the tallest in England, was not a stranger to similar catastrophes. For hundreds of years the local churches were the sole early warning system for the periodic floods that would sweep away crops, cattle, and frequently the unfortunate inhabitants of the low lying fens. Not for nothing was the area around Boston and Spalding known as the administrative County of Holland.

The verger of St. Botolph's (Boston 'Stump') immediately took the age old fenland remedy for warning the inhabitants of impending danger— the massive bells, high up in the tower, were soon ringing the flood warning far and wide. The verger, later in the day when the tide had receded, caught a large flapping fish in the nave of the church, marooned by the receding flood water.

On the golf course Mr G Creamer, the greenkeeper and steward, had a narrow escape from being caught out in the middle of the course, when the break occurred. He could see the huge waves tearing through the gap. The club house, which was raised four feet above ground level, soon had muddy sea water three feet up its interior walls. The silt charged water eventually, when it receded several days later, left a layer of mud nearly two feet thick over much of the fairways and greens. Disconsolate club

118.

members came in a steady stream over the next few days, to recover their muddy bags, clubs and equipment. Mrs Isaac recalled that both she and her husband rushed down to Pudding Pie as soon as the water levels permitted, and managed to retrieve some of the sand boxes on the tees before they were totally ruined.

The Stunned Golfers

The Pudding Pie golfers were stunned by the tragedy. Their golf course by the side of the Witham, was now a muddy lake, with the high areas projecting forlornly above the water. Not only did they have no golf course, but they knew that they could be legally obliged to repair and make good the river flood bank. The committee realised immediately that there was absolutely no prospect of the club being able to raise the large sum of money needed to repair the bank, let alone the equally substantial sum which would be needed to reclaim the course. Boston Corporation were sympathetic to the golfers, but were governed by their auditors, and the strict rules dealing with the spending of public monies. In due course when the waters had receded and the directors of Boston Golf Club Company Ltd had time to study the alternatives open to them, they decided to offer the course to the Corporation in exchange for them taking over the liability of the floodbank repairs. The Corporation, to the great relief of the Pudding Pie directors, agreed to their proposal. Had they refused it would have meant instant bankruptcy for the Boston Golf Club Co. Ltd. What in fact Boston Corporation did was to repair the damage themselves at heavy expense, and then sell the fifty acres to a major timber company, who used it to store large quantities of imported wood, piled high on the old course.

There is another mystery at this point in the affairs of the club. We do know from Richard Tinn, the club's solicitor, that the Pudding Pie deeds were handed over to the Corporation, presumably as a result of them taking over responsibility of making good the repairs to the bank. But if, and when, the club had become owners of the freehold is not known. There is no mention in early newspaper accounts of the club's affairs, of the freehold being purchased, and it is difficult to see how earlier committees could ever have found themselves in a sufficiently strong financial position to purchase the title to Pudding Pie

Farm. Probably the only person who could have saved Pudding Pie course for the Boston golfers, was their old landlord Fred Parkes, but he had moved his trawler business to Fleetwood in 1924, subsequent to the *Lockwood* fiasco. By the time the course flooded he was a multi-millionaire involved in purchasing land and farms all over England, in addition to running his widespread fishing interests, with the help of his son Basil. Had he been on the spot, plugging the flood bank and restoring Pudding Pie would have been exactly the sort of exercise which would have appealed to his entrepreneurial spirit.

GHOSTS AND MEMORIES.

Today the old Pudding Pie golf course lies desolate and covered with heaps of timber. A few yards away from the old fairways, the swirling menacing Witham rushes down to the Wash. What ghosts and memories linger over the old fairways and greens. The missed putts, the lost opportunities to win that coveted trophy. The fabulous Walter Hagan hitting his famous wedge shots inches from the hole and then demonstrating that brilliant putters can sink them on any kind of surface. His lounging but elegant figure, leaning against the bar, regaling his spellbound audience with stories of his exploits on championship courses from all over the world. The indomitable Major Cooper who was instrumental in the club acquiring the Pudding Pie course. Charlie Smith watching all his years of work swept away in a few seconds.

The fenmen who had just lost their golf club however, were not likely to be wasting their time dreaming about ghosts and memories. Their practical, down to earth approach to life, would incline them to be planning where and when they could start up a new course as quickly as possible. Would they succeed in replacing their muddy old course? Time would tell.

THE INTERVAL

The entry in *The Golfing Annual* for 1949 giving details of Pudding Pie, was as follows:

BOSTON GOLF CLUB

> Boston Golf Club Co Ltd. St Nicholas. Tel 2872, Membership 180 Hon Sec Dr J Pankhurst, Professional W Hill, Record 66-C Dawson SSS 70 9 Holes, Visitors 3/- a day. Sunday Play.

This was the last entry for Pudding Pie. There was no entry for the club in the 1950 edition. Thus ended the apparent life of Pudding Pie, a club born in an atmosphere of storm and strife, and seeming to end its life in equally squally weather. The club's life however did not end on the 1st March 1949. Boston Golf Club Co Ltd continued to live as a legal entity. It could well have done however, with a golf course to back up its paper qualifications. The old course had provided the Boston golfers with twenty-six years of golf. How long would it be before a replacement could be found? Meanwhile the surrounding clubs once more came to the rescue of the Boston club. Woodhall Spa, Rauceby, and Surfleet, immediately offered the Boston players facilities at their courses at reduced rates. The problem of golf in 1949 therefore was solved for those members who could get to these nearby courses. But what about the future?

The committee held a series of meetings to discuss what could be done. There were two problems. The club had very little capital— only slightly above £200. Secondly they faced the old problem that had limited Fred Curtis and Major Oliver Cooper— the high price and the scarcity of land to purchase, or to rent, in the Boston area. There was never any suggestion that the club should be wound up. The committee along with other interested club members continued to meet and hold informal discussions on how to set up another golf club.

THE PROBLEMS

They faced an even greater problem than did Frank Curtis back in 1900. The possibility of setting up a limited 'six months' course' was not feasible in 1949, given the developments that had taken place in the game since then, and the rise in member's expectations. It would have to be a good nine hole, full year course, with prospects of enlarging it to eighteen holes not long after starting up. Anything else would not have been commercially viable. That meant at least fifty acres, with additional land adjacent and likely to be available.

Had Boston been nearer the wolds, fifteen miles up the road, there would have been much less of a problem. On the grade one, double cropping silts around Boston, comprising some of the most fertile and sought after land in the country, it was a very different kettle of fish.   There was however no shortage of keen well connected members, willing to assist the club to find and set up a new club. A further problem was that Britain was in a period of financial turmoil, with one balance of payments' crisis following another.   Money was scarce and expensive to borrow. It was difficult enough for a thriving business to get cash from a reluctant bank manager, let alone an almost bankrupt golf club.

Time slipped by and the committee members became more and more frustrated.   The Boston Corporation at that period owned many small farms which they let out. They were sympathetic to the Pudding Pie committee members. Perhaps they could help the club in its present difficulty. Several meetings were held between committee and council members to investigate the possibility of obtaining a Council farm to turn into a golf course.   Despite several promising starts, all of the possible sites on investigation had one or more major drawbacks.

Boston was not the only club to suffer from flooding. In 1953 there was a major flood disaster all along the East Coast, resulting in millions of pounds of damage. Sandilands golf club including the club house was completely flooded. Much of the course was under water for several weeks.   Prompt action by the club in building a new sea wall saved the situation, but in the process fourteen of the greens were destroyed and the course had to be virtually rebuilt.

Seacroft golf club suffered, but to a lesser extent. This disaster highlighted the true distinction between real 'links' courses like Seacroft, Sandilands, and the inland courses like Boston which gave themselves the title of 'links'.

The indigenous grasses of the seaside course are bred to stand up to the salt water and soon recovered from the flooding, unlike the greens at Pudding Pie and later Cowbridge which were wiped out by the salt water.

Meanwhile other clubs in the county were making steady progress. Woodhall was now in the top echelon of clubs in the country and regularly played host to major prestigious events. Seacroft was also becoming recognised as an outstanding club. In 1960 the English County Championship was held there and in the same year Eric Brown and Bobby Locke played Max Faulkner and Ken Bousefield in a charity exhibition match. Between them they had won five Opens.

122.

Whilst Boston golfers were recovering from the tragic flooding, the professional golf scene was getting back to normality after the end of hostilities. The 1950s saw the arrival of a host of great overseas golfers competing for our Open. The winners in the fifties were Bobby Locke, Max Faulkner, Bobby Locke, Ben Hogan, Peter Thomson, Peter Thomson, Peter Thomson Bobby Locke, Peter Thomson and Garry Player. Bobby Locke, the South African golfer, was one of the best ever putters, despite a style that offended all the purists of the day.

Peter Thomson, the Australian super-golfer, was one of the best iron players of the period and this, combined with an extremely astute golfing brain, brought him a host of victories. Surprisingly he never had quite the same success on the American circuit, probably because he felt happier playing in Britain.

Ben Hogan, who only competed once in our Open, was arguably the best ever striker of a golf ball to date. Possessed of a super-human concentration and dedication, he was described by Bernard Darwin, golf correspondant for The Times and one of the best judges of golfing ability, as always giving him the impression that he could score whatever was required to obtain victory. His meticulous preparation and resulting scores of 73 71 70 68 for his victory at Carnoustie confirmed to his British fans his world superiority in the field of professional golf.

POWER GOLF

32. Ben Hogan, thought by many to be the greatest striker of a golf ball to date.

Henry Cotton was coming to the end of his illustrious career by the '50s, having won our Open in 1934, 1937 and 1948. Another of the great American golfers, 'slamming' Sam Snead, had won his only Open at St Andrews in 1946, but in the '50s concentrated on the American circuit, winning the US PGA in 1951 and the US Masters in 1952 and 1954.

THE SEARCH

GOLF BY HENRY COTTON

33. Henry Cotton: possessed of tremendous concentration and dedication. He won the British Open in 1934, 1937, and 1948.

Life must however go on after calamities and the Pudding Pie committee, realising that the wooden club house was beginning to deteriorate, sold it to the Boston Aero Club for a modest sum, and they dismantled and removed it to a site on the edge of Boston. There it stands today and, smartly painted, it continues providing warmth and shelter for its new owners.

When Pudding Pie flooded in 1949, one of the most disappointed players was a sixteen year old schoolboy who lived with his parents in a house on Spilsby Road. He had recently been introduced to the game by his father, and he would frequently bicycle down to the course to play and practise. He was heartbroken when the course flooded. The effect this had on his son certainly reinforced the determination of the father to find a new course. Bryan Cooper and his son Philip, were therefore constantly on the look out for a suitable site for a replacement to the Pudding Pie course. Bryan was a local farmer who owned Caytoft Farms Ltd, a large arable farm near Boston. He was the son of Sam Cooper, an agricultural merchant and one of the prominent early Boston golfers. Sam was the brother of the redoubtable Major Oliver Cooper. So Bryan and his son were well bred to take a major role in the future of Boston golf.

On their trips to play golf at Woodhall, and on other journeys through the surrounding countryside, Bryan with his expert farming eye, prodded on by his son, were therefore two of the most active searchers for a potential new Boston golf course. The Boston Corporation also continued trying to be of assistance. Several of their farms were the subject of discussion between them and the golf committee. Perhaps it was an arrangement that had been reached, when the Pudding Pie committee handed over the deeds of Pudding Pie to the Corporation.

Eventually one of their farms on Punchbowl Lane on the edge of the town became vacant and looked promising. However another development had just occurred. The Coopers on their Woodhall outings regularly passed a stretch of land at Cowbridge, on the north of the town, that interested them greatly. It was a small grazing farm situated two miles north of Boston. It lay on the southern edge of the old East and West fens, a massive block of 40,000 acres and the last of the fens to be reclaimed by the fen drainage engineers. Sir Joseph Banks, the famous Lincolnshire land improver, provided the drive to reclaim this area and the engineering skills came from John Rennie. The task was completed in 1813.

Aqueduct Farm

The farm that interested them was appropriately called Aqueduct Farm and it was bounded by two major drainage channels, the Cowbridge and Stonebridge Drains. In one of the best examples of fen drainage engineering, the Stonebridge Drain flows over the Cowbridge Drain—the aqueduct which carries the catchwater from the Lincolnshire Wolds down to the Haven (the Witham outfall) and out to sea. This was one of the means devised to avoid the hitherto regular flooding of the adjacent low lying fens. This farm was owned by a Mr George Barton who originated from Sheffield and who had settled in Boston. He had built up a successful business propagating roses. and rented land around the town to plant the rootstock on which to bud his plants. Roses respond well to farmyard manure and to provide this commodity he had purchased a small farm to graze the cattle that would provide this. The stock were grazed in the summer on permanent pasture, and then wintered in traditional covered fold yards. There was a small cottage type farm house. The farm was therefore a subsidiary enterprise to the rose business. It was situated just off Horncastle Road, but had a difficult access, with

34. The aqueduct where the Stonebridge Drain flows over the Cowbridge Drain. This is adjacent to the farm which takes its name from this famous example of fen drainage engineering.

a long journey of several hundred yards over a farm track, from Willows Lane. Mr Barton had recently died in 1961 and the farm was coming on the market.

Bryan and Philip Cooper saw the potential of Aqueduct farm for a small golf course. It only extended to 52 acres but it had however several advantages to their knowledgeable eyes. It was under permanent pasture and had been rather neglected in recent years because of Mr Barton's poor health. It had a run down set of buildings, and it had very poor access. All of these qualities they hoped would help to keep the efficient arable farmers from around the area, bidding up the price. It had moreover some adjacent land in the form of two large islands, formed by the junction of the two canals, that could well become available in the future to extend the course.

THE BID FOR AQUEDUCT FARM

There followed a series of meetings and telephone discussions between the Coopers, various members of the old Pudding Pie

126.

committee and one or two other keen golfers who had come into the area since 1949.

Augustus Isaac, or Gus as he was popularly known, Martin Middlebrook, Ron Peck, Dick Giles, Gerry Hopper, Lionel Robinson, William Sinclair, John Leake, Gilbert Buchner, Bill Jackson, Bill Chapman, Mr Oldham, F Merry Cave, Hubert Frost, Ray Ringrose, E Chapman, Leslie Clarke, Brian Morris and of course Bryan and Philip Cooper, together with other interested members added their voices and suggestions to the debate. There was ample room for discussion because it was a major undertaking they were contemplating, with ample room for a serious financial mistake.

The cost of setting up a golf club in 1961 was very much more involved than the old system used in 1900 of renting a couple of fields, borrowing an old hand pushed mowing machine, and then holding the opening match the following day. Golfers' expectations were very much higher, and so also were start up costs. But the main problem to be in a position to bid for Aqueduct Farm was obtaining the capital required of around £10,000. There were several bank managers friendly to the club and involved in the discussions, but even they were finding that the current credit squeeze made that sort of money for that sort of venture, simply unavailable.

Once more it seemed that all was lost, and Boston would have to wait even longer before it could boast of having its own golf club. Had it been a Lincoln Club there would have been no problem. In the past, wealthy benefactors of that town had helped their club out in similar circumstances. However on this occasion Boston was especially fortunate, and once more it was the Cooper family who saved the day.

Encouraged by his son and using his own capital Bryan Cooper made up his mind to acquire Aqueduct Farm for the Boston Golf Club. The sale was held on a Wednesday afternoon in the Assembly Rooms, Boston, by Messrs Simons and Ingamells, Auctioneers. Ray Ringrose, the club's solicitor, was given the delicate task of doing the actual bidding on behalf of the Coopers. They were all naturally apprehensive. Their limit of £10,000 was a great deal of money in those days. Had they all known that Franz Buitelaar an ambitious young Dutchman, who was subsequently to build up one of the largest wholesale meat businesses in the county, was also after Aqueduct Farm, they would have been even more nervous. When the bidding approached £9,000 they were much relieved to see it slow down. Their final bid of around £9,000 was successful. Boston Golf Club was back in business. There was no more delighted young golfer around at that instant than Philip Cooper. His father, like most fathers when put on the spot by their enthusiastic offspring, had other things on his mind. £9,000 in those days was a veritable fortune and equivalent to around £200,000 at 1990s' prices

At a meeting attended by a group of the interested golfers, held at Lloyds Bank, Boston on the 8th November 1961, Bryan Cooper offered it to Boston Golf Club Company Ltd, still alive and kicking, and his offer was gratefully accepted. Another historic day had dawned for the club. The thread of continuity unbroken since 1900 was about to continue for Boston golfers. Brian Morris accepted the post of Hon Sec. The following day, the 9th November 1961, another meeting was held of an ex officio Committee of Management. Mr Gus Isaac reported on the financial position of the existing Golf Company. There was a balance of around £100, which would be available to help out on the new course. Not much, but it could so easily have been a hefty deficit. Ron Peck gave a report on the likely costs of starting up Aqueduct Farm, the number of members that ought to be aimed for, and the annual subscription that might be required.

It was agreed to hold a public meeting on the 22nd November, to seek support, and help raise the funds to get the club started. The public meeting, held at the Peacock and Royal Hotel, Boston, attracted a large attendance. It was chaired by the Mayor, Councillor T Balderston, who outlined the situation.

128.

Chapter Eight

The New Course At Cowbridge

COUNCILLOR T BALDERSTON ADDRESSED the large gathering: 'Aqueduct Farm at Cowbridge, two miles north of Boston and extending to forty-seven acres, has been purchased with a view to laying out a twelve hole golf course initially, with the prospect of a further six holes to be added in the future. A committee has been formed to carry out these plans and it is as follows: Chairman A W Isaac, the Hon Sec B Morris, Hon Treasurer E Chapman, the committee: G Buchner, B Cooper, P Cooper, F Merry Cave, H Frost, R Giles, G Hopper, W Jackson, R Killick, J Leake, M Middlebrook, F Oldham, R Peck, R Ringrose, L Robinson, P Reynolds, W Sinclair and G Smith. The objective of the meeting was to assess the likely membership and to seek financial assistance to get the club off the ground.'

He told the meeting that:

'. . . the money required would be £9,000 for the purchase of the course, £4,000-£6,000 for the course layout and clubhouse, and the running costs would require a further £2,000-£3,000. The entrance fee would most likely be £5 and the annual subscription £8 for men and £6 for women. He appealed for financial help from those who were in a position to give it. Gifts of £200 or over would attract life membership. Debentures in units of £10 would attract 5% interest and stock could be purchased in the Boston Golf Club Co Ltd in units of 1. The Hon Treasurer E T Chapman took the names of those wishing to join and provide funds. There was a good response to the chairman's appeal for members, and it was decided to proceed as quickly as possible with the plan to get the club up and running. Forty seven acres had been purchased and a twelve hole course would be laid out and opened early in 1962.'

There was a tremendous amount of work and planning required to turn Aqueduct Farm into a good golf course. The chairman and committee started off by setting up four sub committees to plan the work and ensure it got done. These were: A course layout committee, a finance committee, a domestic

129.

35. *Martin Middlebrook, a founder member of the Boston course at Cowbridge. He was the first paid-up playing member with a £3. joining fee and £8. for the first annual subscription. He has gone on to become a well known author of war histories.*

commitee, and an entertainment committee. The elected committee members were allocated amongst these sub committees, and because of the work load most were on two or more. The most important as far as getting the course planned and laid out, was the layout committee, and, fortunately for the club, Bryan and Philip Cooper were especially interested in this work and agreed to serve on it. They had a particular interest because they must have felt to some degree that the course belonged to them, as indeed at the start up it did.

THE WORK ON THE NEW COURSE

Leaving their farm work to get on as best it could, they set men and machines to knock the course into shape. How much these few months really cost Caythorpe Farms is a subject that the Coopers would probably rather forget. In terms of actual labour costs and foregone profits from farm work not done, they were substantial. The top priority was of course the greens and tees. The finance committee had the worry of raising cash to pay for the heavy start up costs. Because of the late starting date the first subs had to be reduced to £6 for men and £4 for women.

These sums should be considered in relation to the average miminum farm worker's wage. This was what set the standards for an agricultural area like Boston, and in 1962 it was £8.12s.0d. a week for forty-six basic hours. Following the open meeting, there was a period of frenetic activity, as the committee and members got down to the task of getting the course and buildings into shape. Boston may not have had the wealthy benefactors possessed by Lincoln but where the fenmen were unbeatable was in a situation where jackets had to be taken off, and a great deal of work, skilled and unskilled, carried out. They had a priceless advantange over the Pudding Pie course in that they were dealing with lighter and better drained soil.

All low lying fens however require a comprehensive tile and ditch system to move the water away. Drainage is an ongoing job that never ceases at Cowbridge. Fortunately the sticky mess that confronted the Pudding Pie committee was absent on the mainly permanent pasture of Cowbridge. There was another priceless advantage over the 1900 and 1922 situations. The social changes that had taken place during the course of the century had given Cowbridge a broad spectrum of members that could tackle any job, from electrical wiring, to bricklaying, plastering, joinery or anything else that required doing. Frank Curtis's members would simply not have known where to start had they been faced with the task at Cowbridge. This was just as well for the Cowbridge committee since money was scarce at the time.

Aqueduct Farm at the takeover was all grassland. This was also a great advantage. Many years later it would take Peter Pearson two years to reseed, and get established, land added to the course that had previously been in an arable rotation. This was not a problem facing the Cowbridge committee. The fertile silt at Cowbridge supported grassland that could provide first class fairways, as well as fatten a bullock to the acre.

Good management soon began to improve the areas cut out for fairways. Initially it was planned to employ a Surrey golf architect to plan the new course but shortage of money persuaded the committee to cut out this cost. Bryan and Philip Cooper spent a great deal of time on course planning and, following that, on the supervision of the work. Many evenings at their house at Spilsby Road, the kitchen table was strewn with maps and plans of the course layout. Everyone on the committees, and indeed everyone with an interest in the club, could and did put in 'their ha'penny worth' in those early days, but the course planning and field work was carried out by Bryan and Philip Cooper, their farm workers and the ground staff.

THE GROUND STAFF

Two ground staff were immediately taken on. Mr Morley, known as 'Wag', and George Cuppleditch. Both were experienced farm workers who, under the direction of the Coopers and the layout committee, started to get the greens into shape. Wag Morley had worked for Mr Barton at Aqueduct Farm and his knowledge of the farm proved invaluable. Wag Morley is still alive and well today in 1997—and will be 81 in September. He retains a vivid memory of the early days at Cowbridge and indeed much of his life was interwoven with the Boston Golf Club. He was born in 1916 in Kendrick's farm cottage at Frithbank within sight of the Cowbridge islands. When his mother died in 1918 in the horrific 'flu epidemic which killed thousands of people that year, he went to live with his grandmother at Cowbridge Hall. A golfer standing on the tenth tee today has a large field behind him as he tees off. Fifty yards down towards the railway in the corner of that field, stood Cowbridge Hall, a large imposing residence which has long since been demolished. In 1928 his father bought the cottage and three acres on the large island fifty yards past the tenth green and Wag was still living there when he started as greenkeeper in 1961 on the newly opened Cowbridge course. He had invaluable experience for his new post, having been stockman and in charge of Aqueduct Farm since 1949.

When he went to work there the farm was owned by George Horace Barton, the Sheffield businessman who continued to live in Sheffield whilst running his rose nursery business in Boston. He owned two blocks of land, ten acres on Sibsey Road, just north of the present Pilgrim Hospital, and a further twelve acres in two fields down Tollfield Road. On this area he had a dozen workers planting out root stock which would be grafted with buds to grow into rose bushes which he sold all over the country.

For this large enterprise he required large quantities of farmyard manure and to produce this he had purchased Aqueduct Farm. There he had around forty cows of mixed breeds running with a Lincoln Red bull to produce beef stores. Wag would drive these to Boston market which was held every week opposite the present Red Cow tavern. The cows and calves were wintered in the covered yard which was later converted into the golf club lounge. By spring there would be five feet of solid farmyard manure which laboriously had to be dug out and carted away for the roses. Aqueduct Farm was divided into five fields, three of which were grass, and two arable growing corn and

132.

mangolds. In 1956 the arable fields had been grassed down. Hence Boston golf club, in 1961, took over a farm which was largely permanent pasture—a fact of inestimable value to the golfers.

When 'Wag' started as greenkeeper Bryan Cooper provided him with a small French made two stroke tractor (four wheeled) together with implements for work on the course. At the same time he provided him with a 14" Atco petrol mower to cut the greens. Later Mr Cooper purchased two 18" Ransome mowers which were a vast improvement. The greens were cut every other day in the summer and his first task each day was to whisk the dew off all the greens with a large bamboo cane and rake all the bunkers. Reg Killick, a butcher in Boston, was the first member in charge of greens and he was most helpful to Wag in his new post. He had George Cuppleditch as his assistant. The field drainage was in a poor state and one of his early tasks was to lay drains to some of the wetter areas. He left however in May 1968, after asking the committee for a wage increase—he recalls he was earning around £7 a week—and was informed the club could not afford to pay him any more. A hard worker with wide experience of field work he provided invaluable help to the Boston club in the few years he was head greenkeeper.

The club was also greatly indebted to Bert Locke, a bowling green expert from Skegness, who spent much time with his specialised equipment improving the greens. His scarifiers, rakes and specialised mowers, capable of pleasing the choosy bowlers of Skegness, soon started to improve the indigenous grasses where they were sufficiently good enough to be improved. He had a lifetimes' experience in bowling green management, and after inspecting the situation, came to the conclusion that most of the greens could be improved as they lay, given suitable management of the old permanent pasture.

This cost reducing idea went down very well with the committee. It turned out to be rather too optimistic for some of the greens, as time went on, but nevertheless his help was invaluable. John Grant who farmed at Sibsey provided men and equipment and concentrated on digging out and sanding the bunkers over the course. Geoffrey Bradley from Fishtoft provided lorries, men and trailers to cart sand and carry out the hundred

133.

and one haulage tasks required in the laying out of the course. Dick Needham, another arable farmer from Sibsey, provided tractors, trailers and men to help push on with the conversion of a small grassland farm into an adequate golf course.

Messrs Levertons from Grantham, and Boston Tractors, assisted by loaning tractors and heavy earth-moving equipment for the considerable amount of work required to construct bunkers, make up roadways and tracks, and remove derelict buildings. Gerry Hopper, soon to be elected to become the first captain at Cowbridge, was instrumental in persuading local firms to help out with equipment. A start was made to purchase equipment for the club's own use. A set of gangmowers, and a tractor, were among the first of many such implements.

GETTING THE COURSE IN SHAPE

It must be remembered that whilst all the work was going on in the first year, to lay down the new twelve hole golf course, the land and the course still belonged to Bryan Cooper's farming company. There had been no legal transfer of the land nor the lease to the club. He, his son, and his men, spent a great deal of time and money on the course during this period. The Cooper family of course got an immense amount of fun out of the whole project as did all the members of the committee and many of the club members who put in a great deal of work on the course and buildings. Philip recalls how he and his father would spend hours walking around the course, investigating and arguing about the merits of alternative layouts. This would be followed by a session on their kitchen table with maps, pins, string and plasticene laying out the endless possibilities of greens and fairways on the new course.

The original plan of improving the greens from the existing pasture had to be amended as the committee saw how they were developing. On some holes, such as the present first, the existing sward did improve sufficiently to be left, but the present eighteenth in front of the clubhouse was reseeded. This area near the old farm buildings required a great deal of work, following its use as a dump for the old foundations. After these were buried it was levelled and reseeded. The green finished up with a large slope which is still there, and has left it one of the most testing on

134.

the course, and the graveyard for many aspiring cup winners. Many, many winning speeches have been mentally cast into the adjacent pond, after three or more putts on this hole. For the ongoing pain and occasional pleasure this green has given members, they can thank the famous T H Bowman or 'King' Bowman as he was then known. A member and official of the Seacroft golf club, winner of the Lincolnshire Amateur Championship on six occasions, an English international player in 1932, and one of the best ever Lincolnshire golfers, he was looking over this green with his son Murray, also a fine golfer, and Philip Cooper. Philip was contemplating whether to take some of the slope and difficulties out. The 'King' who could putt up the side of a house persuaded him to leave it be. T H Bowman was an influential member of the Seacroft club for many years and in 1947 was appointed course manager. Murray was equally prominent in the affairs of that club being a committee member, chairman of the greens' committee, and later company chairman at Seacroft: they were frequent visitors to the new Boston course.

Most of the other greens were returfed within the first two years. Turf was cut from the excellent permanent pasture on the far edge of the field running alongside the Stonebridge Drain, which is now the sixth hole. Whilst these were being improved the members used temporary greens, cut out alongside those being improved. The Greens' committee received a great deal of expert advice from the technical advisors of three companies Messrs Fisons, Sinclairs, and Johnsons, well known national fertiliser and seed firms. The committee decided that whilst they were laying down the greens it would be sensible to lay on water at the same time. This together with the pump required to draw water from the adjacent drains cost £400, a heavy expense at the time.

THE COTTAGE

The committee knew from the start up, that the farm house, or cottage as it was called, and the farm buildings would present problems. It was a small typical fenland farm cottage, two rooms up, two down. The thrifty fenmen always believed in spending on the land first, and so the interiors of the farmhouses on the smaller farms were invariably spartan. Aqueduct Farm needed

135.

new sewerage and plumbing throughout and required a complete electrical rewiring. The other buildings consisted of an open fronted crewyard for the cattle, and a cartshed where the implements and waggons were stored. After inspecting this set up, the committee decided that the best thing they could do, was to bulldoze the lot into a large hole and start building elsewhere. There were two problems however to this idea. The club had no money, and there was no really suitable land nearby to build on without impinging on the course. The money problem was worrying. When Bryan Cooper purchased the farm, it was intended to be a short term loan to the club, but the current balance of payments crisis facing the Macmillan administration, and forcing them into a tight money policy, would not go away. There was no money to be had, despite the efforts of the banking members of the committee.

36. *Looking over the sixth green. The original farm house at Aqueduct Farm is the building with the high pitched roof directly beyond the golfer. The professional's shop has been built on to the right of the farm house.*

136.

To make matters worse, the valiant efforts of the committee to persuade the members to provide gifts or loans, was not getting the response that they had hoped for. Unlike Lincoln for example, Boston was not a wealthy area, and any money owned by the members was largely tied up in their businesses. In November 1962 it was reported that the members response to the request for loans to the building fund had been disappointing. Fortunately for the club the membership was growing steadily towards the target of 300. By June 1962, 127 men and 64 ladies had joined the club. Green fees were fixed at 3/6d for weekdays and 5/- at the weekends.

Whilst they were deciding what to do with the buildings, the club used the cottage as a clubroom. The men used the two downstairs rooms for a lounge and changing rooms. The ladies had the use of the two upstairs rooms. The lady members put in a great deal of work turning the cottage into as pleasant a clubhouse as the situation allowed. They decorated the rooms, put up curtains and provided much of the furniture. They also worked out a rota and provided light refreshments for the hard working members and players. Everyone got 'stuck in' and thoroughly enjoyed themselves, in the process of turning Aqueduct Farm into a reasonable golf course.

THE TWO ISLANDS

The committee had considered the possibiltity of building on one of the two 'islands' adjacent to the course. These were bounded by the West Fen Drain and the Cowbridge Drain. The eighteen acre island was owned by the Church Commisioners and the nine acre island by the Witham Fourth Drainage Board. This was one of several Statutory Boards set up to administer the drainage of large blocks of farming land around Boston, which would have very quickly reverted to marsh and ponds in the absence of good drainage management. A local butcher, Bert Platt, who had built up a large and successful business, had the grazing tenancies on both islands, and used them for his sheep and cattle. An approach was made in 1961 to Mr Platt, and the Witham Fourth Board, to allow the club to take 1.3 acres on the nine acre island to build a new clubhouse.

Permission for this was obtained from the head landlords, the tenant, and the planning authorities, but when the committee got down to working out the costs, it was soon realised that, given the financial situation of the club, the development was not a reasonable financial proposition. It was therefore decided to make the best use possible of the existing buildings with a programme of repair and adaptation. At the same time the committee applied to the Witham Fourth, for permission to replace the pedestrian bridge over the Stonebridge Drain, with a more substantial steel and wooden structure that could carry cars. This would then be part of a larger programme to construct an access road onto the B1183 Horncastle Road and cut out the present long muddy approach road from Willows Lane.

The programme to improve the cotttage and buildings was started immediately. Ron Peck, a committee member who owned a large building firm in Boston, was asked to draw up plans. He had started to modernise the cottage, and his bill for £470 was on a 'cost only' basis. The club was fortunate that much of the work done on the new course, was on a free, or cost only basis. Over the next few years, the members would put in hundreds of hours work in their spare time, on a wide variety of jobs, including renovating the old cottage and farm buildings.

THE OLD COMPANY LIQUIDATED

Meanwhile the committee, advised by their solicitors, Ringrose and Co., decided to liquidate the old Pudding Pie Company Limited and form a new company. It had served its purpose and its small but useful assets would assist the new company to get up and started. There was no break in the continuity of the old company and its successor. The Boston Golf Club Company Limited therefore disappeared to be replaced with the new company, The Boston Golf Club Ltd. There was little difference in the name, but legally the new company was a totally different entity. Mr McClement from Messrs Ringrose announced in September 1962, that the incorporation of the new company was now complete and the old company liquidated. The assets and liabilities were now transferred over to the Cowbridge club.

The Boston golf club, from its birth in October 1900 to the re-start at Cowbridge in 1962, had successfully overcome the trauma of the 1949 flood. The old Limited Company had maintained an unbroken life until the new company had taken over. Like Belton Park it had survived a gap that could easily have killed it off. It was very fortunate to have done so, on this and the other life threatening situations it had encountered. It had been a close run thing. It would have required only a blink at the wrong time, for Ray Ringrose to have missed the bid at the auction for Aqueduct Farm, and it would then have gone to Franz Buitelaar. In any event it was something of a miracle for Bryan Cooper to have spotted Aqueduct Farm, and to have had the cash and motivation to make the successful purchase. There were not many occasions when the young Dutchman would come second in that sort of a situation. Had he put in the last bid, would Boston golfers ever have had a golf club of any description? He consoled himself by purchasing another local farm, Fishtoft Grange, at a later date.

SETTLING DOWN

In May 1962 G S Hopper, Gerry to his friends, was elected the first captain of the Cowbridge club. A good all round sportsman he ran a successful family jewelry business in Boston and adjacent towns. Terry Squires, son of Ron Squires, professional from the Sleaford club, accepted the post as the club professional. A slim young man with a smooth elegant swing he was a contempory and friend of Tony Jacklin. He became the club's longest serving professional in due course. The Boston Ladies' golf club had also got into its stride under their first Cowbridge captain, Mrs Jane Coney, and her committee. This was: Mrs E Cheshire, Mrs Flo Reynolds, Mrs M Pilcher, Miss 'Trot' Weightman and Mrs K Walt. It was 'full steam ahead' for the new club. The conditions in Boston and the country in 1962, were of course vastly different from those experienced by Frank Curtis and his committee at the start of golf in Boston in 1900. Were they easier or more difficult?

THE CHANGES

The past sixty years had seen the two greatest wars in human history, where millions of people had lost their lives and whole continents had been in turmoil. Britain in 1900 still had one of the largest empires ever acquired by one country, but by 1962 most of this had disappeared, with Australia and Canada being given Dominion status in 1907, and the great sub-continent of India given its independence in 1947. There had been great social upheavals brought on by all those traumas, and these had seen the end of much of the class differences that had bedevilled British society, including the expanding sport of golf. There had moreover been great improvments in the standard and quality of life for most of the population of Britain, including better housing, medical services, and the opportunity for most people to have the time, and income, to indulge in the new forms of leisure such as golf.

The expectation of life had risen to around seventy for men and seventy-five for women. The Cowbridge treasurer could look forward to having a large group of older but healthier veterans to help pay the ever rising costs of the club. The horse had been replaced by the internal combustion engine, and the car allowed everyone far more choice of where they could spend their time, including where they might choose to play golf. In 1905 there were 15,000 cars on the roads. By 1962 this had risen to 8 million. More golfers could travel by car to their golf club. But they could just as easily carry on to the next club if they thought it was superior to their own. Life for women had seen even greater changes. Gone were the double figure families, and the electric washing machine and other labour saving gadgets had released them from kitchen bondage. Certainly, many more supplemented the family income with a job, but all these changes meant more women could, if they wished, play golf.

THE PROFESSIONAL SCENE

Some of the changes were however two edged. By 1960 many families had a television set. Golf competitions played on the best courses were regularly televised, and club members were not slow to want the best for themselves. Club comittees were caught in a cleft and frequently painful stick, with members wanting better and better facilities, but resisting the inevitable rise in annual subscriptions these would involve. The changes in the professional golfing scene in the '60s generally had a beneficial effect on the amateur scene. The advent of the super stars, highly skilled, highly paid golfers who made fortunes from their lucrative

140.

sponsorship of golf equipment, gave the game a tremendous amount of publicity.

ARNOLD PALMER BY MARK McCORMACK

37. *Arnold Palmer: The first of the golfing multi-millionaires.*

More youngsters and adults wanted to emulate them, and this increased the demand for golfing facilities. Arnold Palmer won his first British Open in 1961, and thenceforth the modern Triumvirate of Palmer, Nicklaus, and Player, would dominate the golfing scene for the best part of the next twenty years. The increase in interest in the game brought dozens of other great golfers on the scene, all capable of winning the top events. Peter Thomson, Roberto di Vicenzo, Tony Lema, and Bob Charles were some of the great foreign golfers who would win our Open in the sixties. Tony Jacklin with his win in 1969 was the only British winner.

GOLFING MILLIONAIRES AND THE MAJORS

Of all these players, one of them stands head and shoulders above the rest for his impact on the modern game of golf. Arnold Palmer, by 1959, had already won The United States Masters which had started up in 1934 under the guidance of Bobby Jones on the great course at Augusta. It was by then evident that he was a golfer of supreme ability and possessed the charisma of a superstar. He was already sought after by firms wanting to use his name on their products. Heinz Ketchup paid him five hundred dollars a year and two other firms supplied him with free golf balls and free golf shirts. In that same year a brilliant young lawyer, Mark McCormack, already a friend of Palmer, agreed to represent him in managing his business affairs. The effect was dramatic. Within two or three years Palmer was a dollar millionaire from agreements negotiated by McCormack for use of his name. McCormack's skill as a marketing man achieved this, and soon he was representing other top golfers and had completely revolutionised the market value of not only his own stable of stars, which included Jack Nicklaus and Gary Player, but also the other top golfers of the period. Palmer, Nicklaus and Player became the modern Triumvirate as they competed for victory on the golf circuit.

The great wealth of the very best golfers had another effect on the golfing scene. To them winning prize money became secondary to proving their place amongst the great golfers of the present and past. Four of the world tournaments were recognised to be of superior importance. These were the US PGA, the US Open, the British Open and the US Masters. All the great golfers of the world strove to win these championships. The winner had proved himself the best golfer amongst the cream of world talent. Gradually the status of the world class golfers began to the measured not by how much money they had won on the circuit, but by the number of these four tournaments— the Majors— that they had won. All these developments had a tremendous impact on the reborn Cowbridge club.

THE FORMAL COURSE OPENING

The course layout committee consisting of Bryan and Philip Cooper, Gilbert Buchner, Gerry Hopper, Reg Killick, Ron Peck, Gerry Smith, Peter Reynolds, Dick Giles and Lionel Robinson, supported by the ground staff, the other committee members, and innumerable club and outside helpers, saw all their efforts come to fruition on 2 June 1962, when the Boston golf club course at Aqueduct Farm was formally opened. The Mayor, Councillor R Jenkins, conducted the proceedings, and there was an exhibition match between Bryan and Philip Cooper, who drove off, and the captain and vice captain, Gerry Hopper and Peter Reynolds. There followed a well attended and thoroughly enjoyable barbecue.

The course consisted of twelve holes 3,754 yards in length, and the players continued on to another six holes, to make up the eighteen hole course of 5,885 yards, with a par of 73, and a possible SSS, yet to be ratified, of 70. The area extended to forty-nine acres together with 8.8 acres of land making up the verges of the waterways. The membership was then 142 men, 71 ladies,

142.

38. The Mayor, Councillor R. Jenkins, formally opens the Boston Golf Course (12 holes) congratulating Bryan Cooper on his efforts as the original purchaser of the course.

nineteen Juniors, and ten non-playing members. There were seven life members.

THE CLUB LOUNGE

Meanwhile work proceeded with the buildings. Ron Peck prepared plans for the conversion of the buildings. The covered area of the cattle yard would be converted into a lounge and bar. The cart shed would have a new floor, and then new walls built, to convert it into a men's locker, and changing rooms.

RABBITS SECTION

In September 1962 an important development took place—a Rabbits' section was formed. Golfers who play to a handicap of seventeen or less are 'Golfers'. Above that magical figure they sprout a tail and become 'Rabbits'. As we shall see later the definition of who comes into what category is not quite as simple as would first appear.

143.

This section would develop steadily to become arguably the most important and largest group in the club, setting the standards of behaviour for the bulk of the membership. J. Stanford was the first chairman. The secretary and chairman of the Skegness North Shore Rabbits section attended the first meeting and provided most useful advice on how best to proceed in planning future events. Gerry Hopper and Terry Squires also attended. The first committee members were: Messrs Trigg, Haughton, Bland and Meades with J. Stanford as their first captain.

MEMBERSHIP OF THE GOLF UNIONS

By October 1962 the club had made sufficient progress to feel able to apply for affiliation to the Lincolnshire Golf Union. The ladies' club at the same time applied for membership of the Ladies' Golf Union. The president of the Lincolnshire Golf Union, J Blow, wrote to Brian Morris in early 1963 explaining that he would: 'like to visit the smaller clubs in the Union,' and he was invited to attend the AGM held on 15th May 1963. At this meeting he outlined the objectives of the Union.

> There are currently twenty-two affiliated clubs in the county. A programme of inter-club matches is arranged each year, together with a County Championship match. There is a Voucher Scheme in operation, whereby members of affiliated clubs can purchase a £1 voucher that allows them to play at any of the twenty-two clubs on a weekday.

With typical green fees of the period being around 3/6d, a day this was a highly attractive way for members to play, at a reasonable cost, most clubs around the county. Would that an equally attractive, widely available, scheme be put into operation today. It would have great attraction for the club golfers, if less so for the club secretaries. The new honorary treasurer, G Holland, manager of the National Provincial Bank and an enthusiastic club member, noted that £800 had been contributed by 30 members for the building fund, but commented that much more was required.

Following the successful application for affiliation to the County Union, a provisional Standard Scratch Score of 70 was

144.

issued to the club. This was eventually reduced to 68, with a par of 73, for a course length of 5,885 yards. The letters from the Union confirming these figures mentioned the shortage of hazards and bunkers, as being one of the reasons for the reduction. The club was included in the 1964 county fixture list. Frank Curtis and Major Oliver Cooper would have been overjoyed to have their club given the honour of county membership. It meant that the Boston golf club had 'arrived' and could now be included in the list of 'real' golf clubs in the county— a feat which thus far had eluded the earlier Boston clubs. Despite the tight finances, the committee pressed on with the acquisition of essential machinery for course maintenance. In March 1964, two sets of gang mowers and a second-hand tractor, were purchased from Messrs Gratton's at a satisfactory price. There was a fund raising effort started up to help pay for these. The ladies' section worked especially hard to put on a range of activities to raise cash and swell the development fund.

THE MEN'S LOCKER ROOM

Shortly after the formation of the Rabbits section, their chairman, Bill Stanford, offered his members' services to carry out the conversion of the cart shed into a men's locker room. This was obviously going to be a rather difficult and expensive job if put to tender and the committee accepted their offer most gratefully. The Rabbits went to their task with a will. Teams of volunteers worked evenings and weekends, begging and scrounging much of the materials from any likely source. They made good progress with this work. By September 1963 the floor had been laid. By that time they had run out of money but with a further advance of £200 they got on with the front wall, windows, and the internal partition. Twelve lockers were installed and a further twelve were in the process of construction.

Meanwhile a temporary 'lean to' was built for Terry Squires against the cottage wall, to use as a shop for his stock of clubs and balls. There was a small workshop at the back, where he could mend clubs and other equipment. Like most temporary buildings it would be in use for much longer that originally planned.

The farm buildings were those of a typical small arable farm built before the turn of the century. There was then little available 'artificial' fertilisers as we know it today, apart from a little Guano— the accumulated bird droppings of centuries— shipped back from South America. The farm yard manure produced by wintering cattle was therefore the principal means of fertilising crops for higher yields or, in the case of Mr Barton, feeding rose bushes. At Aqueduct Farm the cattle had been housed in a covered yard, backing onto a large uncovered yard. They were bedded down with straw and fed on roots, hay and fattening cereals. By the end of the winter there would be six feet or more of well trodden farmyard manure, built up under the stock. The plans involved converting the covered yard into the club lounge. Today, where the fattening cattle used to lie chewing their cud, the members sit down to enjoy their pints, or sip their coffee and eat their cakes in elegant surroundings. They might ocasionally reminisce on how fortunate they are, and think back on the old farm workers who had to dig out these solid heaps of well trodden manure and heave it on to farm carts by hand— one of the toughest jobs going on those old farms.

Much of the lounge conversion was also done by club volunteers. Bill Stanford, Charles Trigg, John Houghton, Jack Dolan, Graham Popplewell and many other members put in hundreds of hours, and saved the club many hundreds of pounds, over these early years. Rodney White did much of the electrical wiring. Ron Peck provided skilled technical advice, and kept a fatherly eye over all the proceedings. The ladies worked equally hard. Mrs Skene made the beautiful curtains which adorned the lounge windows. Many of their husbands were mystified at the sudden disappearance of articles of furniture from around their homes.

Bill Stanford was typical of many members who put in countless hours for the club converting the old buildings into the clubhouse. A manager at a local garage, he was a 12-14 handicap golfer and could turn his hand to any kind of building work

The new lounge was formally opened on Saturday 30th May 1964 by Bryan Cooper, and there were great celebrations and many toasts to the new and elegant room. This development immediately started to improve the membership figures and the

39. The club lounge (after the latest improvements in 1995). The author is standing and looking at the photographer.

club began to resemble the older established clubs of the county. Needless to say it also whetted the appetite of the committee to consider the acquisition of more land to expand the course to a full eighteen holes.

There were of course some incidents that greatly worried the committee. The club could not afford the luxury of a club steward for the first few years and John Bateman of Messrs J Riddlington and Son, the brewing firm, kindly advanced a barrel of beer which was put in a corner of the cottage. This had an adjacent 'honesty box'. This box was very soon renamed the 'dishonesty' box and alternative methods were quickly found to provide liquid refreshments for the weary workers.

Until the conversion of the lounge was completed, members used one of the downstairs' rooms in the cottage which was turned into a 'tea room' where light refreshments could be served.

147.

The ladies' committee put in a great effort to decorate and furnish this room and make it feel attractive. The ladies formed a rota to serve the refreshments. Altogether, the Boston golfers were beginning to feel rather pleased with themselves and their spanking new golf course.

The Purchase Of The Course

The credit squeeze eased off in early 1963 and the local bank managers had been impressed with the progress at the Boston golf club. Both Barclays and the National Provincial Bank were prepared to lend the club funds to purchase the freehold of Aqueduct Farm, from Caytoft Farms. Barclays was chosen to be the club's bankers and a loan of £8,000 over seventeen years, secured on the title deeds of the course, was agreed on, this to be repaid at £500 per year. The purchase from Caytoft Farms was finalised in March 1963. Boston golf club now owned their own golf course.

The club president from 1953-66 was A W Isaac, better known as Gus. His father Robert had come to Boston in 1914 and subsequently had built up a thriving business, Oldrids, which today is one of the best department stores in the county. Robert was a prominent member at Pudding Pie and the club president from 1941-47, Gus' wife Jessie was president of the ladies' section from 1963-67, making the Isaacs the first family to contribute three club presidents to date.

The club started to get a full progamme of club and inter-club matches and competitions arranged. Peter Reynolds was appointed competition secretary in late 1962 and pressed on with this task. Short and stocky Peter could hit the ball vast distances and was extremely competitive. With his own dental practice in Boston, he and his wife Gill, lady captain in 1980, were keen club members.

The cups and trophies from Pudding Pie had been carefully guarded, and were now brought out, dusted down and gently brought into the club's calendar of events. The Sanderson Cup, the Killick Trophy, the Fleet Cup, the Woodthorpe Cup, the Horry Cup, the Cooper Cup, the Hopper Cup, the Hospital Cup, the Carter Cup, the Reynolds Cup the Morley Trophy, the Sutcliffe Tankard and many others, all became the target for the old and

148.

new generation of Boston golfers, including a thriving Rabbit section. The ladies' club also set about planning a busy programme of competitions and events for their cups and trophies. By 1963 the club, notwithstanding the work still being done to improve the greens and fairways, was managing to provide adequate if not wonderful golfing conditions for the members. The Woodthorpe Cup was won by J Houghton, the Anderson Cup by Bill Stanford, the Horry Cup by J Bramley, the Fleet Cup by R Elliott, the Sutcliffe Tankard by R Rhodes, the Hospital Cup by P Dovenden, the Carter Cup by W Bland, and the Cooper Cup by, appropriately, Bryan Cooper.

GOLF UNION MEMBERSHIP

In December 1963 another milestone was reached in the history of the club. The Boston golf club was officially accepted into the Lincolnshire Golf Union and the national body, The English Golf Union. At the same period the ladies became full members of The Ladies' Golf Union. Boston had now 'arrived' as a golf club and had joined the ranks of the 'great and the good'. Henceforth we would be admitted to the priviledged circle of the best clubs in the county. Our best golfers would be allowed to compete against the best in the land, and if they were good enough, they could don the colours of England and compete against the best in the world.

The doors of golfing heaven had opened to the humble fenland course, after 60 years of purgatory and the near threat of a watery grave. Better things, however, still beckoned to provide a challenge for the committee. The Standard Scratch Score for Cowbridge was deemed to be 68 and it was still a twelve hole course: not quite up to the level of the championship course of Woodhall just up the road, with its SSS of 73. Woodhall had the class to attract the most illustrious clubs and competitions in the country, to compete over its beautiful and challenging course, under the benevolent but watchful eye of its owners, the Hotchkin family.

It would not be long however before the Boston golfers began to be seen in county matches. It must be remembered that whilst the old Pudding Pie course was being slowly submerged under heaps of timber, the Boston golfers were playing at other courses around the county. Many of them were excelling at the game,

149.

winning prestigious competitions, and playing in county teams. Gerry Hopper, Peter Reynolds, and Michael Emmett were all honoured in this way. When the Cowbridge course opened up therefore, the new club could put an experienced team in the field immediately. In 1963 Gerry Hopper, Peter Reynolds, and Terry Squires were in a team which won the Lincolnshire Golf Union President's Cup for the second year running. This was excellent publicity for the club. The Rabbits team also started to make a mark for themselves, with an unbeaten record in matches against Sleaford, Surfleet, and North Shore. Our ladies also won the Lincolnshire Ladies' Shield. Mrs Freda Allen was also chosen to play in county matches, and later would be appointed captain of the Lincolnshire Ladies.

The work on the course to build twelve good greens and tees was proving more difficult than was originally envisaged. The chairman of the greens' committtee, Philip Cooper, with the assistance of Gerry Hopper, Bryan Cooper, and other committee members, worked like trojans organising the relocation of problem greens, returfing those that failed to improve from the original sward, and returfing the tees. Endeavouring to do this whilst allowing the members full access to the course was extremely difficult. It was achieved by cutting temporary greens and occasionally closing sections of the course. Getting the best location for the present sixth green proved a major headache.

By the end of the summer of 1964 the greens were generally in satisfactory order. Two holes (one and two) were still the original sward, nine had been returfed and one, the present eighteenth had been reseeded. All the tees had been returfed. By 1965 membership had risen to 232 including eleven life members and forty juniors. The loan account had been reduced to £7,500 and the weekday green fees raised to 5/- and weekends 10/-. Peter Reynolds was the men's captain and Mrs Freda Allen the ladies' captain.

A CLUB STEWARD AND STEWARDESS

In the early days at Cowbridge, refreshments and drinks had been served by members working on a voluntary roster. After a time this became difficult to operate and the committee, in 1964, appointed Mr and Mrs Gilbert as steward and stewardess. With

150.

the completion of work on the cart shed and clubhouse they were able to occupy the cottage. Mr Gilbert was given permission to keep a flock of geese in a large pen alongside the tenth fairway. This was in the best tradition of the fens, with flocks of geese being almost as important as the cattle, on the small fen farms. In earlier times these would be driven along tracks and roads to the town markets, having first been walked over wet tar to protect their feet. Their feathers were traditionally plucked up to five times a year to provide quills for pens, and feathers for the thriving Boston feather bed industry. What would the Animal Rights activists of the present day have had to say about that? Mr Gilbert's geese no doubt escaped these trials and probably only provided the Christmas dinner for his family and some of the club members.

We tend to think of theft as being a phenomenon of the 80's and 90's, but from 1963 onwards the occasional thefts of clubs and money and 'break ins' were noted in the club minutes.

After the hectic activity of the first three years, the club began to settle down to a more normal existence. The first sign of this was when the committee began to feel rather more secure and had time to observe the sins of the members. 'Course etiquette is a matter of concern and clubs and feet are being 'heavily grounded' behind the balls'. At the same time they began to cast their eyes enviously on the two islands bordering their twelve holes.

THE TWO ISLANDS

From the start up at Cowbridge, it was realised that the two islands could play a key role, if and when the club wished to expand to eighteen holes. The club president, Bill Jackson, a local bank manager, was empowered in 1967 to approach Bert Platt, the butcher who owned the grazing rights, to ascertain whether he would be prepared to part with his tenancy. The head landlords were known to be quite happy about the prospect of golf on their land. Mr Platt a shrewd and hardheaded business man knew the value of his lease, both to himself and the golf club. Not unreasonably he let it be known that he did not feel inclined to act the philanthropist. He might consider allowing the club to use the land for a price to be negotiated, but he wished to be able to continue grazing his stock. Now this sort of arrangement was common in the early part of the century on golf courses. Indeed Pudding Pie, Rauceby, Belton Park, and many other courses in the county had allowed sheep and cattle to graze in amongst the golfers. But time had moved on and the 'sixties' golfers were much more fussy. The club gracefully declined this offer.

Bryan Cooper, John Grant, and Geoff Bradley continued to provide men and equipment to work on the course. By 1966 the committee noted many 'mysterious applications of the out of bounds, and lost ball rules.' Clubs and feet continued to be 'heavily grounded', despite the earlier exhortations of the committee. There were complaints about the excessively long rough. During the summer Michael Emmitt, John Bramley, and Bob Barclay played in county teams. Bob Barclay lowered the course record with a gross 70 on Captain's Day. He had come to Boston to play football with Boston United and eventually built up a large insurance brokerage business. He was a fine all round sportsman and was to play a prominent part in the future affairs of Boston golf club.

Kay Buchner had a most successful year as lady captain as had the men's captain, Alan Foster. He was one of the most colourful characters of the period. Tall, dark and dashing he had the ability to get the best out of fellow committee members. Driving up to the club in his Rolls Royce he cut an impressive figure. President from 1970-76 he helped the club prosper in those early days at Cowbridge. The club continued with improvements to the course and the members' accommodation. Terry Squires moved into his new shop. After getting the greens and tees in reasonable working order, the committee were able to start on a task that at Cowbridge would be virtually permanently ongoing— the drainage of the fairways and 'rough'. Boston, unlike the light land courses of Belton and Rauceby, had virtually no problem with drought, except in very exceptional years. The fertile low lying silts however, do suffer in prolonged wet periods and good drainage is essential. They were also able to devote more time to the problem of building good bunkers. John Grant, a well known farmer from Sibsey, and his wife Margaret, were keen members of the club. He put in a great deal of time and effort with his men and machines on bunker construction. To avoid waterlogging on the high water table of the flat fenland these

152.

were 'perched up' as high as possible.

The accomodation road from Willows Lane— the old and very long farm track, which was the only access for heavy lorries, was giving problems because it had not been constructed to take that sort of traffic. Heavy vehicles used it regularly and in wet times it became virtually impassable. The new access road from the Horncastle Road at Kitchen's Bridge, was finally completed in late 1966 and this made life easier for everyone. By 1967 membership had reached 274 and continued to creep up. The committee had temporarily to forget about obtaining the islands and had new tees built on holes thirteen to eighteen, in order that members would not feel that they were playing identical holes.

THE LATE SIXTIES

The club captains from 1966-69 were Alan Foster, Bert Raven, Bill Stanford, and John Leake. The lady captains for the same peiod were Mrs Kay Buchner, Mrs Mary Allen, Mrs E Cheshire, and Mrs Jane Daker. Wag Morley meanwhile had left the club to go to Burghley Park and in 1967 Bob Lakin, who replaced him as head greenkeeper, had his wages increased from £13 to £15 a week. He was assisted by Mr Bontoft. A new Haytor cutter had just been purchased and it was now possible to cut all the fairways in one day, a great improvement on the older machinery. Golf green keepers, like farm workers of the period, were now having to manage and operate more complicated and expensive equipment, a situation now recognised by the club.

To help cover the extra expenses, green fees were raised from 7/6d to 10/- during the week and 10/- to 15/- at the weekend, a steep rise by any standard. The annual subscriptions were also raised to £16 and £18 a year for ladies and men respectively. The new men's toilet block was completed that year. Problems were arising with a subject that was, and remains, a continual problem for every club committee— how to decide a fair and equitable wage arrangement for the club steward. Mrs Gilbert was paid a small nominal salary and expected to make this up from catering profits, a common arrangement. When these do not come up to expectations, as frequently occurs in many clubs, the result is dissatisfied stewards with all the problems that can then arise.

Members in their blissful ignorance, tend to think their steward is making a fortune from inflated meal prices, when the reverse may well be the case.

The men were still using the ground floor of the cottage as a changing room. The next improvement planned was to convert the locker room into a men's changing room thus freeing the ground floor of the cottage. This could then be used by the ladies as their changing room. The ladies were congratulated and thanked by the committee for the 'lovely furniture and fittings now in use in the clubroom', 'a magnificent contribution very much appreciated by all club members.'

Improved Financial Situation

The increased membership was beginning to show through in the accounts. A further indication of this was the comment of the club secretary that: 'because of our improved financial situation we were no longer obliged to do things on the cheap.' In 1970 the men's captain was Brian Morris, a local architect who had carried the heavy workload of club secretary from the restart of Cowbridge in 1961 until 1969 when he relinquished the post. The lady captain was Miss Weightman, 'Trot' to all her friends. She also would work extremely hard for the club for many years, and become president of the ladies in 1993. My wife was especially grateful to Trot for the help she gave her to get rid of the dreaded 'p' on her handicap.

The way the ladies set about organising the game of golf must impress any observer. The formidable Issette Pearson, who started off the Ladies' Golf Union in 1893, three decades before the men would get around to starting up their Golf Union, set a standard that has been kept to by successive generations of the fair sex. One of the differences in their approach to ensuring a fair handicap system, is the 'p' concept. The ladies, when they start off playing the game, have a 'p' inserted after their handicap which indicates that it is a provisional figure and they are in consequence barred from many competitions. Getting rid of the 'p' very soon becomes a matter of life and death to the aspiring champion. The duties of the loving mother, the tender wife, or the cordon bleu cook, are all forgotten until the heavenly non 'p' stage is reached.

154.

Trot took over the captaincy from Jane Daker, who with her husband Derek, served the club for many years in a number of offices. A lasting memory of Boston golf club is of Derek, seated in his favourite seat in the club lounge ready to answer almost any question on golfing matters, and to arbitrate on innumerable friendly disputes between members. Jane was invariably seated alongside him ready to assist in the more difficult cases. Successive match secretaries had compiled an extensive programme of competitions for the members. Dorothy Skinner, ladies' captain and Charles Trigg, the men's captain, had their hands full supervising these hectic lists of events.

The club suffered a serious loss that year when Mr Gilbert died following a serious illness. His wife felt that she could not carry on as stewardess on her own. Meanwhile Mrs Freda Allen, the Hon secretary, intimated that the ladies would be prepared to vacate their lounge in the cottage provided alternative accomodation could be found to take their lockers. They were happy to help the club financially to make these changes. Harry Corns drew up plans to make further improvements to the cottage.

Thus by the end of the sixties, the club had broken the back of the work of settling into the new course. It had been a period of tremendous effort from the Coopers, the committee, ground staff and from a large number of the members, all of whom had given their time and services freely, to help keep down expenses. It had also been a period of great fun and satisfaction, as the rough Aqueduct Farm and its land and buildings, were renovated and improved, to provide much the best golf course Boston had had since the club's birth in 1900.

Meanwhile developments were taking place in other parts of the county. In 1965, Louth golf club started up on the lovely wolds west of the town. An eighteen hole course with an S.S.S. of 70, its pleasantly undulating fairways present a good test for golfers of all abilities.

CHAPTER NINE

THE 'SEVENTIES'

THE 'SIXTIES' HAD SEEN GREAT CHANGES in all aspects of life for the general public and for the golfers. Advances in medicine appeared to have accelerated at that period, allowing more and more golfers to continue hitting the small white ball, when at an earlier period they would have been confined to rocking chairs, with worn out hip joints and clogged up coronary arteries. The culmination came with Dr Barnard carrying out the first heart transplant in 1967. Neil Armstrong set foot on the moon in 1969 and demonstrated the effect of lack of gravity on struck objects. The thought of golf courses extending to 20 miles in length is guaranteed to give nightmares to any overworked club secretary. Despite the occasional balance of payments crisis, the standard of living of the average family crept steadily up and the average working week fell. Both of these factors helped increase the membership at the Boston golf club and the extra revenue needed to pay for the continually improving course.

The 'seventies' saw this progress maintained. Britain joined the Common Market in 1972 and for the first few years British farm profits improved dramatically as the price of their produce rose to the level paid to the small, inefficient, French and German farmers. This helped the economy of Boston and therefore that of the Boston golf club. The decade was less satisfactory for the British professional golfers. British competitions were swamped by a wave of super players, not only from America, but of all countries Spain! John Henry Taylor would have been astounded had he seen the way Severiano Ballesteros would attack his beloved golf courses. Away back in 1905 his view of the continental golfers was: 'the volatile natures of our Gallic neighbours do not exactly fit them for the earlier stages of learning the game thoroughly'. Our Open was won in the 'seventies' by: 1970 – Jack Nicklaus; 1971 and 1972 – Lee Trevino; 1973 – Tom Weiskopf; 1974 – Gary Player; 1975 – Tom Watson; 1976 – Johnny Miller; 1977 – Tom Watson; 1978 – Jack Nicklaus; 1979 – Severiano Ballesteros. the rising young Spanish

156.

star, Only Tony Jacklin among British golfers, with his superb victory in the US Open in 1970, when he left the rest of the field trailing, could claim a 'major'. The publicity, however, gained by the superstars helped the membership of every club in the country.

THE CAPTAINS

The Boston club continued steadily to improve their course facilities under the captains of that decade. These were Brian Morris, Charles Trigg, Peter Pearson, senior, Bert Howes, John Odling, Harry Corns, John Mitchell, John Barnes-Moss, Bob Barclay, and Barry Johnson. Peter Pearson, senior, went on to become a long standing president from 1977-1988. His son, Peter Pearson, junior, would also go on to become an equally long standing chairman of the greens' committee doing sterling work to make the Boston putting surfaces amongst the best in the county. John Barnes-Moss, following a distinguished career in the RAF, became the club's first paid secretary, coping admirably with the ever increased work load, as the membership and facilities increased. Later he helped build up and run the thriving veterans section in the club. Bob Barclay (who also became the club president in 1992, an office which he still holds) contributed substantially to the efforts to increase the course to eighteen holes.

LADIES' CLUB

The ladies' club was also fortunate in the choice of enthusiastic and hard working captains, over the same period. These were: Trot Weightman, Dorothy Skinner, Flo Reynolds, Hazel La Touche, Kath Bradley, May Cott, Nora Royle, Jennie Reynolds, Shirley Greswell and Marion Smith. Flo Reynolds was one of the great club characters who had also played golf at Pudding Pie. Bryan Cooper recalls how she used to tee the ball up on two tees. She had her own style with everything she did. She especially enjoyed the festivities following the competitions. Nora Royle was also the type of person one never forgot. She was the epitome of the fen golfer. No matter what time you met her heading for the course, she had done a double day's work on her small intensive farm, where she grew beautiful flowers and succulent vegetables. She had lost an eye in an accident but it made little difference to her golf. Not a big hitter, Nora was one of those players who never seemed to be doing anything very much, until her opponent would suddenly realise that Nora was several holes up.

The committee continued to worry about the limitations of a twelve hole course. Peter Pearson, the president, suggested at the 1971 AGM, that the club try to acquire land adjacent to the course to expand to a full course. The minutes record that there was a lively discussion and the view was expressed by many of the members that, 'a competently maintained twelve hole course was preferable to a larger course not so easily maintained'. Fortunately however for the club, the meeting, by a show of hands, decided in favour of aiming for the eighteen holes.

Boston golf club has always had a keen and hard working ladies' section, with seldom an ill word between the sexes, excepting the husband and wife teams in the Mixed Greensomes. Then the patience of the men occasionally became strained at the impossible lies provided by their spouses. Like most other clubs in the country however they were reluctant to allow the fair sex into the spheres of management. In 1972 a proposal from the ladies that two of their members be allowed to 'sit in' on the House Sub Committee meetings was rejected.

The acquisition of new and better machinery continued, with the purchase of a powered turf slitter for £100. Mr and Mrs Campling were appointed steward and stewardess in 1972. A new development in the amenities offered to the members was the start up of a bridge club. At the end of the year it was noted that the new stewards had settled in well and were pleased with the new large and well equipped kitchen. Thanks were extended to John and Freda Allen for their work in renovating the ladies' room and for all their efforts the previous winter in assisting with catering.

In early 1973 the stewards expressed their unhappiness with their long hours and with the work of clearing up after the bridge club. No doubt some members would wonder what these bridge players were getting up to. In October 1974 it was reported the the steward and stewardess were leaving— but it was a Mr and Mrs Sharp, who some time earlier had been appointed to replace Mr and Mrs Campling. They must have decided that the goings on at the bridge club and other problems, were too much and moved on to greener pastures.

John Mitchell reported in late 1973 that it was proving very difficult to get sufficient members willing to play in the teams for club and county fixtures.

TREE PLANTING AND OTHER ITEMS

Work to improve the course continued apace and the tree planting and drainage work was making steady progress. The club from the start up at Cowbridge had put in a major effort to ensure that the course would have a large number of carefully chosen, well laid out trees. Philip Cooper played a major role in organising the tree planting operation, including the choice of varieties and locations on the course. Today all that early work has paid off, and Boston now has a course that scenically compares favourably with many of the old Lincolnshire parkland courses. The two groundsmen were now Mr Bontoft and a new appointment, Mr Don Warsop. Don was to prove a good servant to the club for many years to come. The widening and improvement of the footbridge over the Stonebridge Drain greatly improved access to the clubhouse and course. The new ladies' locker room was completed in late 1973. The expenditure on this and other improvments put the club accounts once more into the red. Meanwhile it was decided that Mr Larkin, who was semi-retired but was helping part time on the course, was not needed as two groundsmen with their equipment could cope.

For most golfers an announcement was made in the autumn that had far greater significance in adding to the pleasure of the game than had the introduction of the Haskell ball. 'Players would be allowed to lift and clean their balls on the fairway.' The principal object of this rule is to protect the tender fairways and not to make the game easier for the players. This rule, whilst giving great pleasure to many, gave, and continues to give rise to, some acrimonious disputes. Largely about the difference between two inches and anything up to two feet.

The Boston ladies have always been well known for their good natures. There are however limits to sweet reasonableness. In March 1974 they intimated to the committee that they were unhappy about the price of whisky in the bar. A very serious matter, especially for those lassies having problems with their 'p's and wishing to drown their sorrows.

The club was still trying to purchase land adjacent to the course, and the cost of the proposed bar extension had risen from £800 to £1,100. In August 1974, and following our success in joining the English Golf Union, the club had a visit from the representatives of the R and A who cut the claimed yardage of the men's course by 140 yards and the ladies by 117 yards. Inflation and the realisation by the committee of the increased value of the golf to members, caused them to raise the life membership subscription to £300, a figure that now causes much distress to those of us who were too short sighted to avail ourselves of this astonishing bargain. The club was delighted with the honour accorded to Freda Allen when she was appointed captain of Lincolnshire Ladies in October 1973. The membership increased to around 480 by the end of 1974.

COMMITTEE BUSINESS 1974

At a committee meeting held on 14th November 1974 those attending were the president Alan Foster, captain H Corns, honorary secretary G Redman, the honorary treasurer J Reynolds, the committee: H Eaglen, W Johnson, P Redman, J Cannon, M Norton, J Stanford, R Woodthorpe, D Daker, R Howes, H Rainbow, J Wiggins, J Adams, and M Goodacre. Apologies from J Odling, P Pearson, V Pyatt. In attendance: the ladies captain, Mrs M Cott and the ladies' secretary Mrs M Allen. The president, Alan Foster, said that the sponsored event of 15th September raised £500. Finances were still tight and we were operating up to the limits of our overdraft. Mr and Mrs Sharp, steward and stewardess, had resigned. The loan account was down to £3,500.

The chairman of the greens' committee, R Woodthorpe, reported that it had been a good year with the course continuing to settle down. Mr J Stanford, chairman of the house committee, reported that progress had been satisfactory and apart from the scarcity of cash all was going well. Derek Daker, chairman of the entertainments' committee, reported on the programme for the coming autumn. The secretary reported that eighteen new members had applied to join. We were now up to 480 playing members and until we could extend the course were reaching our limit.

The country was in the middle of another financial crisis with inflation in the region of 20%. This meant that the golf club's costs were rising at a similar rate. The rises were affecting every one and there was great pressure on employers to give wage rises. At a management committee meeting held on 16th January 1975 it was noted that Terry Squires the club professional felt, quite reasonably, that his remuneration should rise to match his costs. He had not had an increase for some time and the value of his retainer had diminished because of the inflation. The committee agreed to raise this to £850 from 1st January 1975 together with 5% of the green fees collected by him. The hope was expressed by the greens' committee that the increase 'would encourage Mr Squires to take more interest in the work of the course'— a euphemism for expecting him to do more of the physical work needed on the course.

The Victorian attitude that golf professionals should cut the greens, look after the fairways, and carry out the odd jobs about the course, was a long time in dying, despite the efforts of John Henry Taylor, Walter Hagan, Henry Cotton, and the British and American PGAs. There is no record that this suggestion was ever acted upon by the Boston professional. Work went on improving greens and tees and planting trees. The president suggested that the old barn, the last remaining of the old buildings, which abutted onto the men's locker room, should be demolished and the area tidied up. This was done, at a cost of £140, later in the year. The club lounge had done excellent service from the early days, but with the increase in membership it was clearly not large enough. Bert Rainbow and Ted Eaglen suggested that the much needed extension should be started as soon as possible, given the escalating costs of building taking place at the time. The membership by March 1975 was: men 343 including twenty-three country members; ladies 83 including three country members, juniors forty-nine. The winter Sunday evening bar sessions would be changed from 5.00 p.m.–8.30 p.m. over to 7.00 p.m.–10.30 p.m..

WET WEATHER CLOSES THE COURSE

'The course will be closed for a week because of bad weather'. Fen courses such as Boston and Spalding occasionally suffered from very wet conditions underfoot, forcing the temporary closure of the course, but they had the advantage in the summer over the light land courses like Belton and Rauceby, of never 'burning up'. The club was indebted in the same year to the County Council for providing three hundred trees for planting around the course. The chairman of the greens' committee, now Mr Cannon, reported complaints of slow play and overcrowding at the weekends. The club received a request from the secretary of the County Ladies for the use of the course for their trials in April 1975. A further club development was the installation of showers in the men's changing rooms. The club recorded its thanks to Mr. Lord of Messrs Fisons for his advice on green and course management.

In June 1975 the club received a shock with the news that their popular professional, Terry Squires, who had by then been in post for thirteen years, might be leaving to take up a similar position at Seacroft. The minutes record that with pressure from the club members, Mr Squires' retainer was increased from £850 to £1,000 together with a petrol allowance of £20 a month, to persuade him to desist from this idea. This reflected the rampant inflation affecting the country, delighting house owners as the real value of their mortgage dropped with the apparently never ending rise in house values. Negative equity was a phrase which lay way ahead in the dim and distant future.

The club meanwhile was increasing in popularity with visiting golfers, and green fees were averaging £6 a day. The Masked Ball held in Boston was a great success. The effect of inflation and the success of the club was reflected in the increase in the cost of life membership, which went up to £400 in September. Mrs Warsop had taken on the duties of stewardess assisted by her husband when he could spare the time from his course work.

The efforts to get additional land were still unsuccessful despite the exertions of the committee. The refurnished, redecorated and enlarged bar, was now in use and much appreciated by the members. At the AGM in October 1975 the members voiced their appreciation of the efforts of the stewardess. In 1976 a new handicapping system was announced for the men. It was to be given a two year trial. Almost since the game started, the National Committee had striven to devise a fair and equitable system of handicapping that would satisfy the average club player and situation. Would this one succeed?

An equally intractable problem was to ensure a fair method of remunerating club stewards for all their efforts. When Mrs Warsop was appointed as stewardess it was agreed to pay her £1,250 together with £250 for her husband's assistance at the bar. In addition she would get an incentive bonus of 20% of the net bar profits. This would be reviewed after six months. The club's landlords who owned banks alongside the drains, the Witham Fourth and the Anglian Water Authority, proposed a modest increase in the annual rent for these banks, from £9.03 to £13.50. The bar takings were up, but there would still be an overdraft of nearly £2,500 by the end of the year. 1975 and 1976 were extraordinarily dry and hot years. The winter rainfall in 1974 and 1975 was also below average and the result was that by the summer of 1976 the soil moisture deficit had soared to well over 6 inches and the water table had dropped almost out of sight.

PROBLEMS WITH THE DROUGHT AND THE GREENS

The fertile silts with their traditionally high water table come into their own in these conditions. Whilst crops and grassland on the Sleaford light Bunter sandstone, and on the thin chalky Horncastle Wolds, suffer greatly from drought stress and can fail, the silts in these circumstances can still grow a moderate crop of potatoes and cereals. The potato crop, a key crop around Boston and the Wash, always fetch very high prices in times of drought and they did in 1975 and 1976 making good profits for the silt farmers. The light land golf courses like Belton Park and Rauceby suffered dreadfully in those years with the fairways almost disappearing. Their irrigation systems saved the greens.

These conditions however caused a serious problem to develop on the Cowbridge course. At the management committee meeting held on 31st March 1977, the chairman reported that 'the greens had suffered a disaster'. In fact on the twelve hole course, greens on the fourth, eighth, ninth, tenth, eleventh, and twelfth holes were largely wiped out. What had happened was that the greens had been irrigated with water from the drains, as was the custom in dry conditions. The salt levels in these however had risen to a level where the irrigated grass on the greens was killed. Around the low lying Wash, high concentrations of salt in the subsoil, together with tidal water getting into the drains, can result in abnormally high salt levels in the water flowing through the waterways. The prolonged drought had aggravated the situation with the water levels of these drains falling sharply.

Instead of putting water with normal levels of around 300-500 parts per million of chloride the greens were dosed with water containing over 1,000 parts per million. Now salt water is a good natural weed killer. Unfortunately it cannot distinguish between weeds and the adjacent crop. At a level of 700 ppm, ryegrass is badly scorched and at 1,000 ppm it is obliterated. A few days after the treatment the poor old greens started to give up the ghost. It was an unfortunate combination of circumstances that caused the problem. To aggravate the situation, the salt water had affected the structure of the top soil, just as had occurred when Pudding Pie flooded in 1920. The members of the greens' committee however, when the problem was diagnosed, very soon mobilised teams of volunteers to re-lay and reseed the greens whilst golf continued on temporary areas cut out alongside. For several months sweating members riddled out heaps of soil and raked and rolled in the grass seed. Helped by the natural fertility of the soil the greens were fairly quickly restored to their former glory, but meanwhile a few committee legs were pulled by members of the various clubs around the county.

THE SIR HENRY LUNN SHIELD

The Boston golfers, however, were beginning to make their mark in County golf. In the Sir Henry Lunn Shield competition, a prestigious County trophy, the Boston team of M Norton, P Redman, P Pearson and M Stancer brought the maginficent shield back to Boston in 1976.

JOHN BARNES-MOSS

John Barnes-Moss took over as captain at the AGM in October 1976. A Squadron Leader in the RAF at Waddington, he had been a keen and first-class golfer since his youth. He proved a valuable acquisition to the club. After his captaincy ended, he became the club secretary and held this part-time post until, in 1980 after the course was extended to eighteen holes and the secretarial workload had expanded enormously, he became the first full-ime

164.

Boston Golf Club - THE SIR HENRY LUNN SHIELD - Winners 1976
M.J. Norton   P.G. Redman   P.J. Pearson   M. Stancer

40. The Boston Golf Club team with the prestigious
Sir Henry Lunn Shield in 1976.

club secretary. This post he filled with distinction aided by his organisational skills, until 1986. In 1988 he became the honorary secretary of the seniors' section and assisted it expand from around twenty to up to sixty members, to become an important and thriving section of the club. They hold a full programme of home and away competitions, competing successfully with the other senior sections throughout the county.

Meanwhile the committee were still maintaining their interest in the islands. Bob Barclay, chairman of the new forward planning committee, had looked into the possibility of finding alternative grazing land for Mr Platt to encourage him to vacate the two islands. He reported in 1977 that the search so far had been unsuccessful. He felt that the prospect of getting the islands appeared to be receding and it would be wise for the club to make the best of what they had at present. In line with this approach the committee would look at the possibility of enlarging the men's locker rooms at a cost of around £5,000. The committee had also considered the possibility of enlarging the clubroom, but the cost of this would be in the region of £20,000 which was more than the club felt it could afford at that point in time.

41. John Barnes-Moss and Frances Grant in a jolly mood.

Meanwhile a new greenkeeper, Mr Harmer, had started to work for the club. At the AGM in Octber 1977 the new captain, Mr Barclay, informed the meeting of a petition submitted by the members asking that money be spent on the course rather than on the changing rooms. By 1977 the membership was 331 men, seventy-two ladies and sixty juniors.

DICK HARDY

In 1974 a new member joined the club. Dick Hardy and his wife Margaret were keen golfers but had played their golf at Rauceby for several years. The family had farmed at Willoughby House on the edge of Boston for generations, growing arable crops and fattening cattle. His father had been a keen member at Pudding Pie and had won several trophies at the old club. When he joined Cowbridge he very soon proved a valuable member. With his knowledge of grassland it was not surprising that the committee would soon pass over to him the golf equivalent of the fakirs bed of nails—chairman of the greens' committee. He held this office for several years and under his direction the course continued to improve. His wife was elected lady captain in 1981 and Dick the men's captain in 1986. However the greatest service he would do for the club took place before this.

166.

CHAPTER TEN

THE COWBRIDGE ISLANDS

AFTER BRYAN AND PHILIP COOPER, the golf committee, groundstaff, and an army of helpers had spent two years of hard unremitting toil changing a rather small, run down grassland farm into a reasonable, twelve hole golf course, their minds began to turn to the future. Should the club expand, or should it improve the existing course? It must be remembered that there were at the time many nine hole courses around the country and there were many in the club who would have preferred the club to remain a small course. At the AGM in October 1971 there was a long discussion on the possibility of expanding the course and the minutes note that: 'many members held the view that it was better to have a twelve hole course that was easy to maintain rather that a larger one that would be more difficult'. After further discussion it was agreed however that the club should aim to move to an eighteen hole course. In fact the committee had been investigating such a possibility ever since 1963.

Many of them felt that the key to the future expansion of the Boston golf club lay in acquiring the two islands abutting Aqueduct Farm. Not only were they the easiest land to add to the course, but they possessed a unique fenland character, bounded as they were by the Stonebridge, Cowbridge, Maud Foster and West Fen Drains. Golf architects of the time were already spending vast sums of money on the new courses then being constructed, digging out ponds, lakes and streams. Boston golf club was extremely fortunate to have had generations of old drainage engineers do the work for them, with the added advantage that they were features that could look back to a history which would make a typical American club green with envy.

The two islands were known as the Medforth or Small Island, extending to nine acres, and a larger one known as the Back or Large Island, which was eighteen acres in size, but included a house and a field, leaving around thirteen acres for possible addition to the course. The history of these islands goes far back in time.   To a period when the early Adventurers, as the entrepreneurs of the period were named, encouraged by Elizabeth I, Henry VIII, and other monarchs, ventured their capital on speculative enterprises such as the drainage of the old fens.

THE EAST AND WEST FENS

Golfers watching their balls disappear today into the West Fen or Stonebridge Drains, join a long list of aggrieved individuals stretching back into the dim and distant past, who were unhappy at the effects these picturesque waterways were having on their fortunes.   Before the fens were drained all the surrounding villages owned common rights, to fish, catch wild fowl, cut peat and harvest withies, on the 40,000 acres of the East, West, and Wildmore Fens. There used to be several duck decoys a few miles up the road where thousands of geese and duck were 'decoyed' each year, by little well trained dogs, up into the long tunnel nets, and then despatched to the London and Birmingham markets. The Adventurers, profiting from turning these areas into fertile farming land, were gaining at the villager's expense and before the work was eventually completed, over several centuries, there were continual and bitter disputes, between the commoners and the improvers.   The early schemes failed because of this hostility, together with the intractable technical problems that faced the early engineers.

SIR JOSEPH BANKS

Sir Joseph Banks, a wealthy landowner from Revesby, one of the most eminent Lincolnshire men of the period and a president of the Royal Society, in 1800 persuaded the local landowners and commoners to accept the proposals of John Rennie the famous drainage engineer to carry out a comprehensive and expensive drainage programme for this area.   In 1801 a Parliamentary Act was passed, to allow the work to proceed at an estimated cost of £28,914.   Employing an army of navvies using only spades, wheelbarrows and horses, the work was completed in five years. 40,000 acres, including the two islands at Cowbridge, were reclaimed from being largely the habitat of ducks, geese, fish, and withies, to become good farming land.   Rennie however had not completely solved the problems caused by floodwater pouring

168.

down from the Wolds to the north, onto the low lying fens and the two islands at Cowbridge.

From that period right up to quite recent times Cowbridge, and the area around, had been subjected to regular and severe flooding. Fortunately for Boston golf club however the most recent major drainage scheme carried out in 1965 on the Hobhole Drain had greatly reduced the chance of flooding. Because of the earlier risk however, the islands had been avoided by the local arable farmers and had been used by livestock men as grazing fields for cattle, sheep, and horses. A small area on the Medforth Island had also been used at the start of the century as a source of brick clay for the nearby brick works over the canal and opposite the present first green.

THE PLATTS

In 1919 a Boston man, Herbert Platt, who had served in the Great War, took over the tenancy of the islands for his expanding business as a horse dealer. The Medforth Island was then owned by the Witham Fourth Drainage Board, the authority responsible for the maintenance of the three fens. The larger island was owned by the Church Commissioners. Boston in those days, like the rest of Britain, was still largely a horse based economy. Heavy breeds like the Shires, Suffolks, Percherons, and Clydesdales pulled the farm ploughs and waggons, and the lighter breeds of Welsh ponies and cobs the traps and carriages of the gentry.

Herbert Platt bought horses from markets all over the country including Ireland. He pastured them on the two islands prior to breaking them in, or selling them on to his clients. The islands were ideal for this purpose, since they were naturally separated from the adjacent arable land by the drains and he was spared the expense of fencing, or disputes with neighbours, whose crops might be ruined by trespassing stock. He had a son Robert, who did not join him, but became an apprentice butcher with a Skegness firm. Robert, or Bert as he was better known, would play a key role in the history of Boston golf club and to understand this role it is worth looking in some detail into his background.

He learned his trade as a butcher spending seven years in Skegness and whilst there he started dealing for himself in pigs

169.

and cattle in a small way. No doubt he capitalized on the experience he had gained whilst helping his father. Having acquired some capital and experience he moved back into Boston and after further expanding his business he took over the leases of the two islands from his father.

He was a shrewd business man and a hard worker and over a period of years he built up a large wholesale and retail butcher's business in Boston, owning two slaughter houses and a shop in Bargate. He was one of the first Boston men to export large shipments of cattle and sheep to the continent. He was probably introduced to this trade by a young Dutchman called Frans Buitelaär, who had come to Boston as a teenager. Bert struck up a friendship with him and together they built up a large export trade to Holland. Bert travelled all over the country to auctions and marts buying cattle, sheep, and pigs for himself and others.

THE DEALER

The life of a large scale livestock dealer in those days was extremely tough and demanding. Bert Platt did dozens of deals in a single day at a major auction. The British livestock industry, then as now, is one of the most complicated in the world. British livestock breeders had started up most of the current breeds of cattle, sheep, and pigs and there were dozens of widely different breeds all with a role to play in this industry. His work involved scrambling in and out of pens of cattle, sheep, and pigs making instant decisions. He needed an expert eye to sort out the myriad crosses of Swaledales, Cheviots, Border Leicesters, Scottish Blackface, Cluns, Suffolks, and a dozen other different breeds and crosses of sheep.

The cattle breeds of this period included beef and dairy Shorthorns, Aberdeen Angus, Herefords, Welsh Blacks, Friesians, Ayrshires, and many others including all combination of crosses of the pure breeds. A cattle dealer needed years of experience to deal with the demands on his skills. One minute he would be buying half a dozen Hereford cross Friesian bullocks, from a hard headed small Welsh farmer. The next minute bargaining for 100 Suffolk cross lambs, from a large south Shropshire arable farmer. He had to be able to recognise at a glance the dozens of different

170.

types of 'ringers' and diseased animals slipped in to hoodwink the unsuspecting buyer. If he 'got it wrong' there was no Ombudsman, nor FIMBRA, nor sympathetic court to bail him out. It was a very tough world where it was very much caveat with a vengeance emptor.

The man who held the key to the future of Boston golf club, had survived and thrived in this sort of environment for all of his business life. Any club representative assigned to deal on behalf of the club with Bert Platt, was taking on someone with unparalled experience of all aspects of dealing, and who was an expert in getting the very best price for anything he might be selling. Not an easy task—and so it proved. From 1963 a succession of golf club committee members tried their hand at persuading Mr Platt to part with the islands. Bert was a pleasant man to try to do business with. Full of anecdotes about his past life and with a fund of amusing stories he was a delight to meet and talk to. Getting him to sign on the dotted line was a different matter altogether, as one delegation after another found out. It must be remembered that, although he was only a tenant of the two head landlords, Bert fully realised that under the 1948 Agricultural Holdings Act, he had full security of tenure and in view of this owned a highly valuable asset.

A tenant of agricultural land in many ways had more legal rights than his landlord, the owner of the property. The main factor preventing him selling the lease of the islands, was that he and his sons would have great difficulty in getting alternative land around Boston and would almost certainly have to pay much more rent for much less convenient grassland.

After a succession of abortive attempts the committee began to acknowledge that they would have to look elsewhere and they instructed a sub-committee to look out for alternative land. The perennial problem facing the club was soon evident. Suitable land was either not available, or if it was only at an exhorbitant price. In June 1977 Bob Barclay, chairman of the forward planning committee, reported that the prospect of obtaining the lease of the islands or other additional land had diminished and the club ought to concentrate on making the best use of what they already owned.

At that time Bob Barclay had been a keen member of Boston golf club for many years and had served on the committee in a number of offices. He was then vice-captain and became captain in 1978. In addition to being a first class golfer holding the club record for the best scratch score, he had been a good footballer and played for Boston United. It so happened that another keen supporter of Boston United was a certain Bert Platt who was also a director of the football club. At that time the chairman of the greens' committee was Richard Hardy, a member of a well known Boston farming family. They farmed at Willoughby House Farm on the edge of town and in addition to growing all the arable crops of the area, Dick and his father were keen stockmen, rearing and selling beef cattle. They were also keen on the sport of kings— horse racing— and had stabled their own racing horses. Bert Platt was a social as well as a business friend of Dick's father and was on friendly terms with Dick. The committee felt that perhaps Bob and Dick given these advantages might charm the lease out of Bert. In late 1977 Bob Barclay and Dick Hardy contacted Bert Platt and asked if they could call on him. The answer being yes they set out one autumn evening for Bert's house in Red Cap Lane.

At that time Bert was approaching the end of his working career and was sixty-five years old. He had started to hand over the business to his sons, John and Andrew, but he was still in charge of the big decisions. Bob Barclay and Dick Hardy were at the beginning of their business careers, Dick as an arable farmer, Bob starting up his own insurance agency business. Neither of them were new to business dealings but compared to Bert they were mere suckling babes. They knew this and so did Bert. It was therefore with a great deal of trepidation that they were ushered into the lounge. The meeting did not get off to a good start. Bert invited 'young Dick and Bobby' to make themselves comfortable whilst he finished looking at his favourite television show. Eventually he got around to asking what he could do for them. By this time of course they were practically speechless. To their great astonishment however, when they broached the subject of the purchase by the golf club of the lease of the two islands, they found he was in a most receptive mood. Bert with

*42. Peter Reynolds, Bob Barclay, Dick Hardy, David Grant,
and Dick Greswell in the club lounge.*

his dealing experience did not dally when he had made up his mind. Quite quickly with very little haggling over price the deal was arranged and agreed. For the sum of £10,000 the Boston golf club could have what they wanted. The golf club contingent could hardly believe their good fortune. As they left the house Bert saw them off. 'Well I hope you lads make the very best use of that big island,' he shouted as they got into their car. 'Excuse me Bert,' said Dick, 'I thought for a moment you said the big island'. 'Yes, that's what I said,' replied Bert. A hurried discussion between Bob and Dick and a scurry back into the lounge. Another frantic discussion and the small island was added to the bargain— for no extra charge.

Bert had obviously intended from the start to let them have the tenancy, but he meant to have his little bit of fun in the process. The price of £10,000 was a great deal of money in 1978 but it was a fair price to Bert Platt for the asset he was handing over, and it was a great bargain for Boston golf club despite the grumbles by many members about the cost of this transaction. It marked a turning point in the fortunes of the club. There is little doubt that the admiration that Bert Platt had for Bob Barclay as a Boston

United footballer and the personal friendship between the families of the Platts and the Hardys had a considerable bearing on the results of the negotiation.

The golf club negotiators had another fright before they could report back to the committee that the deal had been successfully completed. Bert Platt was only the tenant of the two Islands. The landlord of the large island was the Church Commissioners and the small island the Witham Fourth Drainage Board. There was no problem getting permission to transfer the lease from the Witham Fourth. Their headquarters were then in Boston, the board members were friends of many of the farmer members of the club, and it was a satisfactory arrangement to have golfers rather than the occasionally troublesome cattle wandering around the island.

The Church Commissioners were something quite different, and Bob and Dick arranged to meet in Lincoln with the senior church dignitary who handled these matters. One fine morning they set off for the Minster at Lincoln with Bert and his son John. Bert was in top form and regaled the party with his usual fund of anecdotes and dealing stories. After a time it started to dawn on the two golfers that they might have a problem on their hands. Whilst Bert's stories and language might go down very well at a male stag party they were not on their way to that sort of function. They became more and more concerned as the implications dawned on them. If they were not careful the whole deal could quite easily be fouled up at the last minute. They could picture themselves being unceremoniously dumped outside the door of the Minster by an infuriated and scandalised bishop. A hurried discussion outside his lordship's office and they decided that at all costs Bert must be kept out of the proceedings until the transfer was accomplished. Alas that was quite impossible. The bishop and Bert were soon deep in conversation with the two golfers consigned to the sidelines. Gradually their initial horror vanished. Not only was the discussion going rather well, but the bishop had obviously taken quite a shine to Bert and not surprisingly. The language coming from the Boston butcher could well have been that of the bishop himself. He regaled the cleric with tales of his boyhood schooling days at the local church school in Boston and other fascinating anecdotes, soon the pair were getting on like a house on fire. Topped with a glass or two of

174.

rather fine sherry and holding closely onto the signed parchment, they left Lincoln having to drag Bert away from his new friend.

Dick and Bob had under estimated the chameleon like skills of a born dealer. One final word about Bert Platt. Like all big cattle dealers when he had agreed a deal and shaken on it, that was that. There was no need of anything in writing from him, or his solicitor. His word was his bond. In this respect he had a great deal in common with Fred Parkes and it was precisely this quality that got Fred into all his difficulties over the salvage of the SS Lockwood, back in 1922. He had carried out to the letter his part of the bargain and at great expense had floated and salvaged the SS Lockwood. How could any respectable person or organisation avoid paying because of a piece of paper?

However had all this not occured and had Fred Parkes stayed in Boston, the Pudding Pie committee might not have been offered it as a golf course. 'It's an ill wind that . . .' Boston golf club were now the proud possessors of the island tenancies. At an Extra Ordinary General Meeting held at the golf club on 16 March 1978 Peter Pearson senior, the club president, invited the members on this historic occasion to back the committee by supporting the purchase of the lease of the Medforth Island and the Large Island. This was agreed with great enthusiasm by those attending.

THE START OF THE 'VETERANS'

Another event occured in 1978 which was a landmark in the history of the club. The first meeting was held of the 'Veterans'— the over-sixty-years of age golfers.

This took the form of a golf meeting played in threes with the members drawing for partners.

On that historic first meeting Messrs Edrich, Squibbs, Cannon, King, Rainbow, Cook, and Deptford attended and played for a golf ball. Appropriately Messrs King and Cannon tied and each had a golf ball. Membership would from then on grow steadily.

AN EIGHTEEN HOLE COURSE

With the acquisition of the two islands now safely accomplished, the club could press on with the planning and work involved in turning Cowbridge into an eighteen hole course. Both the men's and ladies' committees were soon involved in the task of getting the extra holes ready as quickly as possible. The captain, Bob Barclay, and his committee: C Atterby, J Atterby, D Daker, M Goodacre, J Gill, R Hardy, J Mitchell, H Rainbow, B Matthews, D Smith, H Corns, R Gresswell, R Howes, and P Pearson junior, put in a great deal of extra work, with Dick Hardy and Peter Pearson carrying the main responsibility of turning the islands into a part of the golf course. Donald Steel, a well known golf architect, was called in to advise on the layout, and give advice on how best to proceed with the laying down of the greens and management of the fairways.

It was fortunate for him and the committee that the land was already down to good quality permanent pasture, and the fairways could be left in their natural state. The drainage was also fairly satisfactory.

It was decided to make three holes on the Small Island one a par three, one a par three/four and the third a par four. The large island would have two long par four holes and a par three hole. A great deal of work would be needed to lay out and reseed the greens and build the bunkers. It was decided to put in an irrigation system at the same time as the greens were being reseeded and Peter Pearson was given a budget of £2,643 to do this.

Donald Steel recommended laying the greens down over a stone base to improve the drainage but this would be expensive and it was left to the discretion of the chairman of the greens' committee, Dick Hardy, to decide what was best. In the event the high cost and more urgent improvements did not favour the 'stoning' of the greens. This was a decision which involved the committee in considerable difficulty at the 1995 AGM when two greens were relaid over a stone base at very high cost.

The cost of turning the islands into six extra holes would not be cheap. The committee appealed for donations to a development fund and this raised £6,500. The ladies' section were especially successful at fund raising, under their captain, Shirley Gresswell, and her committee: Mrs M Smith, Mrs G Reynolds, Mrs J Reynolds, Mrs R Street, Mrs M Hardy, Miss T Weightman, Mrs M Cott, Mrs M Allen, Mrs K Bradley and Mrs M Davies. With encouragement from their lively president, Mrs J Coney, who was in her element in this sort of situation, a whole series of events were organised to swell the development fund. Dick Hardy sought

176.

their aid in planning the new holes to ensure that the ladies' tees were placed in the best possible situation. Gone were the days when the Boston lady golfers would leave all the decision to the menfolk.

At the annual summer ball planned for 1980, an event which owed much of its success to their involvement, they made it quite clear in the nicest possible way that they were prepared to give all the help required with the provision and laying out of the food and liquid refreshments, but that did not include the washing and tidying up afterwards. When in 1979 Wilkinson Sword had the audacity to present a trophy that did not include the ladies, they very quickly remedied that rather unfair occurence by persuading Dunhills to donate a salver for a similar event for themselves.

They had a further boost when it was announced that the 1980 British Ladies' Open would be held at Woodhall Spa from July 17-21. Perhaps the time would not be far off, given Boston golf club's rate of improvement, when that event might be held on their own course?

THE BRITISH WOMEN'S PROFESSIONAL GOLFERS' ASSOCIATION.

The early years of the century saw lady golfers demurely swishing at the ball whilst clad in long voluminous dresses covering a whole range of mysterious undergarments. They were all amateurs. Year by year this changed and more and more ladies discovered that they had golfing skills not much inferior to their male counterparts. Inevitably in the latter half of the century some of them decided to make golf their living and became professionals. In 1979, the British Women's Professional Golfers' Association was formed with steadily increasing prize money, played for by better and better golfers. The lengths of their attire appeared to decrease in inverse ratio to their skills. Today the best of them, like Laura Davies, can play against men on equal terms and their tournaments are drawing ever larger audiences. Their stylish and fashionable outfits add significantly to the attraction of their tournaments.

THE OPENING OF THE 'EIGHTEEN HOLES'— AT LAST

The laying out of the new holes came up to everyone's expectation and hardly a word of criticism was heard from any quarter— an amazing situation considering the close attention

43. The opening of the full eighteen hole Boston Golf Club course on 30th March 1980. Mrs Jane Coney and Mr Philip Cooper lead off.

given to the work by several hundred potential golf architects.

The reason for this was that it was generally recognised that the new holes, situated as they were on two attractive— one could say beautiful— islands with wonderful natural hazards all around, had added immensly to the quality of the Boston golf club. On the 30th March 1980, the new eighteen hole course was formally opened when Philip Cooper drove the first ball over the Stonebridge Drain down towards the then tenth hole.

It was an historic moment in the life of the club. It had taken eighty years to achieve the transition from a nine hole winter course to a fully fledged full sized golf club, but Boston had succeeded despite several very close brushes with catastrophe. How proud and delighted Oliver Cooper, Frank Curtis, and all the past committees would have been to see all their past efforts so wonderfully fulfilled.

178.

CHAPTER ELEVEN

THE 'EIGHTIES'

T HE '1980s' WAS A DECADE that saw tremendous changes in all aspects of our lives. In golf it was a period when the domination of the international scene by the super golfers from America, was broken by an upsurge of talent in Europe. The standard of living of the British people, so important to the treasurers of all golf clubs facing ever increasing costs from more demanding members, was as usual greatly affected by the value the international financiers placed on the pound. Jack Nicklaus, the super golfer, was thought to be coming to the end of his illustrious career by the beginning of the 'eighties', but there was still life in the old dog. He won the US Open in 1980 and the US Masters in 1986 giving him eighteen major's—a feat which will probably never be repeated as the standard of international golf continues to rise.

Tom Watson continued to play scintillating golf in this decade winning his third, fourth and fifth British Open titles in 1980, 1982 and 1983 with only one golfer ever bettering that feat—the incomparable Harry Vardon. The British Open victors in the 'eighties' were: 1980 Tom Watson, 1981 Bill Rogers, 1982 Tom Watson, 1983 Tom Watson, 1984 Severiano Ballesteros, 1985 Sandy Lyle, 1986 Greg Norman, 1987 Nick Faldo, 1988 Severiano Ballesteros, 1989 Mark Calcavecchia, 1990 Nick Faldo.

But the great golfing story of the decade was the rise of the British and European stars. Severiano Ballesteros, a youth who came from a humble Spanish peasant home overlooking Santander Bay to star as one of the great charismatic characters in golf, capable of attracting hordes of spectators to see him performing miracle recovery shots from lies left by his rather wayward driving; Bernard Langer, the poker faced German, the first player from that country to leave his mark on international golf; and of course our own Nick Faldo, Sandy Lyle, and Ian Woosnam.

Britain had not won a Ryder Cup match since 1957, when the little Welsh terrier, Dai Rees, captained one of the best teams we ever fielded, including Peter Alliss, Eric Brown, Christie O'Connor, Harry Weetman and the irrepressible Max Faulkner. A succession of failures from 1959 to 1977, persuaded the R and A to include in the 1979 team, players from the whole of Europe, to take on the might of America. The European team were severly beaten in 1979, and again in 1981 at Walton Heath, but were only just defeated by $14^1/_2$ points to $13^1/_2$ in 1983 at Palm Beach, Florida. The Europeans however were victorious in 1985, 1987 and in 1989 the match was halved to the delight of the British public and the disbelief of their American counterparts. The publicity attending these victories of course gave a great boost to every golf club in Lincolnshire and elsewhere. In addition, the top European players carried back over the Atlantic, many of the elite American trophies during that period.

THE IRON LADY— MARGARET THATCHER

Golf, like every other leisure activity, is greatly affected by the general state of trade and industry, wages and the cost of living. After the stop, go, stop, progress of the economy over the previous three decades the 'eighties' were to see an improvement. The 'Iron Lady', Margaret Thatcher, would become Prime Minister in 1979 and following the disastrous inflation of the Wilson Government in 1974–75, when the average wage rose by no less than 26% in a twelvemonth, she came in on a platform of economic reform to control inflation. The gnomes of Zurich liked this fiscal policy and refrained for a time from selling the dear old pound. She was greatly assisted by Britain around this time, becoming a major oil producer.

Everyone's standard of living benefited from all these changes until 1988, when Chancellor Lawson failed to control the massive lending by banks and institutions, causing the boom and then collapse of the property market, leaving many sadder and wiser house buyers with property worth much less than their mortgage— the so called negative equity gap.

A severe depression began to hit all European countries and America, in the late 'eighties'. This was exacerbated by the end of the 'cold war' which severely cut the spending on armaments, so important for the economies of Europe, when President Gorbachev began to dismantle the 'Iron Curtain' in 1985.

180.

Boston golf club however managed to shrug off all those changes and continued to spend on further club improvement. The committee had no problem keeping up the membership levels and the waiting list built up. The recession had bankrupted many firms and many others had given some of their staff early retirement. The 1980s' job losers were fortunate compared to their earlier counterparts. In 1900 anyone losing his job, and in severe financial difficulty, could end up in the workhouse on Skirbeck Road. Matters were rather different in the 'eighties'. Many people losing their jobs were given generous pensions and lump sum payments, which allowed them to continue playing golf and lead reasonable lives.

THE SENIOR CITIZEN'S SECTION

Meanwhile Boston was already starting to benefit from having an eighteen hole course. Green fees rose in line with inflation but the course still attracted an increasing number of visits from other golf societies in and outside the county. Another important development which took place at Boston and other clubs throughout the county was the development of the senior section in golf clubs. The secretary, John Barnes-Moss, in November 1978 reported a request for a morning to be set aside for the 'Senior Citizens', to allow men over 50 to come, draw for partners, and play, one morning a week. This idea was accepted, and by the end of the decade around forty-fifty older players had joined and were also playing inter-club competitions against other clubs in the county.

The members and green staff required better access to the islands, and during 1980 a bridge was built and the existing footpath widened in order to allow cars and tractors to get to the clubhouse and islands.

In early 1980 plans were announced to build a new dining room and extend the club room and locker rooms at a cost of £13,500. The committee felt in a position to increase green fees to £3.50 during the week and £5.00 at the weekend. There were also plans to give reduced annual subscriptions to members who reached the age of 65. At the AGM in October 1980 the house chairman reported that the new clubhouse extension had been built at a cost of £9,000. The old covered cattle yard had now been transformed into an elegant and spacious lounge. Members could look out through a glass frontage on to the eighteenth green and fairway. The decor was planned around beautiful brick pillars and end walls, built from old Lincolnshire bricks donated by Ted Benjamin and Dick Hardy. Ted's wife Marcia presented the club with the substantial brass footrest around the base of the bar counter. The bricks, I am delighted to say, were cleaned and dressed by the author and his wife one cold snowy winter day.

The numerous club trophies were now housed in a spacious mahogany cabinet, with a full length glass frontage, where they could be studied with ease. Around the walls of the dining room abutting on to the lounge were hung the elegant boards containing the names of past trophy winners, captains, and presidents. These were beautfully inscribed by Fred Reed as a labour of love saving the club many hundreds of pounds. Given all these added amenities on the course and in the clubhouse the committee decided the time was ripe for increases in member's charges. Annual subscriptions were increased to £75 for men and £65 for ladies, the combined rates £120 and juniors £25. From the opening of the Cowbridge course in 1962 to 1980 membership had risen from 129 men, sixty-six ladies, and six juniors to 420 men, 105 ladies and sixty-eight juniors, a total of 593 playing members. In 1962 the Annual subscriptions were £8.00 for men and £6.00 for ladies. There had however been unparalled inflation over the period, as seen by the fact that the average farm worker's wage in 1962 was £8.13s. a week, and in 1980 it had risen to £65.00 a week. The men's captains in the 'eighties' were Cyril Foster, Richard Tinn, David Ogden, John Atterby, Fred Bramwell, Don Smith, Dick Hardy, Dick Needham, Brian Skinner, and Sid Swallow. Sid Swallow would also do sterling work as a long standing honorary treasurer. The ladies' captains were Mrs Gillian Reynolds, Mrs Margaret Hardy, Mrs Barbara Holgate, Mrs Marcia Benjamin, Mrs Audrey Skinner, Mrs Minette Davies, Mrs Audrey Dawson, Mrs Freda Bramwell, Mrs Marion Hearth, and Mrs Chris Means.

At the management committee meeting on 27th October 1981, David Ogden the captain, suggested that the lady captain, her vice-captain and the ladies' secretary, be co-opted on to the committee for the coming year, and his suggestion was accepted.

The chairman of the greens' committee was Dick Needham who, with Peter Pearson junior, and Ron Rainbow, had the task of getting the new island greens into good order. Ron Rainbow took responsibility for the tree planting programme on the islands.

THE TREE PLANTING PROGRAMME

Boston golf club, right from the start up of the Cowbridge course, was determined that there would be a comprehensive plan to ensure that tree planting would play an important part in the development programme. Several committee members were given special responsibility for this area of course improvements including Ron Rainbow, Philip Cooper, and John Leake.

By the start of the 'eighties' this plan was bearing fruit literally and metaphorically and the planting programme continued on the islands. The result was that by the end of the decade Boston could boast of having played its part in the improvement of the local environment by having a course that in many ways resembled the beautiful parkland courses of Belton and Rauceby whilst maintaining the charm of a typical fenland scene. Copses of Poplars, Silver Birch, Weeping Willows, Oak, Sycamore, Beech and Elm were planted around the course interspersed with Scotch Pine, Douglas Fir, Ash, Alder, Chestnut, and Lime. A range of species of single trees including Pink Almond, Rowan, Cherry, and Apple dot the course. These, together with the flourishing mature hedges of Hawthorn, provide golfers with a beautiful riot of blossom for much of the year. The autumn spectacle of all possible shades of red and brown, make a walk around the course a delight, and worth, for nature lovers, a considerable part of the annual subscription on its own. The large flat fields of the fertile silts are not well endowed with trees, and the tree-lined fairways of the Cowbridge course stand out strikingly, as one motors past on the way to Boston or the Wolds.

Running a golf club is not all milk and honey. In March 1982 David Ogden, the captain, reported to the committee that the mysterious loss in revenue from bar sales, despite the rise in turnover, could be attributed to: 'ullage and wastage at the pumps'. The committee must have found the correct antidote to cure this unfortunate condition since it did not subsequently arise. In his years on the committee, David Ogden had put in a

183.

great deal of effort using his expert knowledge of building and construction to save the club much expense. The heavy expenditure of the past year and the projected capital requirements, led the committee to obtain a loan of £20,000 from the Midland Bank.

Impressed by the success of the club, and even more so by the highly impressive cash flow, the Midland did not quibble about this large sum. However the club were not taking any chances. At the AGM in October 1983 the Annual subscriptions were raised to £99 for the men and £87 for the ladies. There is no end to the cruelty inflicted by man upon his fellow men or women. In July 1983 Peter Pearson junior, suggested leaving an area of rough of approximately 100 yards in front of each ladies' tee to 'avoid the bad shots prospering'. This was rich coming from PP junior who was aware of bad shots only by hearsay. The committee did receive a jolt in that year when there was a record number of resignations from the club. Despite this in January 1984 the secretary reported a membership of 445 men, 103 ladies, sixty boys, and five girls— a total of 613 playing members.

CHRIS MEANS

The ladies' locker room was enlarged and a shower installed in 1982. This did not work properly for some time and the early users would shoot out rather hurriedly, either frozen stiff or parboiled. Chris Means was elected captain of the county second team in 1984 and went on to become Boston golf club captain in 1989, Lincolnshire captain in 1992 and 1993 and a ladies' county selector in 1982, 1984, 1990, and 1995. One of the best lady golfers to play at Boston, she could hit the ball vast distances and her powers of recovery from her occasional wayward drive almost rivalled the great Ballesteros. This made her a formidable competitor. She played for the county first team in 1979, 1980, 1986, and 1994.

Looking over the ladies' club minutes, one cannot help but take the view that they greatly enjoyed both their golf and committee meetings. The committee meetings seem to have been lively as well as enjoyable occassions. Their honorary secretary, Mrs Gill Reynolds, reported after one of their meetings that: 'Miss

184.

Weightman thanked Mrs Smith for the excellent refreshments served during the meeting which then closed in a noisy manner.' A golf club and course would undoubtedly be a drabber and duller place without the presence of the fair sex members.

ALISON JOHNS

In the middle of the decade a young girl by the name of Alison Johns started to play golf at Boston, and found that she had an unusual facility for the game. Her father Clive Johns was a keen golfer and gave his daughter every encouragement. In 1985 she became Lincolnshire junior matchplay champion and started winning many other prestigious events. She would continue steadily to improve, winning the Lincolnshire ladies' county championship in 1986 with a record qualifying score and won

BOSTON GOLF CLUB

ALISON JOHNS

*Represented Great Britain & Ireland
vs Canada 1989*

*England Full International
1987, 1988, 1989*

*England Under-21 International
1988, 1989, 1990*

*England Junior International
1985, 1987, 1988*

England Schools International 1987

England Under-18 Champion 1987

England Under-15 Champion 1985

Rochampton Gold Cup Winner 1988

Bells PGA Junior Champion 1986

*Lincolnshire Ladies County Champion
1986, 1990*

Midland Girls Champion 1987, 1989

*Central England Foursomes Winner
with Jim Payne 1987*

*Lincolnshire Junior Open Champion
1986, 1987, 1988, 1990*

*Lincolnshire Junior Matchplay Champion
1985, 1987, 1990*

Northern Schools Champion 1985

Turned Professional 1991

CLUB PHOTOGRAPH

*44. Alison Johns and her record.
The outstanding lady golfer from the Boston golf club to date.*

185.

again in 1990. From then on she would win almost every event in the ladies' county calender. She represented England at senior level in the home internationals at Ashburnum in 1987 and gained further international honours in 1988, 1989, and 1990. Her success provided a great boost for the Boston club, and much inspiration for the junior section. Alison decided to use her skills to their best advantage by becoming an assistant golf professional in 1991 and competed on the ladies' professional European tour from her club base in Lincolnshire. Her mother Margaret, encouraged by her daughter's success, became a keen golfer and hard working club member.

A friend and contemporary of Alison, Helen Dobson from Skegness, a member at Seacroft, has also proved to be an outstanding golfer. The Lincolnshire ladies' champion in 1985,1987, 1988, and 1989 she turned professional in 1990 and in 1993 won the Illinois Classic in America and in the same year the European Masters' tournament in Belgium. She is currently playing most of her golf on the American ladies' professional circuit in America since she moved there in 1995.

The British amateur lady golfers had, like their male counterparts, been having a hard time at the hands of the Americans in their early Curtis Cup encounters. From 1960 to 1986 they lost thirteen straight encounters, beaten by a galaxy of talent from over the Atlantic. Following the appointment of a new captain, Diane Bailey, things began to look up for the home team. She tackled the job seriously planning her tactics well in advance and motivating her team into believing that the Americans could be beaten. In 1986 in Kansas in sweltering heat the British team won their first ever victory in America by the handsome margin of thirteen to five. They narrowly retained the trophy in 1988 at Royal St George.

The 'eighties' saw the ladies' European and World professional golf scene go from strength to strength, with the emergence of new European talent to compete successfully against the Americans. The brilliant USA player, Nancy Lopez, won record amounts of prize money in the US including $1.5 million in 1985 and was 'Player of the Year' for the third time in that same year.

The most exciting development for British ladies' golf however, was the emergence of Laura Davies, from West Byfleet in Surrey, as a world class golfer. In 1986 she won the British Ladies' Open. In 1987 she stunned the ladies golf world by winning the U.S. Open, and $55,000. She continued with her successes over the latter years of the 'eighties' and into the 'nineties'.

Whilst there were no male members nor juniors who could approach the success of Alison Johns, Boston had built up a thriving junior membership, with many first class up and coming young players, encouraged by the committee and their hard working organisers. Jeremy Woodcock proved to be a young golfer who did well in junior county events in his early playing days. He would go on to play for the county, and was the Lincolnshire youth county captain for two years. Simon Woods was another successful young player who won many club and county events and played in the county youth team. Mark Stancer showed great promise and eventually became a professional golfer. As more mature players, they continue today to be in contention for a high placing any event they care to compete in.

Reorganisation of the Committees

The business of running Boston golf club in the nineteen eighties had changed out of all recognition to what it had been in the Sleaford Road, Tower Road, and Pudding Pie eras. It was now a very large business with a very large cash turnover. At the AGM in September 1985 a new management structure was proposed, with the large number of small committees being replaced by a business committee under the chairmanship of Bob Barclay, and a golf committee, with Don Smith in the chair. The functions of the old committees would be divided appropriately between these two main committees.

The advantages of being a 'good' golf club were now being seen in all sorts of ways. The finances of the Cowbridge club were being bolstered by sponsorship from business firms 'purchasing' a tee, and the commercial value of this advertisement had risen to £1,000 for a five year contract. The use of the course was also now being sought after by county and other organisations. The Lincolnshire Union of Golf Clubs asked for it to be available for the 1987 Lincolnshire seniors versus Norfolk seniors match, and the Lincolnshire Ladies' County Golf Association wanted it for the Brocklesby cup at their autumn meeting in 1987.

THE PEARSONS

From 1977-88 the club president was Peter Pearson senior, CBE, to distinguish him from his hard working son PP junior. The junior edition of the family had, by constant and dedicated supervision, done much to give the club some of the best greens in the county, in the 'seventies', 'eighties', and 'nineties'. A fine hockey and badminton player in addition to being a very good golfer, he won innumerable trophies over that period. He and his father grow potatoes and cauliflowers on their prime silt farm at Freiston on the edge of Boston. Peter Pearson senior, a highly respected South Lincolnshire arable farmer, has been greatly involved in National Farmers' Union affairs as well as those of the Boston Council. His knowledge of problems involved in large scale vegetable production, earned him a place on the British and European farming committees. As club president he provided much encouragement to the club to improve, in order to bring it up to the level of the other top clubs in the county.

A NEW SCALE OF FEES

The costs of playing golf continued to rise and in 1986 it was proposed to raise the entrance fees to £95 for a single and £160 for a combined membership. The annual subscription for men would go to £118 and the ladies to £104, country membership to £70 and full time students to £10. Cyril Foster suggested that the course was not being used to full capacity and that the present limit of 650 playing members should be increased. This was agreed by the management committee.

TERRY SQUIRES

Plans were in hand to provide a new shop for Terry Squires the club professional, who has been such a good servant to the club having been in the post since the club started up at Cowbridge in 1962. It was decided that the club should hold a 'Benefit Day' for him on the 5th July 1988, to celebrate his 25 years with the club. There were a variety of fundraising activities to enable the club to give him a substantial and well deserved present. Both the men's and ladies' sections worked hard to make it a huge success and this reflected the popularity he had built up with club members

188.

over his years of tenure. The presentation took place on the 8th October 1988. Terry has had a highly successful golf career winning honours all over the country and on the continent.

45. *Terry Squires, Boston golf professional, flanked by his two assistants— 1996. L. to R. Nick Hiom, Terry Squires, Scott Emery.*

He won the Lincolnshire Open Championship on no less than seven occasions and the Lincolnshire Professional Championship on five occasions. In 1969 he won the Midlands Professional Championship. Apparently possessed of the secret of eternal youth, he has not changed appreciably in looks or outlook over several decades. The calendar however does not lie and he is now eligible to compete on the senior circuit, which he has done successfully in recent years.

'SWEET MEMORIES'

The club steward and stewardess from 1985-1989 were Robert and Judy Epton. As the years pass one becomes more and more aware that it is the simple things that contribute so much to what is popularly known as 'the quality of life'. For me the sweets and cakes fashioned in her kitchen, by Judy, came solidly into this category. What did it matter if, in 'The Mixed Greensome', one was heading for the booby prize, with the wife wailing in one's ears about the shame and disgrace of fifteen Stapleford points. A few holes ahead, there waited Judy's delectable sweets, certain to make life worth living for at least a few precious moments. Alas, the best things in life tend to be ephemeral, and in 1989 Bob and Judy departed for pastures new.

THE BOSTON 'RABBITS'

The 'Rabbit' section—the term used to denote those with handicaps of eighteen and over—performed ably in the 1988 Nel-

46. The Nelson Cup winners, 1988.
From L. to R. — John Swithinbank, Terry Dainty, Rob Wilson, Brian Draper,
Dennis Limb, Sean Marshall, George Kent, Mark Catchpole,
Richard Harrison, Tony Tomblin, Barry Molson, Cyril Large.

son Cup, a competition for teams of players from the North Shore, Boston and Seacroft Golf clubs. It had been donated by a Skegness jeweller of that name. The Boston team won this important competition in 1988.

A Full Time Secretary/Manager

The ever increasing workload of running the business of a modern golf club, led the committee into another major step forward. There had been paid part time secretaries, succeeded by full time secretaries, employed in the past, to manage the office business and affairs of the club. John Barnes-Moss had done both, culminating in his fulltime work from 1980-1986. He was succeeded by John Mitchell, another good servant to the club, before his untimely illness and death. The committee decided at this time to appoint a full-time experienced Manager/Secretary and a long standing member, Don Smith, took up the post in 1989.

Don and his wife Marion, had been hard working members, serving on club committees for several years. Don was elected the club captain in 1985 and Marion had been lady captain in 1979. His office is situated off the entrance to the club lounge and there Don and his assistant surrounded by computers and other 'high tech.' office equipment, carry out the 'one-hundred-and-one' administrative jobs involved in running a million pound business with a turnover of many thousands of pounds a month. Keeping several hundred golfers happy is not by any means the easiest job in the world. Don however manages this successfully and in addition nips out of his office from time to time to pick up his clubs and get into the prize lists.

47. Don Smith, secretary/ manager from 1989, on the 18ᵗʰ green outside the clubhouse.

CLUB ETIQUETTE

One of his many concerns is the need to implement the committee policy and cajole members into keeping up club standards which tend from time to time to slip. The subject of correct dress and etiquette constantly recurs in the committee minutes. Golf committees the world over are in a constant state of schizophrenia, torn between the desire to remove from their beloved courses all those members and visitors slouching about in totally unsatisfactory outfits, chopping up their beloved fairways and greens, against the unfortunate need to tolerate them to help reduce the ever increasing bank overdraft.

In 1989 Jane Daker raised, in the ladies' committee, the question of how brief the ladies should be permitted to wear their shorts and sun tops. Now this was clearly a matter to be decided solely by the club's entertainment committee who, knowing the broad mindedness of the members of that august group, would not set any limit to the shortness of these garments. The ladies were also having some difficulty with cancellations by members who had agreed to enter for matches. Mrs M Davies, the captain, suggested that there should be a rule: 'that grandchildren should arrive on the earthly scene before and after the golfing season, to avoid the problems these cancellations cause.' The length of men's socks when playing in shorts came under the eagle eyed scrutiny of the committee. It was rumoured that tape measures had been issued to each of them.

THE LADIES

Notwithstanding these problems, the ladies were continuing to enjoy themselves, with a full programme of home and away matches and exotic social events. The Boston ladies, in common with the ladies section of most golf clubs, put a great deal of effort into the club, in activities which are frequently unobserved by the male chauvinist members, who generally are much too concerned with either getting speedily into the bar, or equally speedily out on to the course, to notice such things as the beautiful floral

JANE HAWKES

48. The 1993 Ladies Am/Am
From L: Jean Flynn, Marina Reed, Madge Dawson, and Marian Bavin
looking forward to a jolly day.

192.

decorations around the lounge. In 1989 the ladies committee started to organise an annual AM/AM event, the proceeds to go to charity. This involved the secretary and themselves in a considerable amount of work, but the Boston ladies are good at organising these sort of functions and they have been outstandingly successful, with this event attracting large entries from all over the county. This has now become a popular annual event. To date they have successfully raised many thousands of pounds for a number of worthy causes. The club each year has a full programme of entertainments organised over Christmas and again the ladies put in a tremendous effort to decorate the lounge for these events. For these and all the other ways in which the fair sex add to the common weal of the Boston golf club, we would like to pay tribute. The club increasingly recognized the importance of the ladies in the life and activities of the club. In 1989 they were allocated their own reserved tee times on Tuesdays for their competitions.

COURSE ENLARGEMENT

Towards the latter half of the decade, the restless spirit of the committee began to manifest itself by contemplating further developments to the course. Boston was now an interesting and attractive eighteen hole course. Why bother to go to the expense and hassle of any further major changes? Many members would be against such a move, since it would inevitably cause annual subscriptions to rise.

To explain what was worrying the ambitious committee members let us look at the list of Lincolnshire golf clubs in the English Golf Union *Golfing Yearbook* for 1985. There is a list of twenty-seven clubs in the county who are members of the English Golf Union. Their 'Standard Scratch Score' rating—the score expected from a scratch player in normal summer conditions of wind and weather, and largely based on the length of the course— varies from 73 for the championship course of Woodhall Spa; 71 for Belton Park, Seacroft, and Normanby Hall; 70 for Burghley Park, Louth, Lincoln, and Sleaford; 69 for Carholme and North Shore; 68 for Boston, Spalding, and Sutton Bridge. Boston is down at the bottom.

The SSS rating is important not just from the viewpoint of

status, but it is also an important measure applied by the best golfers, golfing societies, and golf associations, when they decide where to play or hold competitions. It is an important indicator of how 'good', a particular golf course is. It is not by any manner of means, the only measure of quality. Other aspects of a golf club become well known to the mobile golfing fraternity. The effort a golf club has put into making their course pleasant to play over, from the scenic beauty aspect, greatly affects its popularity. The background and history attached to a club, is becoming increasingly important. The quality and number of artificial and natural hazards on the course to test the skill of players is another. The quality of the clubhouse and club amenities are also of great importance.

The Boston golf club of 1989, despite its SSS of 68, had much to offer from its scenic beauty, its fenland charm and its history including the natural fenland hazards. Its length and layout was especially popular with the higher handicap players who after all make up the bulk of the members. But what about the future? In the 'nineteen-eighties' and especially towards the latter years, there was a great increase in golf club construction, brought on by the general demand for increased leisure activities and by the encouragement by government to take agricultural land out of farming. The Boston golf club committee were determined to make their course amongst the best in the county. To do this they needed a higher SSS and to obtain this they needed more land to lengthen their course and to increase safety distances on some parts of the playing area.

But land around the course was scarce and expensive. The club president, Derek Daker, possessed of a wide circle of friends and aquaintances, found out however that a suitable block of eighteen acres, lying to the east of the course, abutting the fourth fairway and the railway line and farmed by Mr F Bratley, might be available, subject to negotiation. Bob Barclay, who had successfully negotiated the purchase of the lease of the islands, was empowered by the committee to enter into negotiation with the owner, and the purchase was agreed in the latter months of 1989 of the eighteen acres for £63,000. The land was prime silt and the price was fair to both parties. The deal was completed on the 14th February 1990.

194.

CHAPTER TWELVE

THE 'NINETIES'

1990 SAW THE START OF THE DECADE that will culminate at the beginning of the Third Millenium AD and brings this story up to date. It is a little less than a mere hundred years since it all began when Frank Curtis and his committee took the plunge and formed the Boston golf club. It seems safe to say however, that it has been a hundred years that will never again be equalled for its rate of change of the conditions affecting mankind and his environment. It has seen the work-horse powered economy move forward to an era where atomic energy accounts for an ever increasing share of mankind's power supply: where Homo Sapiens has stepped on to the moon: where the mysteries of the gene and the brain are steadily and remorselessly being unravelled.

The age that Boston golfers can expect to reach, and still be able to propel the small white ball around Cowbridge, is also increasing steadily. At the present rate of progress, in a hundred years, there will be centenarians tramping over the course, complete with all new metal joints, pig's hearts, livers, and kidneys, and implanted with genetic material from the world's best golfers. The mind boggles at the changes that could occur a thousand years from now.

IN THE WIDER WORLD OF GOLF

The professional game continues to expand and the best golfers are now super paid super stars with players such as Greg Norman able to command appearance money in excess of £100,000 simply to play at a major tournament. What fee would the incomparable Walter Hagan's agent negotiate today for an exhibition match at Cowbridge?

Undoubtedly the driving force behind the rise in fortunes of professional golfers has been the American Golfers' Union, together with the individual golfers' agents, with the brilliant Mark McCormack leading their field. A first class amateur golfer he started looking after the fortunes of Arnold Palmer and gradually became responsible for the fortunes of many of the best golfers. A master of media management he has transformed the image and fortunes of all golfers and not simply those in his stable.

The PGA of America likewise have a team of outstanding managers. Their official guide would have astonished Harry Vardon and J H Ferguson. It lists every member's scoring average, driving distances, accuracy putting scores, and 'sand saves'. John Daly, in 1994, drove on average 288.9 m, with an average score of 72.83, and had amassed career winnings of $1,187,829 in prize money. In the same period Greg Norman had amassed career winnings of $6,607,562. To illustrate the improvements in recent years of the earning capacity of the best golfers Arnold Palmer amassed the surprisingly low total of $1,904,668 in his wonderful career.

MICHAEL HOBBS

These figures relate only to prize money. If one adds on appearance payments, commercial sponsorship payments, and the other additions that they earn, the figures become almost unbelievable. Are they worth it? These are free market earnings and paid for by commerce and the public. They must be deemed to be worth their income.

Jack Nicklaus the super-star golfer from Columbus, Ohio in terms of successes in the Majors— he had won eighteen by the start of the '90s— stood head and shoulders above his peers. With competition becoming fiercer year by year will his record ever be beaten? He was thought to be coming to the end of his career by the end of the eighties but continued to remain prominent in the top tournaments.

49. Jack Nicklaus from Columbus, Ohio. Winner of the greatest number of 'Majors' achieved by one golfer so far.

The winners of the 1990-96 British Opens were: '90–Nick Faldo, '91–Ian Baker Finch, '92–Nick Faldo, '93–Greg Norman, '94–Nick Price, '95–John Daly, whose fans were delighted to see the big hitting American demonstrate his short game skills to win our major championship, and '96–Tom Lehman.

196.

The Ryder Cup: In 1991 the US won 14 $\frac{1}{2}$ to 13 $\frac{1}{2}$ in America. In 1993 at the Belfry— US won 15 to 13. The European team had their revenge in 1995 when they won in America under the captaincy of Bernard Gallacher.

The Curtis Cup: In 1995 the European ladies won, after a succession of defeats, fielding one of the best ever teams including our super star Laura Davies.

The Walker Cup: The sheer number of top class amateurs produced in America proved too much for our Walker Cup teams who were defeated in 1991 and 1993 but to our great delight the tables were turned when we won in 1995.

AND BACK IN BOSTON

Meanwhile at the start of the decade, there was no halt to the steady progress at the club. Following the purchase of the eighteen acres from Mr F Bratley, for £63,000 in 1990, the committee got down to the task of replanning the course. The land had been used for arable cropping and the fairways and greens had to be ploughed, cultivated and reseeded. Dick Hardy carried out this work and saved the club the considerable expense of hiring contractors.

The indigenous grasses of the fens are ryegrass and other broad leaved species. Whilst these are good for fattening bullocks, they are not as favoured by modern golf architects for reseeding fairways as the fine leaved fescues, indigenous to upland heaths or seaside links. These hold the ball higher and allow a better and cleaner strike. The greens committee decided to reseed the fairways on the new fifteenth and sixteenth holes, with these fine leaved species and the difference from the rest of the course is striking. It will be an interesting experiment to see for how long these interlopers manage to withstand the onslaught of the indigenous grasses. The additional new land involved the club in replanning virtually the whole course. The two par three holes on the islands have been replaced by two new holes on the additional land— a long par four, and a very long par five running alongside the railway line. The course is now safer and longer and the SSS has been lifted from 68 to 71.

Was it all worth the expense and hassle? Many high handicap players preferred the old layout with its six pleasant and shortish

197.

finishing holes facing them after playing back to the clubhouse. For the committee planning the club for the next century however it was almost certainly the best decision.

A PRACTICE GROUND

With all these course and clubhouse improvements effected since 1962 there was one important facility that was still missing. There was no practice ground. Anyone wishing to improve their game was obliged to use part of the sixth or eighteenth fairways. This was unsatisfactory as it interfered with play for members playing these holes. In 1991 the committee started serious negotiations with Mr. R. Sykes, who owned a four acre field on the far side of the Stonebridge Drain, opposite the clubhouse. The deal was completed in June 1992 for £24,000. It was not the ideal shape nor size for a practice ground, but it was on the market and golf clubs have to be careful who they might get as neighbours— a factor which may have influenced the committee's decision to purchase it. The practice field runs up to Brickyard Farm, the site of the old brick works. The extraction of the clay there has left a three acre pond which is now a habitat for large numbers of ducks, geese, and other birds, and has greatly improved the natural environment around the golf club. The Boston course is now a veritable wild-life park. There are always a flock of Canada Geese around, with Pink Feet, Mallards, Brent, Cormorants, Swans, and Great Crested Grebes within eyesight of the players. In autumn and spring great flocks of migrating Pink Feet and Brent Geese come and go over the course, trailing in arrowhead formation, chattering to each other with their unforgettably plaintive cries, as they head for the marshes or the open sea. Over a hundred different species of birds have been identified by experts on the Boston golf course

Improvements continued in the clubhouse and steward's house including showers in the ladies' and gents' changing rooms. Don Warsop who had done an excellent job in leading the team of groundstaff retired at the end of 1992. He was succeeded by Dean Bradshaw a young but promising member of the groundstaff team. The tremendous amount of work carried out on a modern golf course is illustrated by Peter Pearson junior, chairman of the greens' committee, recording that 3,800 acres of greens were cut

198.

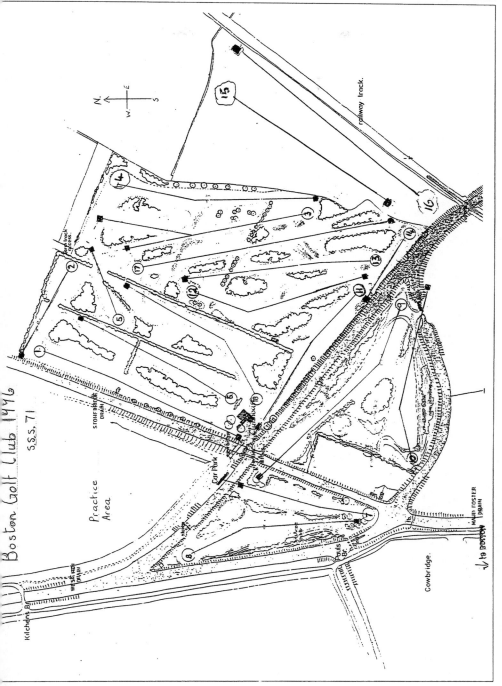

50. Layout of the Boston golf course now extended to 6,490 yards and an SSS of 71.

in 1993. In addition the fairways and greens were all Verti-drained—a specialised machine that cuts small drainage slits in the fairways. Work progressed on the new practice ground to bring it into use.

The problem of the size of the practice area, if not entirely its shape, was solved in 1993 when the field adjacent to the new practice ground was purchased for £27,000 from Mr. T. Taylor. This was nearly four and a half acres in size and doubled the area of the practice ground. A few miles up the road, on the beautiful Lincolnshire Wolds, three times as much land could have been acquired for that price—but that was not where the golf club wanted it, and that is why it cost what it did. The club knew that there was a drainage problem on the new practice field, and in late 1994 a large drainage scheme was completed on half of the new practice area.

THE LADIES

The ladies' section continued to thrive in the 'nineties' under their captains: Marita Jordan, Avril Norton, Margaret Johns, Eileen Mowbray, Ruth Street, Chris Needham, and Frances Grant. They successfully organised their competitions, played adjacent clubs home and away, and twice a year gave the senior members a fright in their hard fought needle matches.

They had been given a good start to the decade when Alison Johns—the most successful golfer to come out of the Boston golf club—won the Lincolnshire Junior Girls Open Championship and the Ladies' County Championship in 1990: a tremendous feat of golf. She turned professional in the following year.

When the club decided to give their popular, long serving professional, Terry Squires a token of their esteem the Ladies decided to hold an Am Am competition (teams of four amateurs) to raise funds for his presentation, they were extremely successful and raised £400. It was so thoroughly enjoyed by all the participants that it was decided to make it an annual event to raise money for charity. It went from strength to strength as the sums raised demonstrate: £400, £1300, £1440, £1400, £2,070, £2,000 and the most recent held in 1995 under the captaincy of Chris Needham no less than £2,600. Various charities have benefited, including the MacMillan Nurses' Appeal, the Multiple Sclerosis Society, Leukaemia Research, the R.N.L.I. Fund, and

200.

latterly Hovenden House, a Cheshire Home,

The ladies' section put their imprint on the club in all sorts of ways. As might be expected with Boston on the edge of the world famous South Holland bulb and flower growing area— of which its neighbour Spalding is the centre— the Boston ladies' section have a large number of flower arranging events and the lounge is decorated all through the summer months with beautiful arrangements of fresh flowers, and in the winter with artistic displays of dried flowers.

THE LADIES ENFRANCHISED

The club, recognising at long last the sterling contribution of the ladies' section, rewarded them at the 1992 AGM by deciding that 'the lady members be given the vote'. From henceforth they could cast their votes at the AGM, and be counted as legally, to use an appropriate phrase, on a par with the men. Unlike some clubs throughout the country the Boston club has always had a first class rapport with the ladies' section. They have however had very little say in the running of the club except that for the last few years the ladies' captain and vice-captain could attend the management committee meetings.

This arrangement appeared to suit most lady members. They had their own committee meetings which were lively and enjoyable. They took an active part in the club activities, particularly on the social side, and they paid annual subscriptions reduced by around 12% despite the fact that many of the ladies play a great deal more golf than many male members. Indeed by 1993 the only restriction they had was that they were not free to use the course on Sunday mornings, because it was felt, rightly or wrongly, that they could play more freely most of the week, whereas the men, tied up with their occupations, had a fairer right to the use of the course on Sunday mornings. From 1992 however the ladies could voice their objections at the AGM to this or any other club matter with which they disagreed. They continued with their programme of matches with the adjacent clubs in the county and in 1994 a team comprising Chris Means, Jane Bratley, Marita Jordan, Francis Grant, Margaret Hardy, Rita Knaggs, Avril Norton and Chris Needham won the county ladies' league. This was an exceptionally fine performance given the

51.

52.

For caption details see opposite page

fierce competition for this major tournament and a first time win for Boston ladies.

In May 1995 a team comprising: Chris Needham, Chris Means, Sophie Hunter, Marita Jordan and Francis Grant won the county ladies' Silver Championship Shield at Seacroft golf course.

What Major Oliver Cooper, who it will be recalled was of the opinion that, 'once the ladies had played nine holes they did not want to go round any more,' would have made of many of the current Boston ladies is something to imagine. Many think nothing of a round in the morning and then, after a pleasant lunch, another in the afternoon.

The ladies committee for 1995/6 was: president Mrs Kath Bradley; captain Mrs Frances Grant; vice-captain Miss Jane Bratley; secretary Mrs Ruth Street; treasurer Mrs Margaret Winn; competition secretary Mrs Chris Needham; handicap secretary Mrs Gill Reynolds; and the committee members: Mrs Josephine Grant, Mrs Margaret Johns, Mrs Barbara Moor, Mrs Pat Usher, Mrs June Frankish, and Mrs Rita Taylor.

1994 had also seen further improvements to the course. The areas around the clubhouse and the approach over the drain bridges were satisfactory but rather dull. Rockeries were therefore constructed in strategic areas, planted up with a selection of Alpines, heathers and other dwarf flowering plants and the beds surrounded with pinky-white magnesium limestone rocks, thus adding greatly to the attractiveness of the clubhouse surrounds. A major programme involving the construction of raised and sculptured tees and pathways around the course, made good progress over the latter half of the year. This was reflected in the greatly increased cost of the course management

---

OPPOSITE PAGE:

Top: 51.—In 1994 the Boston Ladies won the County Ladies' League.
Top from L. - Chris Means, Jane Bratley, Marita Jordan, Fran Grant, Margaret Hardy.
Bottom from L. - Rita Knaggs, Ruth Street (Captain), Chris Needham, Avril Norton.

— — — — —

Bottom: 52.— In 1995 a Boston Ladies' Team won the County Ladies
Silver Championship Shield. Held at Seacroft Golf Club
From L. - Seacroft (Captain) Rosemary Childs, Boston (Captain) Chris Needham,
Frances Grant, Sophie Hunter, Chris Means, Marita Jordan,
County (Captain) Anne Baseley.

53. Past and present Lady Presidents: L. to R. Jessie Isaac, Mary Allen,
Trot Weightman, Jane Daker, Nora Royle, Jane Coney.

of £39,120 in the 1995 accounts much of which could really be regarded as additional capital investment. Tees three, four, five, six, and eighteen were completely relaid by a firm specialising in this work. Irrigation points were provided on them at a total cost of approximately £20,000.

THE JUNIORS

There is a continual flow coming forward each year of young talented players showing great promise. A contemporary of Nick Hiom and Scott Emery, Jeremy Wallhead, another promising young player, has left recently to take up a golfing assistant's post in the county. The day however has gone when all a young professional had to do was to hit a golf ball exceedingly well: nowadays they have to pass written examinations to obtain their professional certificate. We wish him well. The mind boggles at the thought of some of the golfing greats being lost to the game because of the shortage of a little bit of paper. Sophie Hunter is making great progress at the game. She played for the County

Ladies first team in 1996 and has aspirations to make golf her career. The Boston Junior Championship in the 'nineties' was won by N Hiom, J Bradley, N Atterby, N Atterby, J Atterby and B Hinson, B. Simpson.

All of these young players have benefited from the county and national organising of the game for the promising junior players. The English Golf Union for the boys, and the Ladies' English Golf Union for the girls, have a well organised programme of inter-county events where individuals and teams from clubs compete for a range of cups and trophies. At club level the juniors are managed by keen players with a special interest in the juniors. Often they are the parents of keen and promising youngsters, as in the case of Boston where, amongst others, Rex Wallhead, Ron Green, Mike Carson, Margaret Johns, Vic Hunter, Malcolm and Pat Hyde, and more recently Allan Sharpe, have put in a great deal of time and effort organising matches and carting juniors all over the country. Working with the Golf Foundation— the national body for the development of junior golf—they have assisted promising Boston junior golfers to develop.

The Golf Unions have been fortunate to have had a number of extremely keen individuals like Les Pepper, chairman of the Midland Junior Delegation, who has spent thirty years in the service of the juniors, Pat Chatterton, Anne Baseley, Ann Shaw and many others all of whom have been rewarded for their efforts by the success of players like Mark James, Andrew Hare, Alison Johns and Helen Dobson. One of their most recent successes has been Jim Payne, who, if he overcomes his back problems, could be the greatest of them all. It is safe to say that any junior of promise will be spotted and receive every encouragement to fulfil their potential. With special coaching from professionals, Graham Bradley at Blankney and Eric Sharpe at Kenwick Park, they have opportunities for advancement which would have delighted Harry Vardon, J H Taylor and other great golfers of past generations who had special interest in promoting the development of the game.

THE GENTLEMEN IN THE 1990s

The club captains in the early 1990s were P Lawton, T Dawson, P Jordan, R Greswell, R Atterby, A Binks, and N Gleason.

Whilst the men did not have the good fortune to produce a

golfer of the calibre of Alison Johns the standard of the golf continued to improve, with each year a succession of good young players arriving to frustrate the ambitions of the older members in the quest for honours. The club championship winners of the 1990s were: C Hill, C Hill, N Hiom, J Woodcock, J Woodcock, J Woodcock, N. Timby.

Jeremy Woodcock is one of the finest golfers to play at Cowbridge. He has won honours at all levels. He has played for the county on several occasions and will doubtlessly continue to do so for many years.

He was captain of the 'A' team in 1993 and 1994. They did not have the success of the 'B' team however whom Hugh Pinner, a fierce competitor excelling at billiards as well as golf, led to victory in their league in 1991, 1992, and 1993. Included amongst them were B Draper, C Ashton, M Thompson, L Bonner, P Creek,

CLUB PHOTOGRAPH

54. Boston gentlemen's 'B' Team—League winners in 1993.
Standing from L.—Charlie Edwards, Brian Draper, Terry Dawson, Malcolm Hyde, Carl Ashton,
Peter Creek, Rex Wallhead, Jonathan King, Les Bonner, Bob Don-Duncan, Colin Woodcock.
Seated from L. Alan Moor, Don Smith, Hugh Pinner ('B' Team Captain),
Dick Greswell (Club Captain), Gary Willis, Vic Hunter.

206.

I McDonald, J MacDonald, D Edwards, K Vickers, B Newark, D Limb, M Couture, J Whitehead, and H Pinner (captain). Carl Ashton took over the captaincy of the 'A' team and in 1995 they won the East Lincolnshire league. In 1994 a team consisting of David Dawson, Neil Timby and Steve Barrell won the final of the National Toyota Championship at Santa Ponca in Majorca. Two of the most promising younger players, Nick Hiom and Scott Emery, are at present, in 1996, assistants to Terry Squires and who knows what they might achieve under his expert eye.

They have had ample encouragement from Terry who in 1994, 1995 and 1996 had excelled in the senior's professional European tour and won a considerable amount of prize money.

He also led teams of Boston players in Pro/Am competitions including the Notts PGA in Spain in 1990 and 1993.

THE SENIORS

From their start up in 1978 the 'Veterans' have steadily gone from strength to strength. From 1990 their captains have been Roy Sales, Arthur Whittaker, Les Eller, and George Kent.

A sign of the increasing youthfulness of the population in general is the change in attitude of the older golfers. In 1900 anyone fortunate enough to be still around at the age of 60, felt he had almost reached his alloted span and was often looking for the nearest rocking chair. Not so today, where any one about to join Boston seniors had better be prepared to get around the course rather more speedily than many of the younger players. They used to call themselves 'The Veterans', but rightly took umbrage at this connotation of old age. The way medical science is developing, in another hundred years they could well be in line for a rename to something like 'Mature Juniors'.

Today the seniors have a comprehensive organisation of club, inter-club, and open days, giving them the opportunities to spend most of their time playing at courses all over the county, if they so wish. In most clubs they have the use of the course for one morning during the week where, like Boston, they draw numbers from a hat to form random threesomes. This has the great advantage that one can have a delightful chat in between shots, with a range of interesting characters including fighter pilots, diplomats, farmers, plumbers and experts in almost any human activity one can think of. This is especially invaluable when one's game has temporarily disappeared. The seniors appear to be able to acquire an inexhaustible supply of 'characters' and the indigenous fenmen require to be watched carefully. Do not for a moment think you can join their ranks and have a pleasant stress free game of non-competitive golf. On the contrary the older they are the more ferociously keen they become to win. In many ways they are a unique group of men who straddle two centuries with their experiences. Ernest Wilson for example will beguile you with tales of his youth when he was up at the crack of dawn ready to harness his pair of Shires and spend all day ploughing. He can recall his first tractors, or lifting sugar beet by hand and travelling to get a cart load of water for the yarded bullocks. Whilst rattling on with all his fascinating tales, he is sinking putts from all over the green.

The seniors have the excellent arrangement of deducting a shot from one's handicap when one wins the weekly competition thus giving more of their group the opportunity to win a golf ball. One gets used to the idea of marking someone's card with a club handicap of thirty and a Senior's of five or thereabouts. They get additional shots added to their handicaps for all sorts of mysterious reasons. It is a chastening experience playing against a youthful octogenerian such as the inimitable Sid Ayliffe when on getting the occasional birdie he unblushingly claims four Stapleford points. The seniors have gained a certain amount of wiliness in their passage through life. Recently Roy Sales, an inhabitant of Swineshead, a village renowned for the psychological perception of its inhabitants, was heard to say to a senior golfer who was showing some reluctance to partake in the match against the ladies, 'I should play if I were you Jim. It might be your last chance.'

The ladies also have a thriving senior section and the Lincolnshire Veteran Ladies Golf Association organise a list of fixtures with a major spring and autumn meeting, an annual AGM, a luncheon, and matches between the Lincolnshire team and adjacent counties.

THE RABBITS

The 'nineties' have seen the Rabbit section of the Boston golf club go from strength to strength. From their first meeting in

208.

September 1962 they had made steady progress enlarging their membership and range of competitions and activities. There is no common definition of the term 'Rabbit'. Braid, Vardon, and Hagan would probably not have been familiar with the term, although Hagan might well bave come into the category on occasions, on the morning after the night before. It is widely accepted that players with a handicap of seventeen or less are golfers, whilst those over that figure magically change to bunnies. However one defines the term, it is indisputable that the great majority of golfers properly come into the latter category. We must except the ladies however, who operate a metallic system of classification. The Boston Rabbits have been fortunate to have had a succession of first class captains since the start up in 1962. Latterly these have included: R Atterby, R Todd, J Marshall, P Langham, N Smith, T Tomblin, G Kent, T Norton, A Moore, D Hodgson, T Carr, and C Martin. They play for their own trophies including the Hospital Cup, the Cravnic Cup and the Horry Cup amongst others. They have their own Open day and play a comprehensive programme of inter-club matches all over the county.

To attempt to win any of their trophies is a most unnerving experience, since there are always a goodly number of rapidly improving entrants, playing off high handicaps and quite capable of coming in with a net sixty-two or equally miraculous score. This of course wreaks severe damage on the nervous systems of the runners-up, confident of success having played the round of their lives. and then possibly failing even to get into the lower levels of the prize list.

In 1993 the club stewards, John and Heather Dopierala, left for greener pastures after their excellent tenure and their successors, Rex and Mary Baxter, settled into their new posts. By coincidence they had previously been stewards at the Boston Aero Club which has as their clubroom the old Pudding Pie clubhouse. It was sold off after the 1949 flood to the Boston Aero Club and is now resplendent in all its glory on the western edge of Boston.

VAT

Members have been charged VAT on their annual subscriptions for many years and there was much delight when it was announced that it had been decided that this deduction broke tax rules and would be refunded.

Adrian Reynolds, chairman of the finance committee, at the AGM in 1994 explained the background and that the club proposed to deduct the overpayment by members from their annual subsriptions due for the 1995/1996 season.

This was a decision which later would cause much heartache to the committee who saw other clubs persuading the members to allow this sum to be re-used by their clubs for course improvements. Amongst these were Spalding, Burghley Park, and Woodhall Spa.

1995

The club continued to push on with course and clubhouse improvements. Paths were laid down to improve the access to several tees and the first and second greens completly rebuilt by specialist contractors who laid down layers of graded stone chippings underneath the putting surfaces. This was a high cost operation of over £12,000 a green, but should provide free draining surfaces giving several extra golfing days throughout the year on the completion of the programme. In the last month of the year a start was made to cover over the entrance to the ladies' and gentlemen's changing rooms.

THE AGM

During the history of the club, there have been several AGM's which stood out from the remainder. Generally most of these events have been rather dull affairs. The 1995 AGM held on 12 October 1995 in the lounge and dining room of Boston golf club turned out to be one that would be vividly remembered for many years.

In the run up to the meeting there did not appear to be any circumstance that would make it special. There had been no catastrophe such as the mud bath at Pudding Pie or the threatened take over by the Sibsey golf club to make the committee apprehensive. Over the recent years there had been steady improvements made to the course. A block of eighteen acres had been purchased and successfully integrated into the layout to increase the SSS from sixty-eight to seventy-one, making it safer for the players and putting it on a par with the top 25% of the clubs in the county. A practice ground had been added to the course and further improved with the purchase of an adjacent field. Although not the perfect shape it was still much better than that provided by most clubs in the county.

Brian Skinner, the chairman of the management committee, to whom the club owed a considerable debt of gratitude for his share in accomplishing these improvements, could feel particularly happy. He provided in the papers circulated for the AGM a further list of improvements that would be carried out in the near future with a probable cost of £100,000. However £63,000 for the land to extend the course and the additional money required to integrate it into the eighteen holes, had worried many members. The further purchases of £24,000 and £27,000 to provide the large practice ground had added to their concerns

These improvements had necessarily involved a considerable amount of course construction work and mountains of soil and disturbed fairways were dotted over the course. The work had been done in a manner that did not significantly affect play, but there was a certain amount of unsightliness in these areas. In 1995 there had been a series of club burglaries that unnerved some members and there was a sudden unexpected notice informing players that the club lockers were to be removed and not replaced, which annoyed the minority group who would henceforth have to cart their clubs home between games. Murmers about lack of consultation and high handedness began to be heard on the 19th green.

When the members received the notice of the forthcoming AGM it contained the proposal from the committee to remove the ladies', seniors' and rabbits' captains as ex-officio members of the committee. Notwithstanding that included in the proposals was a promise to include representation for these groups, alarm was raised amongst many members about the possibility of loss of power in the management of the club. Members of these groups started to canvas other members to attend the AGM to fight these proposals.

The fears of many members were that the club was running up unnecessary debts. The proposed increases in the annual subscription of around 15% and removing the discount for husband/wife membership would combine to raise many subscriptions by around 30%.

The annual accounts, which are always attached to the AGM literature, did not help to allay members' worries. They are written for tax purposes and are largely incomprehensible to most members. For example, there is no simple way of ascertaining the club's indebtedness.

There was a large turn out at the AGM. Bob Barclay took the chair. He opened the proceedings in a brisk, confident manner, introducing the chairmen of the individual sub-committees to present their reports. It was soon obvious that there were many aspects of the club management that did not please the members as they put their hard-hitting questions from the floor. The proposal to re-organise the committee membership was quickly defeated. The list of course improvements proposed by Brian Skinner, chairman of the management committee, came in for severe criticism and especially the vague proposal to build a bridge over the Cowbridge Drain at the seventh hole. Even the normally imperturable chairman began to wilt under the onslaught. The committee's recommendation to remove the discount for husband and wife membership was passed. The recommendation to raise the annual subscription by around 15% however came in for particularly heavy criticism.

There is no record of any other previous Boston golf club committee ever having their recommendations for the level of annual subscriptions rejected. On this occasion however the unthinkable occured and instead a motion to limit the increase to 5% was proposed and carried. Bob Barclay could not conceal his disappointment at this rebuff. Adrian Reynolds, the honorary treasurer, who had spent many hours calculating the subscription levels required to finance the running of the club and the many developments that had taken place and were being planned, was also visibly disturbed by the success of this proposal and vote. The meeting ended rather untidely amidst a plethora of proposals and counter-proposals which left many of those attending uncertain as to the results of some of the votes. The chairman and the sub-committtee chairmen were obviously extremely unhappy about the whole affair. Many saw it as virtually a vote of no confidence in their stewardship and were seriouly considering block resignations. Given a few days to assimilate the effects of the evening however they decided instead to hold an Extraordinary General Meeting in mid February when more information would be given to the members and further discussions of the propsals for changes to the annual subscriptions could take place. Brian Skinner, and Stewart Binks the outgoing captain, in the meantime tendered their resignation.

On reflection the principal problem had been largely caused by the not uncommon fault of breakdown in communication between the committee and the members. Had the committee made a better job of explaining the excellent improvements they had made and their management of the club finances, and given members more say in development proposals, the AGM would have been a more peaceful affair. Ray Bavin however spoke for many members at the AGM when he pointed out that Boston was traditionally a low wage area with many members on a fixed income. Their fears were that they could be priced out of golf if annual subscriptions rose continually at a much higher level than the rate of inflation.

1995 therefore ended on a rather disappointing note for the hard working committee members, who, despite some sins of omission, might reasonably have expected rather more appreciation for all their efforts from the club members.

The EGM

The Extraordinary General Meeting was held on the 22nd February in the Falkland Suite of the Conservative Club following complaints about the inadequacy of the golf club lounge for a very large meeting. It was an important meeting with the single item on the agenda consisting of a proposal to change the subscription increases decided on at the AGM.

The committee's proposal for an apporopriate 15% increase had been turned down by the members in favour of a 5% increase. The committee felt that this was insufficient for their requirements to manage the club and had called an EGM to get the members' approval for a 10% increase. Adrian Reynolds, the honorary treasurer, Richard Atterby, the new chairman of the management committee, and Don Smith the club secretary, had done their homework, and using carefully prepared charts and tables on an overhead projector they convinced the large gathering that their proposed 10% increase was justified. The motion was carried by a very large majority.

The whole affair of the rather unruly AGM and the following EGM has probably done more good than harm to the club. The committee have learnt that good communications of their plans, with reasons provided for the major charges, is necessary to keep their members happy. In turn the members have found out how difficult a business, managing a modern golf club has become and how much they will have to pay to keep up with their demands for a first class golf club with top rate amenities.

55. *The Boston Golf Club Committee 1996.*

Back Row: Adrian Reynolds (Hon. Treas.), Terry Dawson,
Peter Pearson (Chairman of Greens), Steve Kent, Terry Bacon.
Front Row: David Dawson, Don Smith (Secretary/Manager),
Bob Barclay (President), Noel Gleeson (Captain), John Swithinbank, Ted Eaglen.

HAS THE GOLF IMPROVED

The principal objective in golf is to go around the course in as few shots as one's skill permits. Looking back to the start up of the club in 1900 has the level of golf improved after taking into account the vastly improved clubs, balls and quality of the

214.

fairways and greens? If we look at a typical club competition—the Island Trophy, played on the new course on the 11th September 1994—we can compare the new scores with those common in the early days of the club. These are set out in greater detail in the original manuscript deposited with the club's records for the benefit of anyone wishing to carry out a more detailed analysis. This was a medal competition with a maximum handicap allowance of eighteen. Anyone off more than this, was only allowed eighteen shots. The scores are listed at Appendix D.

There was a field of sixty-eight competitors. The most striking aspect of this competition, compared to those at the start up of the club in the early part of the century, is the great increase in the size of the field. With a men's playing membership today of between 450 and 500 compared to around eighty, this of course is to be expected. The other major difference also to be expected is the lower gross and net scores of the modern golfer. The gutta-percha ball, the primitive clubs, the rougher greens and fairways compared to their modern-day equivalents, accounts for much of this improvement.

There was similarly a large difference between the professional scores at the beginning of the century compared to those of today. J H Taylor won the British Open in 1900 at St Andrews with 79, 77, 78, 75 for a total of 309, whilst nearly ninety years later Greg Norman won at Turnberry in 1986 with 74, 63, 74, 69 for a total of 280, an improvement of 29 shots, or 10% better than J H Taylor's score.

The Island Trophy scores are fairly typical of most club competition scores at the Boston club. They demonstrate how difficult and demanding the game of golf is. That of course is a major part of its attraction.

THE MEN'S HANDICAPS

If we look at the distribution of the Boston men's club handicaps in 1994 these were:

Handicap Range	No of Players	%
0 - 9	39	11
10 - 17	86	24
18 - 28	232	65

Two thirds of the men come into the 'rabbit' or eighteen and over handicap section. How do these theoretical handicaps compare to the scores actually shot in competitions? If we analyse the scores in the Island Trophy, we see that not many players score to their club handicap. This is of course as it should be. The difficulty of the game becomes even more obvious. The SSS for the Island Trophy was 71. Only six out of the field equalled or bettered that figure, with most of the competitors many strokes adrift of their handicaps. There were fifty-four competitors who played to an eighteen handicap of higher— 80% of those entering. Taking into account the fact that only around 15% of the men played, and that these were by and large the better players, it would appear that much more than 80% of members really come into the 'rabbit' category playing to eighteen or higher handicaps. Surprisingly many single figure handicappers— the cream of a golf club— when tested in competitions put in scores that put them comfortably into the 'Rabbit' clasification.

The improvement in the way the game is played is equally strikingly illustrated by the results of a recent Sunday morning medal competition at the Boston club when the leading net results were: D Baker – 67, F Scrupps – 67, G Bennett – 67, J Black – 67, D Hodgson – 67, G Tempest – 68, P Cooper – 68, L Dawson – 68, T Dawson – 68, C Edwards – 69, B Braseby – 69, and M Stanley – 69.

In the early 1900s the old Boston players were winning the monthly medals with nett 80s. How much of the difference is due to equipment, course conditions, and skill change?

THE LADIES' HANDICAPS

A comparison between the ladies scores at the beginning and the end of the century, is even more striking than those of the men. The Cheer Cup results played for in 1993 was as follows:

Miss L Dawson	100	30	70
Miss E Chester	94	20	74
Mrs M Atkins	102	26	76
Mrs J Cowan	101	25	76
Mrs M Johns	95	19	76
Mrs R Knaggs	93	17	76
Mrs R Street	96	20	76

Mrs A Whitehead	101	24	77
Mrs C Tointon	97	19	78
Mrs M Winn	111	33	78
Mrs M Smith	101	22	79
Mrs E Mowbrey	103	19	84
Mrs C Needham	102	15	84
Miss J Bratley	102	18	84
Mrs B Moor	114	29	85
Mrs K Coupland	119	32	87
Mrs C Sherriff	116	29	87

The SSS for the ladies card is 73. These scores resemble those of the men, in that only a small percentage played to their club handicap—in this instance only one player out of the field of seventeen.

The overall average was 79 net or six shots above handicap.

Again this suggests that the course is a severe challenge to the members. Compared however to the lady players of the 1900 era the scores are very much better. There are two likely reasons for this. Firstly the standard of ladies' golf has risen. They most probably work harder at the game today than did the early lady golfers, and this together with better golf balls, equipment, apparel, and of course better coaching, has dramatically improved their scoring.

The second probable reason is that their hadicaps appear to be more accurate than those of the early Boston ladies. In 1900 the Boston Ladies' golf club was not then a member of the English Ladies Golf Union, a further sixty years would elapse before this invitation would arrive. They did not therefore have the beady eyes of Miss Issette Pearson, and her formidable organisation, calculating an accurate SSS for their course, nor allocating an accurate personal handicap for the individual lady members.

The attitude of players to their club handicap merits a lengthy psychological analysis which no doubt in this analytical age will shortly be forthcoming. To suggest to many ten handicap players that they really come into the rabbit category is to risk severe retaliation.

On the other hand Miss Dolbey with her 163 playing off thirty for a net 133 in 1906 might well have been overjoyed at instantly gaining six or more shots.

These results are no reflection on the handicapping system since this is designed to reflect the best form of a golfer. Nor do these results necessarily suggest that golf courses should be designed to accomodate the 'rabbits' rather than the low handicap players. Golf after all has to be a challenge and golf committees are entitled to aim for a course that will stretch their members and attract visiting societies and individual golfers. In any event by strategic placement of front and back tees, it should be possible to keep everybody happy.

But where these figures are important, is that in a typical major club like Boston, with its very large capital value and a turnover fast approaching a quarter of a million pounds, future committees will inevitably be looking more closely at the commercial implications of running their clubs and will be using and analysing this and other sorts of data much more than did their predecessors. They will want to know what their customers, viz. their members, visiting societies and individuals prefer, in all aspects of course and club amenity, in order that they can supply these, keep them happy and run a successful business. They will also want to know the peak and off peak periods of their course usage so that they can make the best use of a very expensive acreage of real estate. They will try to make certain that there is no 'breakdown of communication' between committee and members.

A HIGHLY SUCCESSFUL BUSINESS

Despite the worries expressed at the 1995 AGM, the accounts for the year ending March 1995 illustrate just how large and successful a business Boston golf club has now become, compared to the restart in 1962. The capital worth of the club when Bryan Cooper purchased Aqueduct Farm, was just over a hundred pounds of cash in the bank account of The Boston Golf Club Co Ltd. By March 1995 however, just over thirty years later, the 'Tangible fixed assets' made up of the land, buildings and machinery, had jumped to no less than £252,256. The club owns around eighty acres freehold of the very best land in the country, together with twenty-two acres leasehold on the islands. Valuable as the land is for its straight agricultural potential, its value

218.

56. The 'Captain's Board' hanging in the dining room of the club.

G. S. Hopper '63-'64; A. P. Reynolds '65; F. A. J. Foster '66; H. J. Raven '67; J. W. Stanford '68; J. F. Leake '69;
B. R. Morris '70; S. C. Trigg '71; P. J. Pearson '72; R. E. Howes '73; J. E. Odling '74; H. Corns '75;
J. D. Mitchell '76; J. D. Barnes-Moss '77; R. A. Barclay '78; W. B. Johnson '79; C. F. J. Foster '80; R. W. Tinn '81;
D. W. Ogden '82; J. R. Atterby '83; F. C. Bramwell '84; D. E. Smith '85; C. R. Hardy '86; R. Needham '87;
B. Skinner '88; S. Swallow '89; P. Lawton '90; T. J. E. Dawson '91; P. J. Jordan '92; R. A. Greswell '93;
, J. Atterby '94; A. S. Binks '95; •••• D. E. Smith—Secretary; R. A. Barclay—President; T. R. Squires—Professional.

multiplies when the golf club aspect is taken into consideration. Its worth then would be measured in many hundreds of thousands of pounds. The purchase of the eighteen acre area alongside the railway for £63,000, and the two practice fields for £51,000, at the start of the decade, increased the total indebtedness including hire purchase debts to around £100,000 by the end of March 1995. No doubt the club may wish to carefully phase capital expenditure to allow the high cash flow to reduce this figure over the next few years. Meanwhile the current assets less liabilities are a healthy £191,546 and the reserves— the nett worth of the club— a much understated £111,907.

Employing ten staff and with a total wage bill approaching £100,000, the value of the club as a source of employment, as an addition to the quality of the local environment, and as a valuable leisure amenity to the town of Boston is considerable. Nothing in this life however remains static— the seventies and eighties witnessed a great increase in the number of clubs springing up around the country. Around Boston we now have new eighteen hole courses at South Kyme and Horncastle, and nine hole courses at Kirton Holme and Hubbert's Bridge. Sadly the nine hole course at Holbeach is no more, having vanished under a housing development. Who knows how all these new clubs will develop? Will they act as 'feeders to the Boston golf club', or will one of them improve and expand and challenge Boston's position as the premier club of the area? That will depend on how successful the Boston committees of the future fare, in providing the quality and amenities of course and clubhouse, at the price needed to satisfy and hold on to their 'customers'. The evidence to date is that they will, but one thing is quite certain: they must not take their future success and prosperity too much for granted.

CHAPTER THIRTEEN

GOLF CHANGES IN THE COUNTY

BOSTON HAS NOT BEEN THE ONLY CLUB in the county to have made solid progress in recent years. There have been many striking developments in several aspects of the game in the county over the last decade. The principal clubs have all continued to improve the facilities on offer to members and visitors

BELTON PARK GOLF CLUB

Belton Park golf club has made good use of the additional nine holes constructed in 1979 and it is always a delight to travel from Boston to their Open events. In 1984 Belton House and Park was sold to the National Trust, who immediately set about major repairs to the clubhouse. It requires some effort to remember that it was only in 1975 that the club were given permission to erect fences to keep cattle and sheep off the course— the club has made great strides since those days. The committee had settled down to managing their twenty seven hole course under the new owners— The National Trust— by the beginning of the 1990s. Designed in three loops of nine holes the new layout allowed several permutations of playing an eighteen hole round. The National Trust will provide as near as certain future guaranteed golf for the members.

This beautiful parkland golf course has long been a favourite of golfers throughout the county. With half of the course on a sandy, very free draining, soil and the other half on a good loam it has been playable when other heavier courses including Boston have been waterlogged. In very dry summers however the course, like Sleaford, burns badly. An ambitious programme has been planned over the next few years progressively to irrigate the fairways and a large lake will be constructed to provide the water required.

The club members voted for the VAT refund to be retained by the club for course improvements and this sum will help towards this most worthwhile improvement.

Let us hope the National Trust will continue to be benevolent landlords and not prove too greedy with future rent assessments.

One of the largest developments has taken place just up the road from Belton Park, at Belton Woods, where the De Vere Hotel Group now offers a wide range of hotel and leisure facilities, including the choice of three golf courses. Set in beautiful surroundings this has added greatly to the amenities of the area and deserves the success it is gaining.

LINCOLN

The three Lincoln clubs have improved member's facilities and are thriving; one could not envisage a more pleasant or interesting day out than a round of golf at any one of them followed by a sightseeing or shopping expedition around the lovely city of Lincoln.

In 1985 Lincoln Corporation opened a course at Millfield. A nine hole par three course it offers a useful training ground for aspiring golfers or for a family outing at moderate cost.

THE SPALDING GOLF CLUB

If the Boston golf club has made striking improvements to its course in the 1990s its neighbouring fen club at Spalding has kept pace with developments to their course.

Having built a modern golf clubhouse in 1984 for around £100,000 they decided to enlarge the lounge and changing rooms and this work was carried out in 1993. They then turned what might have been the disaster of the loss of a significant area of the course with the building of the new A16 trunk road into a triumph with the splendid integration of a thirty-three acre block to replace the area lost.

The planning and execution of this work, which involved excavating and landscaping a large lake and constructing nine new or revised holes, was a monumental task. The credit for its success was due to the hard work and planning skills of John Spencer the club professional, Tony Ward the head greenkeeper, Joe Price the then club steward, and the greens' staff. Messrs Overton kindly loaned a large scraper and equally large digger. For several weeks these machines and the Spaldng staff worked like demons transforming the flat fenland into a beautifully landscaped golf course. It has now been laid out to become one of the most attractive courses in the county.

222.

The early '90s were however not all cakes and ale for the committee. Like Boston, some of the members began to feel that the committee was becoming rather extravagent and out of touch with the members. The rise into indebtedness of the club gave many cause for concern.

An Extra Ordinary General Meeting was held in June 1994 when questions regarding the management of the VAT reimbursement and the future plans and developments of the course were thoroughly discussed. This has 'cleared the air' and committee and members can now look forward to enjoying their golf at a modest cost on a most pleasant course.

BURGHLEY PARK AND SLEAFORD

Burghley Park and Sleaford also continue to thrive. They have developed their courses to the stage where it is difficult to see where any future improvements can take place, but doubtlessly their management committees will try hard to disprove this.

THE BLANKNEY GOLF CLUB

Another club which witnessed great changes in the early 1990's was the Blankney golf club situated on the Jurassic limestone heath, halfway between Lincoln and Sleaford on the beautiful and historic Blankney estate.

Every golfer has his favourite golf course or courses. For my choice the two which have given me greatest pleasure and enjoyment to play over are Hawkstone Park— the north Shropshire course where Sandy Lyle learned his trade— and the Blankney golf course. English parkland golf courses, generally constructed on large estates, include many of the most beautiful in the country and many have fascinating histories: None more so than Blankney. The club house, lounge and changing rooms, situated in the village of Blankney, were extensively renovated in the early 1990s whilst retaining the attractive original exterior. All the village houses and buildings have most evidently been planned and constructed by a great estate. For half a century Harry Chaplain, Viscount Chaplain of St Oswald's, Blankney, was the Lord of the Manor. Member of Parliament for thirty-eight years, sitting in cabinet as Chancellor of the Duchy of Lancaster and later as the President of the Minister of Agriculture, he still found time to indulge in his great loves of hunting and racing. Master and owner of the Blankney Hunt for much of his life, he and his friends hunted over the limestone heath, frightening the life out of a large number of foxes, but no doubt to the great relief of the local rabbit and hen populations. His exploits on the turf were legendary. He astonished the racing world by purchasing two colts for the colossal sum of 11,000 guineas in 1865. His perserverence eventually paid off when he purchased for 1,000 guineas a colt he named 'Hermit'. This was to win for him the Blue Riband of the Turf— the Derby— on 22 May 1867. This horse did part of its training on the site of the present golf course. There is a stranger than fiction story connected with his Derby win. In 1864 the arrangements for his marriage to one of the reigning beauties of the 'Season', Lady Florence Paget, were well advanced, when, a few days before the ceremony, she eloped with the Marquis of Hastings— a rather disreputable young noble of the period. A heavy gambler on the Turf, Hastings had very large bets on the 1867 Derby and, when Hermit won, he confessed to having lost £120,000— worth many millions of pounds at today's values. This ruined him,

Alas Harry Chaplain's unstinting hospitality, his heavy costs incurred in his hunting and racing life and exacerbated by the heavy expenses of fighting parliamentary elections, all combined to run him also into heavy debt. He was obliged to sell the Blankney Estate in 1897 to the Earl of Londesborough. Fortunately for local residents of the area who were interested in the new sport of golf, the Earl had also taken up the game. He laid out the first golf course at Blankney around 1900.

Shortly after the end of the Second World War the Londesborough family sold the estate to the present owners— the Parker family— who were large and successful farmers. The new owners were also keen to assist the Blankney golfers and have given them every assistance to improve the course, putting in a great deal of capital to do so. In 1992, the Blankney Estates Ltd— the Parker family business— offered to take over the financial and administrative management of the club. There was a 98% vote by the members to agree to this proposal. The golf club, however, would continue to operate and administer all golfing matters through the management committee. It was also agreed to reduce

224.

membership to 600 by natural wastage. The Blankney Estates also offered to maintain subscription rates at the present level with adjustments for inflation, for a five year period. The current programme of course improvements, involving upgrading of most of the holes under the guidance of Cameron Sinclair, a golf architect, continues.

This change of management has worked admirably to date with the Blankney Estates contributing much capital to improve the club and proving helpful and considerate landlords. The Blankney golf club is a jewel amongst Lincolnshire clubs with its beautiful course and its memorable and historic background. Let us hope it continues to serve the interests of the Blankney golfers into the indefinite future. It would be tragic if it were ever to encounter the same fate as the old Sibsey club.

KENWICK PARK GOLF CLUB

In 1992 a new golf club was started up in the beautiful wolds, two miles south of Louth. The development company behind this venture used an entirely new concept in its financing and management to any other club in the county. It was laid out at Kenwick Estate and 190 acres of this rolling parkland was used to construct a major eighteen hole course designed by golf architects and possessing a large range of amenities, including an elegant and attractive club house, a large purpose built practice ground, and a handsomely stocked 'pro shop' with modern teaching facilities.

Kenwick Park golf club allowed members to own a financial share of the club by purchasing 'units' each consisting of 4,000 X £1 nominal value ordinary shares and one debenture of £500 capital value sold at full value. The first block of 200 units was thus sold at an offer price of £4,500 per unit. With only 650 units offered for sale, playing membership is restricted and the bulk of these were taken up by 1996, but the price, driven by demand and inflation, had then risen to £7,000 a unit. These units will change in value with demand, and can now be sold on the open market if the owners, for example, wish to move from the area, or give up golf.

Having purchased a unit the owner then has the choice of a range of different types of membership. Most have opted for the full seven day annual subscription of £558 inclusive for 1996.

By purchasing a unit the shareholder has a stake in what is likely to become an increasingly valuable asset with access to a high quality golf club with a full range of attractive amenities.

The club belongs to its members, who exercise full control through a board of directors elected by its shareholders.

This is an exciting new development for golf in Lincolnshire and great interest is being taken in its progress.

THE LIMESTONE GOLF COURSES.

The large area of the county on the Lincolnshire Heath and Wolds provides ideal free-drainage and picturesque countryside for the construction of first class golf courses.

There is a life enhancing quality about limestone country, the beautiful white rocks that mingle with the rich brown soil give the overlying grassland an attractive greenness. This quality is missing from the dour black Millsone Gritsoils of the Pennines and the heavier soils of the Midlands boulder clay deposits.

In 1925 the Market Rasen club started up and has gone from strength to strength. Today it offers a first class test of golf in beautiful surroundings. Its SSS of 69 illustrates that it is not necessary to be 71 or 72 to test the skill of the golfer. The first hole, with its daunting carry for the men over some very rough 'rough' is the start of an exhilarating day for visiting golfers.

Louth golf club, dating from 1965, with an SSS of 71 and 6,477 yards long, has developed into a good test of golf amongst the rolling limestone wolds. With a fine club house and dining room it also has the added attraction of facilities for squash. Just up the road is the interesting old market town of Louth built round the magnificent late Gothic church of St James, whose spire dominates the skyline.

Horncastle golf club dates from 1990 and is situated not far from the charming small Wolds town of Horncastle. In addition to offering modestly priced golf on its 5,782 yard SSS 70, golf course, it has a first class lounge, fishing facilities on its well stocked lakes, and a six hole par three mini golf course. In conjunction with the Admiral Rodney Hotel in Horncastle it offers golfing and leisure breaks for golfers and their families.

THE SEA-SIDE LINKS COURSES.

Seacroft, North Shore, and Sandilands have all survived and are thriving. Seacroft is rightly regarded today as one of the best 'Links' courses in the country and is regularly host to major golfing events. Helen Dobson, one of our best ever young lady golfers, who learnt her game at Seacroft, went on to win most of the prestigious amateur competitions in the country. She turned professional, and is now working hard to establish golfing fame and fortune on the international circuit.

North Shore owned by Mr Robin Mitchell has illustrated the difficulties private ownership can provide for its members. He is of course entitled to do almost what he pleases with his course subject to planning or other restrictions for any developments he might consider. A range of alternative contracts have been offered to members varying from an orthodox annual subscription plus joining fee, down to a 'Pay and Play' contract. With the course providing a pleasant mix of links and parkland golf and with excellent adjacent hotel faciliities it is popular with its members and with the large number of holiday golfers attracted to its amenities.

Sandilands and the Grange and Links Hotel, offer good links golf at reasonable prices. It also is highly popular as a golfing holiday centre. Jim Payne, who has recently burst into the top ranks of professional golf, learnt his game here and holds the amateur course record of 66.

These three courses make Skegness a mecca for 'links' golf enthusiasts and add to the reputation of Lincolnshire as a top golfing county.

SOUTH KYME GOLF CLUB

At the start of the 1990s an eighteen hole golf course opened at South Kyme, ten miles west of Boston. Laid out on a hundred and forty acres of flat fen land previously farmed by the owner, Mr E Maplethorpe, the course is ideal for beginners and yet is sufficiently long— 6,597 yards off the white tees—to provide a challenge for experienced golfers. Thousands of trees have been planted and with three well placed but picturesque water hazards the course scenery is improving yearly.

There is a pleasant club house, a practice ground, and the resident golf professional, Peter Chamberlain, provides lessons for all grades of golfers.

The 1996 joining fee was £100 and the annual subscription £268 inclusive. With mid-week green fees of £10 for eighteen holes and £5 for nine holes, South Kyme offers good golfing facilities at reasonable cost.

NINE HOLE COURSES

There has been a striking number of nine hole courses constructed all over the county in the last decade, and time will tell as to whether these will stay as they are—a simple and cheap way of giving an increasing number of people the opportunity to start playing the game—or will some grow and challenge the existing clubs?

Two such courses have been built nearby.

KIRTON HOLME GOLF CLUB

In 1992 Kirton Holme golf club opened as a nine hole course owned and run by Taina and David Welberry. A family run concern the work of establishing the course was largely carried out by the owners and friends With a target membership of 350 it now has a comfortable club house offering drinks and light meals.

In 1993 it was affiliated to the Golf Union allowing it to issue official handicaps. With a yardage of 5,768 yards it offers a good game of golf to low and high handicap players.

The course has been steadily improved over the years and is now well established and the tree planting programme continues apace.

In 1996, with a low joining fee of £20 and an annual membership of £180, with low daily and green fees and an attractive associate membership scheme it brings golf within the reach of most families. It also provides a first class training ground for golfers who might wish to move on to a large course. With the cost af a day's golf at major clubs becoming higher and higher, clubs like Kirton Holme play a valuable role in providing golf for a wide range of incomes and abilities.

Boston West Club

In 1995 another nine hole course opened four miles west of Boston. Like Kirton Holme the land had been farmed and the owners, Richard and Josephine Grant, had golf club architect Michael Zara design this steadily improving course. Off the back tees it measures 6,346 yards when doubled up to an eighteen hole round. An attractive club house has been constructed where meals and drinks are available. There is also a twenty-bay driving range. Already 15,000 trees have been planted. A very well equipped sports shop is run by an independent company, 'Discount Pro Shop'. There are four lakes on the course and it is an interesting and challenging test of golf.

Clearly this is a course which may one day, at the present rate of progress, challenge Boston golf club for its premier position in the area. Whether it does expand to a full eighteen hole course will depend on future economics. It will certainly keep the Boston golf club committee 'on its toes'.

Green fees are at present £5.50 mid-week and £6.50 at the weekend for nine holes.

Joining fees in the region of £117.50 and subscriptions around £235 including VAT are very good value for money given the facilities available.

If Boston does not in the next century produce some world class golfers it will certainly not be the fault of the golf managers in the area.

The E. G. U. Woodhall Spa Development

In 1994 the English Golf Union—the controlling body for amateur golf in Britain—announced ambitious plans for an £8M. golf training centre in Woodhall Spa. The plan was to purchase Woodhall Spa Golf Club—high up the list of the best 100 golf courses in the world—along with adjoining land and develop it into a thirty-six hole National Centre for the men's amateur game in Britain. In addition to constructing a second eighteen hole course, there would be indoor and outdoor training areas, conference facilities, and new offices for the E.G.U.

The Union chose Woodhall Spa after a long study of all the possibilities. The idea had the blessing of Neil Hotchkin, the owner of the Woodhall Spa course and a past president and long time adherent of the aims and philosophy of the English Golf Union.

This work is well under way and will give a tremendous boost to Lincolnshire as a centre for British golf.

The £8M. would be financed partly from the cash reserves of the Union and the remainder by a loan from the Union's bankers. There would be an increase in the per capita levy on affiliated golfers lifting this from £1 to £3 from 1996 onwards allowing the loan to be repaid over ten years.

Lincolnshire golfers especially should obtain great benefit from the training facilities right on their doorstep.

57. The new Headquarters of the English Golf Union at Woodhall Spa.

THE LINCOLNSHIRE UNION OF GOLF CLUBS

The tremendous growth in the popularity of golf in the county is strikingly illustrated in the report of the ninety-seventh annual meeting of the L.U.G.C. convened at the beginning of 1996 at Woodhall Spa. This can be clearly seen if we compare it to the first A.G.M. held in 1900 at the Albion Hotel in Lincoln. Then there was a handful of clubs representing a thousand members: by 1996 there were representatives from forty-seven clubs with a membership of 17,500 golfers. A further six clubs had been affiliated during 1995. These were Humberston County club,

Southview, Pottergate, Humberston Park, Boston West, and Thorney Lakes.

The county first team had had a disasterous year in 1995 losing seven matches and winning one. Paul Streeter (Sleaford) played for the English team and won the County Match Play Championship whilst James Crampton (Spalding) won the Berkhamstead Trophy and retained the County Championship for the third consecutive year. Mr C. Woodcock (Blankney) was elected president and the county captain for 1996/7 will be D. Price (Belton Park).

FIRST CLASS GOLF IN LINCOLNSHIRE

Lincolnshire is now one of the best counties in Britain for golf facilites. The Royal and Ancient *Golfer's Handbook* 1995 lists twenty-eight courses in the county covering a very wide range of golf club settings. These vary from the majestic parkland courses of Blankney and Belton, the beautiful limestone settings of Market Rasen and Louth, the heathlands of Woodhall Spa and Lincoln, the historic fenland courses of Boston and Spalding, to the magnificent sea-side links courses of Seacroft and North Shore.

Furthermore the cost of Lincolnshire golfing is modest compared to many parts of the country with many clubs having arrangments with adjacent hotels to provide reasonably priced golfing holidays.

The Boston golf club committee will no doubt plan to remain in the top echelon of clubs in the county. They will, like all the other clubs, have to work hard to maintain the position as the younger clubs continue to expand and improve.

231.

Appendix A

Club Captains

Ladies		Gentlemen	
1900	Mrs A. Black	1900-1901	F. P. Curtis
1901	Mrs A. Black	1901-1902	F. P. Curtis
1902	Mrs A. Black	1902-1903	F. P. Curtis
1903 - 1919	NOT KNOWN	1903-1907	Rev. H. Garvey
		1908-1911	NOT KNOWN
		1912-1914	W. Kitwood
		1915-1919	R. Bottomley
1920-1922	Mrs MacTaggart	1920-1924	Maj. O. Cooper
1923	Mrs S. Cheavin		
1924	Mrs O. Cooper		
1925	Mrs H. Mawson	1925-1927	A. Parry
1926	Mrs. A Parry		
1927	Mrs P. Arch		
1928-1930	Mrs W. Kitwood	1928	W. Cheer
1931-1933	Miss B. Francis	1929	W. Cheer
1934	Mrs J. Bowman	1930	T. Tyson
1935	Mrs W. Hamer	1931-1933	R. Osmond
		1934	P. Ostler
1936	Mrs P. Arch	1935-1937	W. Horry
1937-1949	NOT KNOWN	1938	S. Margerson
		1939	R. Reynolds
		1940-1941	J. Arch
		1942-1945	L. Robinson
		1946	C. Dawson
		1947-1949	G. Buchner

1949 — NO COURSE — 1962

Ladies		Gentlemen	
1963	Mrs J. Coney	1963	G. S. Hopper
1964	Mrs J. Coney	1964	G. S. Hopper
1965	Mrs F. Allen	1965	A. P. Reynolds
1966	Mrs. K. Buchner	1966	F. A. Foster
1967	Mrs M. Allen	1967	H. J. Raven
1968	Mrs E. Cheshire	1968	J. W. Stanford
1969	Mrs J. Daker	1969	J. F. Leake
1970	Miss T. Weightman	1970	B. R. Morris

	LADIES		GENTLEMEN
1971	Mrs D Skinner	1971	S. C. Trigg
1972	Mrs F. Reynolds	1972	P. J. Pearson
1973	Mrs H. La Touche	1973	R. E. Howes
1974	Mrs K. Bradley	1974	J. E. Odling
1975	Mrs E. Cott	1975	H. Corns
1976	Mrs N. Royle	1076	J. D. Mitchell
1977	Mrs J. Reynolds	1977	J. D. Barnes-Moss
1978	Mrs H. Greswell	1978	R. A. Barclay
1979	Mrs M. Smith	1979	W. B. Johnson
1980	Mrs G. Reynolds	1980	C. F. Foster
1981	Mrs M. Hardy	1981	R. W. Tinn
1982	Mrs B. Holgate	1982	D. W. Ogden
1983	Mrs M. Benjamin	1983	J. R. Atterby
1984	Mrs A. Skinner	1984	F. C. Bramwell
1985	Mrs M. Davies	1985	D. E. Smith
1986	Mrs A. Dawson	1986	C. R. Hardy
1987	Mrs F. Bramwell	1987	R. Needham
1988	Mrs M. Hearth	1988	B. Skinner
1989	Mrs C. Means	1989	S. Swallow
1990	Mrs M. Jordan	1990	P. Lawton
1991	Mrs A. Norton	1991	T. J. Dawson
1992	Mrs M. Johns	1992	P. J. Jordan
1993	Mrs E. Mowbrey	1993	R. A. Greswell
1994	Mrs R. Street	1994	R. J. Atterby
1995	Mrs C. Needham	1995	A. S. Binks

APPENDIX B

CLUB PRESIDENTS

LADIES		GENTLEMEN	
1900-1919	None or Not Known	1900-1914	W. Garfitt, Esq., M.P.
1920-1923	Lady Weighall	1915-1920	NOT KNOWN
1924-1928	Mrs M. Bottomley	1921-1923	Counc. E. Richardson
1929-1931	NOT KNOWN	1924-1934	Ald. T. Kitwood
1932-1937	Mrs W. Kitwood	1935-1940	NOT KNOWN
1938-1949	NOT KNOWN	1941-1947	R. Isaac
1963-1977	Mrs J. Isaac	1947-1949	G. Robinson
1978-1980	Mrs J. Coney	1963-1966	A. W. Isaac
1981-1983	Mrs F. Reynol	1967-1969	W. Jackson
1984-1986	Mrs M. Allen	1970-1976	F. A. Foster
1987-1989	Mrs J. Daker	1977-1988	P. J. Pearson, C.
1990-1992	Mrs N. Royle	1989-1991	D. Daker
1993-1995	Miss T. Weightman	1992	R. A. Barclay
1996-	Mrs K. Bradley		

CLUB SECRETARIES

LADIES		GENTLEMEN	
1900-1908	Miss F. South	1900-1902	Rev. H. Garvey
1909-1912	NOT KNOWN	1903-1906	B. B. Dyer
1913-1917	Miss Poole	1907-1910	W. Bedford
1918-1924	Mrs M. Bottomley	1911-1913	C. Wood
1925-1926	Miss E. Gilliatt	1914-1919	A. Norman
1927-1930	Miss N. Carter	1920-1944	M. Bottomley
1931-1934	Mrs A. Cheer	1945-1949	Dr. J. Pankhurst
1935-1949	Mrs J. Coney		

1949 — NO COURSE — 1962

LADIES		GENTLEMEN	
1962-1969	Miss T. Weightman	1962-1969	B. R. Morris
1970	Mrs J. Daker	1971-1977	G. W. Redman
1971-1974	Mrs F Allen	1978-1985	J. B. Moss
1974-1976	Mrs M. Allen	1986	J. Mitchell
1977-1978	Mrs B. Mitchell	1987	D. E. Smith
1979	Mrs J. Johnson		
1980-1983	Mrs S. Greswell		
1984-1986	Mrs M. Hardy		
1987-1988	Mrs M. Davies		
1989-1990	Mrs M. Johns		
1991-1992	Mrs J. Taylor		
1993	Mrs C. Toynton		
1994	Mrs R. Knaggs		
1995	Mrs R. Street		

Appendix C

The Woodthorpe Cup, September 1927

C. Clayton	36	plays	C. Dawson	24
L. Robinson	20	"	G. Robinson	20
M. Clifton	18	"	N. South	28
Mrs Parry	26	"	Mrs J. Circot	36
G. Hutson	24	"	M. Bottomley	18
J. Tebbutt	28	"	A. Chambers	18
Miss B. Francis	36	"	N. Carter	27
Miss T. Francis	36	"	R. Isaacs	20
F. Foster	28	"	C. Rastall	19
T. Carter	22	"	W. Wright	24
Mrs Hamer	23	"	Mrs Colam	36
F. Smith	24		bye	—
P. Ostler	16	"	H. Hutson	14
W. Killingworth	24	"	Mrs W. Cheer	26
Mrs L. Towell	30	"	T. Stamp	24
H. Haines	24	"	S. Sutherland	24
Mrs D. Arch	26	"	C. Anderson	24
P. Arch	10	"	H. Bettinson	24
J. Arch	7	"	A. Parry	18
J. Pearson	28		bye	—
Mrs T. Carter	36	"	G. Barclay	24
P. Ryesdale	28	"	Mrs. R. Linley	36
E. Turner	24	"	J. Inwood	24
Mrs L. Enderby	36	"	H. Trevitt	24
H. Senior	24	"	W. Cheer	18
Mrs Tyson	36	"	A. Clift	24
Mrs J. Pearson	36	"	A. Oliver	24
L. Slingsby	28	"	T. Tyson	16
Mrs W. Kitwood	36	"	C. Bozman	22

APPENDIX D

THE ISLAND TROPHY SEPTEMBER 1994

C. Latham	(1)	78	10	69	
C. Edwards	(2)	79	10	69	
C. Johns	(3)	82	12	70	
K. Sale	(4)	88	18	70	
M. Holland	(5)	88	18	70	
S. Emery		75	4	71	Lowest gross
A. Green	(6)	90	18	72	
N. Hollingsworth		87	15	72	
M. Scrupps		90	18	72	Best Rabbit
G. Willis		80	8	72	
S. Long		89	17	72	
A. Atterby		88	16	72	
J. Fairman		91	18	73	
R. Atterby		90	17	73	
N. Atterby		90	17	73	
M. Hyde		86	13	73	
N. Sharpe		84	10	74	
L. O'Dea		84	10	74	
K. Vickers		86	12	74	
J. Simpson		89	15	74	
R. Lenton		93	18	75	
M. Whitehead		91	16	75	
A. Dawson		85	10	75	
H. Eaglen		89	13	76	
B. Newark		88	12	76	
B. Pigney		93	17	76	
E. Porter		89	13	76	
D. Gooch		94	17	77	
C. Woodcock		92	15	77	
M. Couture		93	16	77	
I. Jones		94	16	78	
A. Moor		90	12	78	
N. Tooley		96	18	78	
D. Smith		92	14	78	
P. Cooper		91	13	78	
D. Edwards		88	10	78	
R. Williamson		96	18	78	

236.

B. Braseby	89	10	79
T. Carr	97	18	79
J. Wilkinson	92	13	79
V. Dalton	97	18	79
D. Hodgson	97	18	79
L. Bonner	90	11	79
R. Loveley	97	17	80
G. Bennett	97	17	80
J. Allen	95	14	81
D. Limb	93	12	81
J. Harley	97	16	81
C. Martin	99	10	81
R. Gresswell	91	10	81
R. Woods	89	8	81
V. Hunter	92	11	81
H. Cartwright	99	18	81
G. Day	94	12	82
B. Draper	95	13	82
M. Long	91	8	83
N. Gleeson	94	11	83
J. Davenport	98	15	83
M. Holmes	99	16	83
D. Turner	97	13	84
A. Robinson	101	16	85
D. Brogden	99	13	86
A Moxon	101	13	88
P. Kelly	103	15	88
D. Sharpe	104	16	88
D. Roberts	106	18	88
R. Brackenbury	101	10	91

INDEX

See also pages 232-237 for names appearing in the Appendices as they have not been included in the index.

Newark, Brian, 207
Newsam, Mr. W., 14
Newton, Mr. W., 40
niblick golf club, 9
Nicholson, Mr., 9
Nicklaus, Jack, 6, 141-2, 156,
179, 196
Norman, Mr. A., 46, 47
Greg., 179, 195-6, 215
Normanby Hall G. C., 193
North Shore G. C., 43, 45, 47,
Norton, Avril, 201
M., 160
T., 14
Terry, 209

O

O'Connor, Christie, 180
Odling, Mr. F., 114, 157, 160
Ogden, David, 182, 183
Oldham, Mr., 127, 129
Oldrid's Park, 41
Open Championship (British Men's)
16, 29, 30, 61, 74, 75, 99,
142, 157,
winners, 76, 156, 179, 196
British Ladies', 177
Open, USA, 30, 61, 75, 142
Ostler, Mr. P., 48, 50, 78, 91
Oswestry G. C., 92

P

Palmer, Arnold, 141, 196
Pankhurst, Dr. J., 110, 114
paraffin lamps, 50
Parkes, Fred, 44, 53, 54, 56, 68,
120, 179
Parkers Messrs., 224
Parry, Mr. A., 58, 70, 74, 79, 92
Parsons, Mr. F., 45, 50
Payne, Jim, 205, 227
Peacock, Mr., C., 39
Peacock & Royal Hotel, 3, 23, 35, 44
Pearson, Issette, 17, 18, 154, 127

Pearson, Mr. F., 104
Peter, Junr, 8, 157,
160, 176, 183, 188, 214
Peter (Senr), 157, 188,
W., 88
Mr. W., 88, 95
Peck, Mr. Ron, 110, 114, 127, 129,
138, 142, 146
pensions, 22, 96
Pepper, Les., 205
Perseverence Pig Club, 28
pigeon shoot, 40
Pilcher, Mrs. M., 130
Pinder, J., 46
Mr. W., 38, 45
Pinner, Hugh, 207
Platt, Bert, 137, 151, 169-72, 174-5
Player, Gary, 123, 141-2, 156
Playle, Mrs., 87
plough boys, 42
Pooles, Miss, 38, 41, 44
Miss G., 41, 44
Miss M. 44
Popplewell, Graham, 146
population, G.B., 21
Porter, Mr. W., 48
Poyser, Mrs., 84
Price, Joe, 222
Mrs., 38, 41, 42, 44
Nick, 196
prices, 103
Pridgeon, Walter, 41
Prince of Wales, 6, 99
Pudding Pie, 44, 55, 56, 66
deeds, 119

R

Rabbits (golf), 143, 150, 189-90, 216
railways, 44
Rainbow, Ron, 160, 175-6, 183
Rainey, G., 25, 35
Ransomes, Messrs, 46
Rastall, Mr., 91
rationing, 107
Rauceby (Sleaford) G. C., 39, 59, 71,
85, 95, 102, 105, 108, 121, 152,
163, 193

246.

matches, 39, 41, 61, 71, 101, 104, 106, 114
Ray, Ted., 30, 61
Reckett, Dr., 3
Redman, G., 160
  P., 160
Reed, Fred, 182,
  Marina, 192
Rennie, John, x
Revill, Miss M., 27
  Mrs E., 27
Reynolds, A., 77
  Adrian, 212-4
  David, 115
  Flo, 139, 157
  Gill, 182, 184, 203
  Jennie, 157, 176
  Peter, 115, 129, 142, 148, 150, 173
  Robert., 89, 101-2, 106, 110, 115
Richardson Mr. (Spilsby), 24
  Miss Bertha, 38
  Councillor, E., 58, 60, 91
Ridley, Mr. H., 85
Ridlington, Messrs, 147
Ringrose, Mr. R., 127, 129, 139
Roberts, Mr. S., 100
  Cup, 91
Robertson, Mr. W., 104, 114
Robins, George (Junior), 48, 50, 60, 66, 71, 93
  George (Senior), 48, 49
Robinson, Mr. (Spilsby), 24
  George, 46, 48, 50, 58, 70, 114
  Lionel, 110, 114, 127, 129, 142
Rogers, Bill, 179
Romans, 56
Rothery, Mr. H., 101-2, 104, 106
Rowing Club, 87
Royal and Ancient Golf Club, 3, 15-6, 160
Royle, Nora, 157, 204

S

Saint Andrew's G. C., 74
Saint Botolph's Church, 118
Sales, Roy, 207, 208

Sandilands G. C., 23, 74, 84, 94, 122, 227
sandbox, 14
Sarazan, Gene, 9, 75, 79
Saul, Messrs., Auctioneers, 44
Savage Mr. M., 40
Saville, Mr. R., 102, 110
Scarborough, The Earl of, 15
scarlet fever, 41
Scott, Capt. G., 46
  Lady Margaret, 18, 30
  Lawrence, 43
Scrimshaw, Mr., 50, 51
  Mrs., 89
Scrupps, Fred, 216
Seacroft Golf Club, 5, 24, 47, 52, 85, 87, 108, 122, 193, 227
  golfing events, 93, 122
Senior, Mr. H., 87
servants, 42
Sharp, Mrs., 158
Sharpe, Eric, 205
Shaw, Ann, 205
  Mr. S., 4
Sheehan, Dr., 104
sheep, 58, 60-1, 152, 170
Sherriff, Mrs., Chris., 217
Sherwins, Messrs., 48
Short, J., 3
Shove, Mr. J., 38, 40
Sibsey
  Golf Club, (East Lincs. G. C.), 62, 67, 69, 70
    AGM, 77
    competitions, 77, 78
    ladies, 77
    Mr. Caudwell's death, 85
    professional, 62, 73
  Trader, 64, 85
Sidorn, Mrs., 84
Simpson, B., 205
Sinclair, Mr. W., 127, 129
Sinclair's, Messrs., 135
Skegness, 5
Skene, Mrs., 101, 146
Skinner, Mrs. D., 155, 157
  Audrey, 182
  Brian, 182, 211, 213
  Mr. T., 39